THE STORY
OF THE
COSMOS

GENERAL EDITORS
PAUL M. GOULD AND DANIEL RAY

HARVEST HOUSE PUBLISHERS
EUGENE, OREGON

Cover design by Faceout Studio

Cover photo © Vadim Sadovski / Shutterstock

The Story of the Cosmos
Copyright © 2019 by Paul M. Gould and Daniel Ray
Published by Harvest House Publishers
Eugene, Oregon 97408
www.harvesthousepublishers.com

ISBN 978-0-7369-7736-4 (Trade)
ISBN 978-0-7369-7737-1 (eBook)

Library of Congress Cataloging-in-Publication Data is on file at the Library of Congress, Washington, DC.

Printed in China

19 20 21 22 23 24 25 26 27 / IM-SK / 10 9 8 7 6 5 4 3 2 1

To him who spoke the world into being
and sustains it by his loving hands.

From Dan

Thanks to the Sandlin, Valerius, Hughes, Krygsheld, Barlowe, and McCarty families; to Paul personally for taking a chance with me; to our team of contributors; to Dr. Michael Ward and Dr. Holly Ordway for being patient with me as my professors at Houston Baptist University; to my mom; and to all the staff at Harvest House.

From Paul

Thanks to Terry Glaspey for taking a chance on a book exploring the connection between science and story, astrophysics and fantasy! And thanks to our editor, Steve Miller, for a stellar job of cleaning up the manuscript and bringing it to life. It is no small feat to help scientists, philosophers, artists, and apologists speak with one voice! Finally, thanks to the contributors to this volume—an all-"star" cast. Each individual essay is a *thread*; together, this volume forms a cord connecting the natural order to the sacred order.

CONTENTS

Part III: Evidences Pointing to the Creation of the Cosmos

CHAPTER 1

The Heavens Are Telling of the Glory of God

DANIEL RAY

T he heavens are telling of the glory of God and the expanse is declaring the work of His hands."[1] This is the opening verse of what C.S. Lewis believed "to be the greatest poem in the Psalter and one of the greatest lyrics in the world."[2] Written by Israel's ancient King David nearly 3,000 years ago, the prologue of the nineteenth Psalm holds true today more than ever. Within our present age of sophisticated ground- and space-based telescopes, perhaps there has been no greater affirmation of David's hymn than what astronomers have uncovered about the universe in just the last half century.

But increasingly it seems the formal sciences of the universe now explain everything with little or no reference to God and his glory. After all, we have been told by the brightest minds that we inhabit "an insignificant planet orbiting a nondescript star,"[3] that we have been "dethroned" and now must humbly come to grips with our "insignificance in relation to the rest of the universe."[4] Popular astrophysicist Neil DeGrasse Tyson believes man to be cosmically "insignificant."[5] Carl Sagan once described human beings as "inconsequential, a thin film of life on an obscure and solitary lump of rock and metal."[6] Bertrand Russell said we were merely "accidental collocations of atoms."[7] The question of human significance in the cosmos, however, is not finally a purely scientific question. When God is factored out of the equation, however, nearly anything goes. Brannon Braga, one of the producers of the newly revised 2013 and recent 2019 remake of Carl Sagan's 1980 PBS series *Cosmos*, which Tyson himself hosts, said in a speech given in 2012 that "religion sucks, isn't science great, and how the hell do we get the other ninety-five percent of the population to come to their senses?"[8] John G. West notes that the 2013 *Cosmos* series "portrayed religion as the enemy of science, claimed that science shows how life organized through unguided processes, and even compared climate-change skeptics to Nazis."[9]

But are these purveyors of disenchantment correct? Is there really nothing special about the cosmos or our place within it? We believe the cosmos is telling a rather different story—a story of hope, love, and purpose. Even more, we find a storyteller inviting us to enter into a divine drama—and a divine dance! For those who have eyes to see and ears to hear, the cosmos does indeed declare the glory of God.

Consider the iconic Hubble Space Telescope, which floats more than 300 miles above Earth taking some of the most hauntingly surreal images of the universe ever seen by human eyes. The breathtakingly beautiful light sculptures the telescope has uncovered since it was first launched in 1990 have captured the imaginations of generations of young and old alike. As the official Hubble website puts it, "Astronomy has always been a preeminently visual science, going back thousands of years to the early sky watchers. Hubble's jaw-dropping views of far-flung planets, nebulas, and galaxies have redefined the universe for whole new generations."[10]

Hubble has helped translate the luminous vernacular of the heavens for little ones in a most remarkable way. Former Space Telescope Science Institute director Bob Williams shared in a 2011 interview that he believed beauty had become one of the most significant aspects of the telescope's legacy, including beauty as seen through the eyes of children. "The fact though that Hubble produces beautiful images that children like to see is very important for the *funding* of Hubble. Of course that is important for we scientists."[11]

Williams also mentioned the results of a survey which revealed that "pictures from the Hubble Space Telescope occurred more often than dinosaurs on the walls of the classrooms of America. That is quite an accomplishment."[12] "Let the children alone and do not hinder them from coming to Me," Jesus reminds us, "for the kingdom of the heavens belongs to such as these."[13] How remarkable that the legacy of one of the most advanced telescopes ever built seems to affirm this ancient truth. As David proclaims in Psalm 8, "From the mouth of infants and nursing babes, Thou hast established strength…" And funding for a space telescope, we might add!

Taken by the Hubble Space Telescope's Wide Field Planetary Camera 2 in December of 1995, this image features some 3,000 galaxies (*galaxies*, not stars) in a "blank" spot of sky just off the handle of the Big Dipper.[14] It is the first image of its kind ever taken. (Courtesy of NASA)

As director, Williams took a few risks with Hubble. During the Christmas season of 1995, for example, he and his team decided to point Hubble at a very small starless spot of sky and take pictures of it—*for ten days*. Considering Hubble's operational costs, this involved a serious investment. Williams believed, however, more existed in that apparent nothingness than met the eye. Hubble's images delighted the astronomical community. Formally known as the Hubble Deep Field, the "blank" spot contained some 3,000 galaxies of all shapes, colors and sizes, like presents under the tree on Christmas morning. As Williams said in a press conference shortly after the images were released to the public, Hubble found "a myriad of galaxies. There are large ones and small ones, red ones and blue ones, very structured ones and also very amorphous ones. Most of these galaxies were never seen before Hubble. But we don't know the significance of all this yet."[15] Though the myriad galaxies did not audibly say anything to astronomers, they knew there lay before them a great mystery worthy of careful investigation.

Nearly a decade later, Space Telescope Science Institute (STScI) director Matt Mountain gave the order for Hubble to go even deeper. As the psalmist extols, there really "are no words"[16] to describe the astounding glory of what Hubble's mirrors uncovered. In another tiny area of sky within the southern constellation of Fornax (fittingly, the "Furnace"), the Hubble team extracted perhaps the most breathtaking and iconic images of the heavens seen by man. *Ten thousand galaxies* radiated in the deepest image of the universe ever taken known today as the Hubble Ultra Deep Field. Dr. Anton Koekemoer, who served as the primary imaging specialist for the Deep Field, believes these images

> can be thought of as "landscape portraits" of the cosmos, using Hubble as our camera, which we then make available to the world. The variety of colors and shapes in our images are generally intended to appear as they would if they could be seen directly by the human eye, and I sometimes describe these as revealing "God's artwork on a cosmic canvas." The images also often convey much of the scientific results directly, as the shapes, sizes, and colors of the galaxies, stars, and glowing gas clouds all reveal the astrophysical processes that are at work. So there is often an elegant connection between the images themselves and the scientific results that we can obtain from them.[17]

Koekemoer believes Hubble's images can provide sources of inspiration for everyone, regardless of their scientific knowledge or religious beliefs.

> Just contemplating the sheer scale of the universe, as well as the beauty revealed in all our astronomical images, can leave anyone with a profound sense of awe and wonder, regardless of one's perspective on religion. From my own personal viewpoint as a Christian, I would say that we can appreciate even more deeply how the writers of Scripture were inspired thousands of years ago to write: "the heavens declare the glory of God, and the skies proclaim His handiwork" (Ps. 19:1). Contemplating the scale of the universe can

also lead us to ponder the ultimate significance of our own human-ity by comparison, as stated so eloquently by the Psalmist: "What is humankind, that Thou art mindful of us?" (Ps. 8:4). Yet the very next verses provide an answer to this question, by showing how pre-cious we all are to God. When we consider the universe from the viewpoint of religion, by contemplating God as its creator, faith can be deeply enriched and broadened as a result.[18]

Koekemoer sees no conflict between his Christian faith and scientific endeavors.

[It]is quite possible to contemplate the grand scale of the universe, as revealed by modern astronomical science, from the perspective of faith where God is viewed as its creator, as revealed by scripture, and that science and faith can be fully reconciled in this context. Sci-ence can be said to describe the physical mechanisms and processes in the universe, while the Christian faith considers God as the agent responsible for its creation and discusses the purpose of our own lives in that context, which is not really a question that can even be posed in a scientific setting.[19]

We are enamored by the luminous sparks of light twinkling[20] throughout the heavens, light which God has wondrously forged by his hands. As the psalm proclaims, "Of old hast thou laid the foundation of the earth; and the heav-ens are the work of thy hands" (Psalm 102:25 KJV). The galaxies of the Hubble Ultra Deep Field remind me of a few lines from a Henry Wadsworth Longfel-low poem about a village blacksmith:

And children coming home from school
    Look in at the open door;
They love to see the flaming forge,
    And hear the bellows roar,
And catch the burning sparks that fly
    Like chaff from a threshing-floor.[21]

"There is no speech, nor are there words; their voice is not heard," Psalm 19 continues, yet "their line has gone out through all the earth, and their utter-ances to the end of the world" (Psalm 19:3-4 NASB). It is a voice that ceaselessly draws our eyes heavenward.

Another "blank" spot of sky in the constellation of Fornax, the Furnace. The Hubble Space Telescope captured this field of some 10,000 galaxies, the deepest image of the universe taken to date. This is a composite of images in several different wavelengths of light.[22] (Courtesy of NASA)

You do not need a space telescope, or even a regular telescope, to appreciate the night skies. During the fall and winter months in the northern hemisphere, you can see for yourself the ancient rectangular constellation of Orion, with his massive shoulder star, Betelgeuse, and his radiant blue-white foot, Rigel, defensively poised against the intimidating visage of Taurus and his pulsating orange-vermillion eye, Aldebaran. Though this massive star appears only as a tiny speck of pulsing light you can easily cover with the head of a pin, in an up-close-and-personal sense, Aldebaran is some 38,000,000 miles in diameter, more than 40 times larger than our own Sun![23]

And just behind the V-shaped cluster of stars that comprise the head and horns of Taurus is the lovely little basket of blue stars called the Pleiades. This dazzling cluster of stars is mentioned specifically in the pages of the Bible[24] and has influenced countless farmers, poets, authors, scientists, and even a Japanese auto manufacturer. In her book *The Seven Sisters of the Pleiades,* Munya Andrews notes, "Many cultures have emphasized the collective, bunched nature of the Pleiades star cluster," pointing out that they appear twice in the Book of Job, "where they are referred to as *Kimah,* a Hebrew term for 'cluster' or 'heap'...The Pawnee Indians of the North American plains look on them as symbols of unity and pray to these stars to teach people how to be as united as them."[25]

In *The Hobbit,* J.R.R. Tolkien mentions the Pleiades cluster, "known in the ancient days of Middle-earth as Remmirath, 'The Netted Stars.'"[26] In Japan, the Pleiades are known as *Subaru,* which means "unite." The car manufacturer of the same name has as its emblem the familiar cluster of celestial sisters.[27] The nineteenth-century English poet Alfred Tennyson penned these famous lines about Orion and the Pleiades:

> Many a night from yonder ivied casement, ere I went to rest,
>   Did I look on great Orion sloping slowly to the West.
> Many a night I saw the Pleiads, rising thro' the mellow shade,
>   Glitter like a swarm of fire-flies tangled in a silver braid.[28]

The heavens speak to us in a simple yet deeply profound iridescent prose we can all understand but one that is also intensely mysterious. The humblest child, the most insightful poet, and the most erudite astrophysicist can all understand and appreciate what the skies proclaim. "Day to day pours forth speech," David said, "and night to night reveals knowledge" (Psalm 19:2 NASB). Our investments in studying the enigmatic texts of cosmos do not merely "suggest" the universe is declaring something inestimably valuable and beautifully mysterious; the discipline of modern astronomy *tells* us plainly the universe itself is a message of weighty significance. We cannot help but "listen." As astronomer Brian Penprase describes,

> A clear, dark, starry night sky brings out intense feelings in even the most sophisticated city dweller. These feelings vary among individuals, but for most they are intense and connect us to something sublime and transcendent. The night sky calls to us and humans over the years have responded with their star tales, their monuments, their theories, and their observatories with gleaming polished glass.[29]

Our collective wonder and awe about the heavens are part of what David means by "the glory of God." The word translated "glory," in Hebrew, is *kabod,* which is derived from a root meaning "heaviness."[30] Glory, as it is used in the Old Testament, is thus a kind of weighty honor, like something a president or king would have. A potentate's glory may be impressive, but *God's* glory is far above and beyond any earthly magistrate's. His radiance is not something at which a man can look directly and survive the encounter—thus it is necessary for him to be concealed from us. God's raw, unmediated glory is "dangerous and powerful,"[31] at once both luminously lethal and iridescently life-giving.

To truly know the heavens as they were intended to be known, one must be willing to dance a little bit. Long before there was *Dancing with the Stars*, the eighteenth-century English astronomer William Herschel discovered *binary stars*—two stars gravitationally bound to one another in an orbital dance of glory. Herschel's careful observations of 848 double stars, with the help of his sister Caroline, "was the first step on the road to a proof that there are stars moving around one another in gravitational orbits."[32] Fittingly, Herschel also served as a composer and organist in the English resort town of Bath, where many a dance scene takes place in Jane Austen's beloved novels. "It is *your* turn to say something now, Mr. Darcy," says Elizabeth Bennet in *Pride and Prejudice* as she twirls about with the reticent aristocratic bachelor. "*I* talked about the dance, and *you* ought to make some kind of remark on the size of the room, or the numbers of couples."[33]

As part-time work, I have had the distinct pleasure of serving as a DJ at several weddings. I can tell you from firsthand experience that when the more reserved friends and family members decide to get out on the dance floor (usually when I play "YMCA" by the Village People or Harry Belafonte's "Jump in the Line"), one's concept of reality undergoes something of a paradigm shift. "Oh my goodness, Uncle Fred is *dancing*—no way!" No one up to that point had ever seen Uncle Fred dance, but the sight inspires other reluctant guests to at least try to spell YMCA with their hands and arms.

This is a lot like how we make discoveries and maybe a little how science *really* works. There is that first step we take outside of our everyday experiences and see something most people do not, and, well, we dance. And a dance always begins with a single step. Who knows how a single step in your life might change the course of mankind? Fifty years ago, Neil Armstrong took "one small step" and forever altered our perception of ourselves in the cosmos. His mother, Viola, recalled Neil's love of the heavens began at an early age:

> As I look back, I can see how the pattern of his life has all dovetailed together. I believe God gave him a mind to use and maybe destined him to the work he has been doing. As a child and as a young man

he loved and was completely fascinated by the heavens and God's great creation. It seemed as if the heavens were calling him—so great was his undying interest. He has been fine and good, a scholar, a thinker and a diligent worker…His thinking is big and his thoughts are far reaching. He seems to be inspired by God, and speaking his Will. For this I am over and over thankful.[34]

We might picture the universe itself as a kind of regal ballroom, lovingly created and adorned by Christ himself, the grandest of stages for the most enigmatic and beautiful story ever told. And we have all been invited. Within its spacious canopy is a splendid array of stellar chandeliers, elegantly hand-carved balustrades, and exquisitely ornate frescos that add to the atmosphere of our terrestrial tête-à-têtes, interludes, and even our missteps. Those who catch a glimpse of Christ's kingdom dance a little differently, and the world takes notice, for better or for worse.

> We might picture the universe itself as a kind of regal ballroom, lovingly created and adorned by Christ himself, the grandest of stages for the most enigmatic and beautiful story ever told.

Think of the universe as the world-famous Palmer House Hotel in Chicago. It is the oldest continuously operating hotel in the United States, originally built by the wealthy business magnate Potter Palmer as a remarkably lavish wedding present for his bride Bertha in 1871. Two weeks after the stunning architectural masterpiece had opened for business, however, the great Chicago Fire of 1871 completely destroyed it. Palmer, though devastated, resolved to rebuild. Out of the ashes of the Great Fire came the illustrious present-day architectural masterpiece, which the hotel website now calls "A House of Stars."[35] Under the 24-karat-gold chandeliers of the hotel lobby the footsteps of innumerable cultural luminaries have trod—writers, actors, actresses, musicians, athletes, and presidents. They have clustered together under the vaulted firmament of Palmer's monument of love and enduring hospitality. This is another facet of biblical glory, as *kabod* can also refer to one's renown and wealth. By comparison, however, the "weightiness" of God's unending vault of riches makes earthly glory but a vapor.

Though himself not a professing Christian, theoretical physicist Roger Penrose suggests that we need to broaden our imaginations when it comes to the universe if we ever hope to truly understand it. Science needs to be more willing to embrace the possibility that the universe is more like a fantasy story, one that takes into consideration things like Uncle Fred's unexpected dancing to the Village People at his niece's wedding. As Penrose observes, "There are some key aspects to the nature of our actual universe that are so exceptionally odd (though not always fully recognized as such) that if we do not indulge in what may appear to be outrageous flights of fantasy, we shall have no chance of coming to terms with what may well be an extraordinary fantastical-seeming underlying truth."[36]

C.S. Lewis believed our emphasis on a purely scientific and mathematical understanding of the cosmos actually did end up emptying the universe of its glory, though only through our darkened imaginations. Lewis believed that by our penchant for excluding everything else but the numbers from our explanations about the universe, we have ultimately emptied the heavens of their glorious meaning. "By reducing Nature to her mathematical elements," modern naturalistic models of the universe "substituted a mechanical for a genial or animistic conception of the universe. The world was emptied, first of her indwelling spirits, then of her occult sympathies and antipathies, finally of her colours, smells and tastes."[37] As this emptying took place, the increase of artificial lighting in modern cities soon rendered the stars nearly invisible to most of us. "Thus the effect of the mechanical view of the world was to exile God from nature and the universe," writes theologian Terence Nichols. Such a view "severed the unity of God and nature that we find in the Bible."[38] Lewis desired to restore that unity. He was intimately aware of what the contemporary models of the universe had done and were doing to man's understanding of himself.

Lewis was *not* saying, however, that math is bad. By no means. He was implying that man substituted God with math. What was once attributed to God as an explanation for the existence and sustaining power of the cosmos is now mostly attributed to mathematical laws.

But a purely mathematical approach to the universe overlooks our very human endeavors in trying to better understand the incredible light show going on above us night after night. Science, after all, is a human endeavor and is often a lot messier than we might think. Astronomer Johannes Kepler, for example, could not have published his three laws of planetary motion in the early seventeenth century had he not first painstakingly wrestled the all-important data from the hands of a bombastic Danish astronomer with half a nose and penchant for controversy and keeping his research a secret. As science writer Jim Baggot describes it:

> Whenever historians examine the details of scientific discoveries, they inevitably find only confusion and muddle, vagueness and error, good fortune often pointing the way to right answers for the wrong reasons. Occasionally they find true genius. Theorizing involves a deeply human act of creativity. And this, like humour, doesn't fare well under any kind of rational analysis…The knowledge that science can be profoundly messy on occasion simply makes it more human and accessible; more Kirk than Spock.[39]

The late physicist John Archibald Wheeler, who coined the term *black hole*, said in an interview shortly before his death in 2008, "The world is a crazy place, and the way it's organized is truly crazy. But, we have to be crazy enough to see what that way is if we're really going to understand this physical world. It's not just a matter of nice, simple formulas."[40]

Part of that understanding comes through our efforts of creating, an innate desire that cannot finally be explained by nice, simple formulas. In our artistic expressions—in poetry, literature, music, or art—we try to capture the luminous essence of eternity placed within each of us.[41] As theologian Abraham Kuyper observed, "At creation, a sense of this divinity that is located in the form and appearance of things was created within human beings, such that one of the features of our creation according to God's image consisted in the sense of beauty." But, he notes, "This sense of beauty was darkened by sin, and would have been lost entirely if common grace had not preserved it for us."[42] "For us Christians, therefore, art exists in direct connection with our expectations of eternity," Kuyper explains. "With trembling hand, as it were, art reaches out toward the glory that through Christ will one day fill heaven and earth." Kuyper believed that "art lets us behold only scattered images that help us gauge and grasp something of what will appear in the kingdom of glory."[43]

NASA recently announced the discovery of a massive ring of black holes located in a galaxy far, far away.[44] They are not exactly sure, however, if the gems which comprise the ring are black holes or binary stars with one of the pair being a neutron star. Whatever they might be, these objects are emitting extraordinarily intense X-ray light. The remarkable discovery of this ring came about through both the Hubble Space Telescope and the Chandra X-Ray Observatory. Stop to consider this for a second: Medieval folk would have thought the idea of giant telescopes floating about in the heavens taking pictures of invisible light as nothing short of magical, truly the work of a multitude of modern-day wizards! In NASA's press release about the discovery, they briefly compared the ring to the ring in Tolkien's *Lord of the Rings*, which of course raises a very interesting question: Was this ring of X-ray-emitting objects *meant* to be found? What is the meaning of this incredibly powerful light?

> For a moment the wizard stood looking at the fire; then he stooped and removed the ring to the hearth with the tongs, and at once picked it up. Frodo gasped…he now saw fine lines, finer than the finest pen-strokes, running along the ring, outside and inside: lines of fire that seemed to form the letters of a flowing script. They shone piercingly bright, and yet remote, as if out of a great depth.[45]

A fitting description of astronomy. Of course the ring in Middle-earth was forged for evil purposes, but what can be said about NASA's newly discovered ring? What is the proper interpretation of the light shining down on us from the heavens? Who will read the script for us? And how in the world is it we have come to be able read the cosmos in the first place? Was our universe intentionally designed—finely tuned, we might say—for us to discover it? As physicist Freeman Dyson wrote in 1979, "The more I examine the universe and study the details of its architecture, the more evidence I find that the universe in some sense must have known we were coming."[46]

Each of these essays is but one facet of the glorious story of the cosmos. Each essay retains the unique perspective of their authors as they have come to understand, appreciate, and enjoy the splendor of the heavens. As you enter into the story yourself, ultimately, we hope you take your Maker by the hand and see his glory.

And dance with the One whose love moves the Sun and other stars.

PART I:

EXPLORATION
OF THE COSMOS

CHAPTER 2

A Glorious Resonance: The Intelligibility of Nature and the *Imago Dei*

MELISSA CAIN TRAVIS

The chief aim of all investigations of the external world should be to discover the rational order which has been imposed on it by God, and which he revealed to us in the language of mathematics.[1]

JOHANNES KEPLER

In his poetic essay entitled "Man, the Priest of Creation," Scottish theologian T.F. Torrance wrote, "It is in and through the universe of space and time that God has revealed himself to us in modes of rationality that he has conferred upon the creation and upon us in the creation."[2] Torrance, though not a scientist himself, was awestruck by the surprising fact that the natural world is intelligible to mankind, and he attributed this nature-mind harmony to divine intent. In his short yet incredibly rich book *Christian Theology and Scientific Culture,* he explained that were this harmony absent, the scientific enterprise would be impossible:

> …the universe is characterised throughout by a unitary rational order. If the universe were not everywhere inherently and harmoniously rational, it would not be open to consistent rational understanding and interpretation…There could be no science without belief in the inner harmony of the world or without the belief that it is possible to grasp reality with our theoretical constructions.[3]

Reflecting upon the fathers of modern science, Torrance marveled, "What deep faith in the rationality of the structure of the world, what a longing to understand even a small glimpse of the reason revealed in the world, there must have been in Kepler and Newton!"[4]

It is a curious thing that Torrance didn't (at least in these particular works) offer more than this passing, offhanded mention of Johannes Kepler (1571–1630), a renowned German mathematician and astronomer whose genius was driven by the idea of grand harmonies—including the harmony of the heavenly bodies in their dance around the heavens, as well as the one between the creation, the mind of God, and the human intellect. Kepler wrote,

> To God there are, in the whole material world, material laws, figures and relations of special excellency and of the most appropriate order…Those laws are within the grasp of the human mind; God wanted us to recognize them by creating us after his own image so that we could share in his own thoughts.[5]

Kepler's words poetically communicate a specific (and decidedly Christian) understanding of fundamental reality: God created the cosmos according to a preconceived rational plan and, in light of the fact that nature is intelligible to us, the mind of man must be in some sense analogous to the mind of the Maker. In other words, the *cosmic resonance* between the material world, mathematics, and the mind of man is explained by the tripartite harmony that exists between the archetypal plan in the mind of the Maker, the material manifestation of this plan (the copy), and man's intellect (part of the image of God). It is because of this astounding arrangement that we are able to access some of the most complex secrets of the cosmos.[6]

As we will see, the Keplerian idea of a tripartite harmony of archetype, copy, and image has intellectual roots that go back to ancient Greek and early Christian thought about the natural world and man's place in it. The rise of modern science (which included mathematical laws of nature) has beautifully affirmed this harmony, and even though enormous progress has been made in the physical sciences since Kepler's time, this affirmation has persisted. In light of the discoveries of great scientists such as Max Planck and Albert Einstein in the early twentieth century as well as the work done by renowned contemporary physicists such as Roger Penrose, the tripartite harmony enjoys unprecedented vitality as an explanatory paradigm for the observed cosmic resonance that contemporary thinkers (some non-theists included) find absolutely remarkable.

In other words, it seems that theism is the best explanation for the wondrous order and intelligibility of the cosmos.

This phenomenal portrait of stars taken by the Hubble Space Telescope lies at the heart of our Milky Way Galaxy. Stars of all shapes, sizes, compositions and colors, just as the apostle Paul declared, "star differs from star in glory" (1 Corinthians 15:41 ESV). "The image is a composite of exposures taken in near-infrared and visible light with Hubble's Wide Field Camera 3."[7] (Courtesy of NASA)

A Brief Intellectual History

The observation that there is a special relationship between mathematics, matter, and mind is rooted in some of the earliest philosophical thought of the Western tradition. Philosophers of the Pythagorean school, which was based upon the alleged oral teachings of the shadowy figure Pythagoras of Samos (c. 570–495 BC), believed that numbers are the divine essence of physical reality, constituting a "world soul" of which human souls are fragments.[8] The Pythagoreans perceived a mystical interconnection between number, mind, and the material world, an idea that became pervasive in Greek philosophy, mainly due to the influence of Plato (c. 429–347 BC), who believed that the material world is an imperfect copy of the perfect, abstract Forms that served as its pattern.

In his *Timaeus* dialogue, Plato communicated his cosmology of rational archetype, material copy, and the perceiving human mind through the words of a Pythagorean character for whom the dialogue is named. In an extended monologue, Timaeus explains that the beauty and intelligibility of nature are a result of the work of a benevolent craftsman who brought order out of chaos by framing the universe according to the eternal, rational Forms. He says that the cosmos was "crafted in reference to that which is grasped by reason," meaning the abstract ideas the human mind is able to contemplate by reasoning from our experience of the sensible world.[9] He goes on to say, "God invented and gave us sight to the end that we might behold the courses of intelligence in the heaven, and apply them to the courses of our own intelligence which are akin to them."[10] Through the words of Timaeus, Plato highlighted the connection between the rationality of nature and the human ability to grasp it; he explained its existence by positing a transcendent intelligence.

A few centuries after Plato, elements of his philosophy became integrated with Jewish thought about God, the intelligibility of creation, and the doctrine of the *imago Dei*. An excellent example is found in the work of Philo Judaeus (c. 20 BC–AD 50), an Alexandrian Jew and Middle Platonist[11] who recognized the rational structure of the material world and, like Plato, believed that it had been organized according to a preconceived plan. A major difference in Philo's thinking was that he saw this cosmic blueprint as being situated in the mind of God:

> As therefore the city, when previously shadowed out in the mind of the man of architectural skill had no external place, but was stamped solely in the mind of the workman, so in the same manner neither can the world which existed in the ideas have had any other local position except the divine reason which made them...[12]

Philo argued that the "idea of ideas, the Reason of God," what he called the *logos* ("word" or "reason"), pervades nature, accounting for its physical structure as well as man's rationality. Significantly, Philo related this to the Jewish doctrine of mankind: that we are beings made in the image of God. In other words, because God's intellect is reflected, to a finite degree, in his image-bearers, we are naturally inclined to detect signs of his intelligence in his workmanship. It seems likely that Philo saw the compatibility between the Greek concept of *logos* and the Hebrew notion of the creative "word" of God, which is found in passages such as Psalm 33:6—"By the word of the LORD the heavens were made, and by the breath of his mouth all their host" (ESV)—and realized how well the Hellenistic philosophy harmonized with Scripture on this point. Philo's writings went on to influence some early Christian theologians who identified Philo's *logos* with the *logos* in the apostle John's Gospel—Jesus Christ, the eternal Word through whom all things were made (John 1:1-3).[13]

> Because God's intellect is reflected, to a finite degree, in his image-bearers, we are naturally inclined to detect signs of his intelligence in his workmanship.

After the dawn of Christianity, several prominent philosophers and theologians wrote about the implications of the rationality of the world and man's ability to discern it. St. Augustine (354–430), Bishop of Hippo, who was well educated in Greek philosophy, called the spectacle of creation "a great book" that is open before us:

> Look carefully at it top and bottom, observe it, read it. God did not write in letters with ink but he placed what is created itself in front of you to recognize him in; he set before your eyes all these things he has made. Why look for a louder voice? Heaven and earth cries out to you: God made me.[14]

In addition to the evidence of God's wisdom and power in the creation, Augustine affirmed that there must have been a rational plan that predated the formation of the material world. However, he pointedly argued that this plan "must be thought to exist nowhere but in the very mind of the Creator" because it would be sacrilege to believe that God used a self-existent (Platonic) model, one that was ontologically independent of God.[15] In his commentary on Genesis, Augustine mentioned the numerical concepts of measure, number, and weight, "in which…God has arranged all things," but insisted that because there was nothing outside of God before the original act of creation, the immaterial mathematical design must have existed "in him" as ideas.[16] As for mankind's capacity for appreciating the orderliness of the physical world, Augustine explained that the soul of man is illumined by God in a manner that makes this possible.[17] It is because we are made in the image of God that we are able to detect his self-revelation in the created order.

During the medieval period (roughly the fifth through fifteenth centuries), there was continuing interaction between Christian thought and Platonism. Plato's *Timaeus* became central to the higher education curriculum and, as a result, there was a scholarly emphasis on the mathematical rationality of nature and the fitness of the human intellect for comprehending it.[18] An ongoing theological and philosophical theme was the proper understanding of the relationship between the rational plan behind creation and the mind of God. For example, in his *Metalogicon*, John of Salisbury (c. 1120–1180), bishop of Chartres, critiqued the Platonic doctrine of self-existent Forms, saying that if such things exist, they must have somehow originated with "him by Whom all things have been made."[19] He argued that all truths, including mathematical ones, directly depend upon the mind of God for their existence. He echoed Philo and Augustine when he said, "God is number innumerable, weight incalculable, and measure inestimable. And in Him alone all things that have been made in number in 'weight,' and in measure, have been created."[20] Concerning the intellectual abilities that set mankind apart from all other creatures, John said, "For God, breathing life into man, willed that he partake of the divine reason."[21]

Centuries later, major discoveries made during the scientific revolution took the conversation about the intelligibility of nature to unprecedented heights. Geometric models of the universe had been in use for more than a millennium, but through the work of natural philosophers of the sixteenth and seventeenth centuries, it was becoming evident that the interconnection between mathematics and nature went far deeper than spatial descriptions of observed celestial movements. Man's understanding of the cosmos changed dramatically not only from geocentrism to heliocentrism, but also in terms of the mathematical language that could be used to describe natural phenomena such as gravitational force and planetary motion.

At the beginning of this particular trajectory of discovery was Nicolaus Copernicus (1473–1543), who, at the very end of his life published his magnum opus, *The Revolutions of the Heavenly Spheres*, which presented a mathematical model for a heliocentric rather than geocentric cosmos. The idea of heliocentrism was not new, but the overwhelming consensus in the academy was consistent with Aristotle's ancient cosmology—a physical model in which Earth rested at the center of the universe and the Sun, Moon, planets, and stars were embedded in crystalline spheres that carried them in perfectly circular revolutions. The version used at the time of Copernicus was Ptolemy's, which was a complicated mathematical model designed to harmonize naked-eye astronomical observations with the assumptions of geocentrism and circular orbits of the heavenly bodies and produce (roughly) correct predictions about their changing locations in the sky. Copernicus's treatise was not the result of new astronomical observations and analysis that pointed to heliocentrism; rather, it was an attempt to simplify and streamline the cumbersome mathematics of the long-reigning geocentric Aristotelian-Ptolemaic system. Copernicus believed that more elegant mathematical descriptions were more likely to be true; his was a model born of certain aesthetic sensibilities about the relationship between nature and mathematics.

More than a half century passed before heliocentrism was taken (by some) as a legitimate hypothesis about the actual structure of the universe. Interestingly, the two natural philosophers who became famous for their work on the model—Galileo Galilei and Johannes Kepler—found it compelling long before they had any supporting observational evidence. They favored it for aesthetic and mathematical reasons. In Kepler's 1597 correspondence with Galileo, he commented that Galileo was "following the lead of Plato and Pythagoras, our true masters."[22] Indeed, allowing mathematics to lead one's thinking about physical reality was a very Pythagorean-Platonic thing to do, but Galileo and Kepler were also intent on the compilation and analysis of observations that supported the truth of heliocentrism. Fortunately, Kepler had direct access to reams of astronomical records gathered over many years by his late mentor, Tycho Brahe, and he incorporated this data into his mathematical model. Galileo, on the other hand, built his own telescopes and was the first to document supporting evidence (though not definitive proof) of heliocentrism, including the phases of Venus and the moons orbiting Jupiter.

To be sure, Galileo has since enjoyed much more time in the spotlight of history, largely because of his infamous run-in with the Roman Catholic Church. However, it should be noted that Galileo's precommitment to the perfectly circular planetary orbits of the Aristotelian-Ptolemaic model resulted in an incorrect model, even if it did have the Sun at the center. It was Kepler who, through ingenious mathematical work, discovered that by representing the planetary orbits as ellipses rather than circles, the empirical data could be much better reconciled with the heliocentric theory, and the predictive accuracy greatly improved. His work transformed the ancient field of astronomy into a sophisticated theoretical science; his mathematical laws of planetary motion were a giant leap forward in our understanding of celestial mechanics. Both Kepler's and Galileo's discoveries about the physics of planetary and terrestrial motion respectively constituted powerful evidence of the fundamentally mathematical nature of the cosmos and were vital to the groundbreaking physics of Sir Isaac Newton.

As aforementioned, Kepler was thoroughly convinced that God had intentionally ordered the universe in a way that it could be comprehended by mankind. This belief was quite evident in his private letters to fellow scholars and other associates. In a letter dated May 15, 1596, addressed to Baron Sigismund von Herberstein, Kepler said that "God, like a human architect, approached the founding of the world according to order and rule and measured everything in such a manner, that one might think not art took nature for an example but God Himself, in the course of His creation took the art of man as an example."[23] Kepler expressed his conviction that God created the cosmos according to a rational plan and that the mind of God and the mind of man must be, at least in some respects, analogous. Otherwise, the mathematical investigation of nature would be impossible. Kepler had no patience for those who would say that it is presumptuous to imagine that God's mind is anything like man's. He wrote, "Only fools fear that we make man godlike in doing so; for the divine counsels are impenetrable, but not his material creation."[24]

Kepler's perspective on God's natural revelation was shaped by the fact that the world can be described by rational laws accessible to man, a creature specially equipped to glimpse the divine plan of creation. In a letter to his beloved former astronomy professor, Michael Maestlin, Kepler wrote, "God, who founded everything in the world according to the norm of quantity, also has endowed man with a mind which can comprehend these norms. For as the eye for color, the ear for musical sounds, so is the mind of man created for the perception...of quantities."[25] He connected this idea with the Christian doctrine of man in a passage from his work *Conversations with Galileo's Sidereal Messenger*, in which he wrote that geometry "shines in the mind of God" and that a "share of it [mathematical understanding] which has been granted to man is one of the reasons why he is in the image of God."[26]

The Pythagorean-Platonic influence in Kepler's thought is evident, but, unlike the pagan thinkers who came before him, Kepler was in possession of much more dramatic evidence of the deep rationality of nature, and he was convinced that the mathematical plan for creation resided not in some nebulous realm of Forms, but in the transcendent mind of the Maker—whom he identified as the Judeo-Christian God.

Cosmic Resonance in Twentieth-Century Physics and Cosmology

In the early decades of the twentieth century, physics and cosmology enjoyed another leap forward thanks to great scientists such as Max Planck and Albert Einstein. Their work strongly reinforced the convictions held by Kepler and other giants of the scientific revolution: that the material world is fundamentally mathematical and intelligible to man in a way that demands a higher explanation. Rather than undermining Kepler's explanation—the tripartite harmony of divine archetype, material copy, and the image of God in man—growing scientific knowledge served to further support it. Planck, a theist, and Einstein, who rejected the idea of a personal God, both recognized that naturalism falls far short of explaining the resonance between mathematics, nature, and mind.

Max Planck (1858–1947) was a German Nobel Prize-winning theoretical physicist known for his contribution to quantum theory (in fact, he is thought of as the father of the field). Planck held firmly to the belief that science and faith are compatible and even complementary enterprises, and he was fascinated by the seeming congruence between the mathematical structure of the material world and human rationality. He wrote a series of essays that were collected and published posthumously under the title *Scientific Autobiography and Other Papers*, and the first essay, "Scientific Autobiography," opens with these words:

> My original decision to devote myself to science was a direct result of the discovery which has never ceased to fill me with enthusiasm since my early youth—the comprehension of the far from obvious fact that the laws of human reasoning coincide with the laws governing the sequences of the impressions we receive from the world about us; that, therefore, pure reasoning can enable man to gain an insight into the mechanism of the latter.[27]

Like Kepler and others previously mentioned, Planck pondered the uncanny resonance between the rational structure of nature and the mind of man. In the closing essay, "Religion and Natural Science," Planck gave a rather Keplerian expression to the persistent ideas about design in nature and man's ability to discern it. He said that nature is "ruled by definite laws which are independent of the existence of thinking human beings; but these laws, insofar as they can all be comprehended by our senses, can be given a formulation which is adapted for purposeful activity."[28] In other words, the mathematical ordering of nature makes the activities of the human scientist possible. Planck stood amazed by man's scientific aptitude; he marveled that "we, tiny creatures on a tiny planet, are nevertheless capable of knowing though not the essence at least the existence and dimensions of the basic building blocks of the entire great Cosmos!"[29]

Albert Einstein (1879–1955), Planck's colleague and fellow recipient of the Nobel Prize in physics, is best known for his mathematical theories of special and general relativity, but he was also a participant in the public science and theology conversation. Einstein was a secular Jew who rejected organized religion and any conception of a personal higher power, but he refused to be labeled an atheist and was not convinced that pantheism was a correct characterization of his worldview. In any case, it is clear from many of his statements that he perceived some sort of transcendent intelligence in the mathematical structure of the universe and found it astonishing that human beings are equipped to decipher even a small portion of it: "We see the universe marvelously arranged and obeying certain laws but only dimly understand these laws. Our limited minds grasp the mysterious force that moves the constellations."[30] He expressed his "rapturous amazement at the harmony of natural law, which reveals an intelligence of such superiority that, compared with it, all systematic thinking and acting of human beings is an utterly insignificant reflection."[31] This statement shows a strong consonance with Kepler's tripartite harmony—mankind's intellect having a kinship with the divine that makes the order of creation scientifically intelligible.

Indeed, Einstein was awestruck by the inherent mathematical rationality of the cosmos and its accessibility to the human scientist and repeatedly used the word *miracle* when he discussed this. He pointed out that the kind of order exhibited by the universe is *discovered* rather than imposed upon it by the human mind, and that opaque disorder in nature would have been far less surprising:

> [O]ne should expect a chaotic world which cannot be grasped by the mind in any way. One could (yes *one should*) expect the world to be subjected to law only to the extent that we order it through our intelligence. Ordering of this kind would be like the alphabetical

ordering of the words of a language. By contrast, the kind of order created by Newton's theory of gravitation, for instance, is wholly different. Even if the axioms of the theory are proposed by man, the success of such a project presupposes a high degree of ordering of the objective world, and this could not be expected *a priori*. That is the "miracle" which is being constantly reinforced as our knowledge expands.[32]

Einstein mused, "How can it be that mathematics, being after all a product of human thought independent of experience, is so admirably adapted to the objects of reality?"[33] In his famous essay entitled "Physics and Reality," he said this about the universe: "The fact that it is comprehensible is a miracle."[34] Curiously, Einstein refused to consider the arguably theistic implications of this cosmic resonance, and preferred to regard it as an impenetrable mystery; he said, "Oddly enough, we must be satisfied to acknowledge the 'miracle' without there being any legitimate way for us to approach it."[35]

The Ongoing Quest for a Naturalistic Explanation

In response to what Einstein saw as a hopeless enigma, some contemporary thinkers have sought a naturalistic explanation for the mathematical cosmos and its intellectual accessibility. Physicist and philosopher of science Roger Penrose (a non-theist) is convinced that (1) some degree of mathematical Platonism must be the case in light of the objectivity of many mathematical truths, and (2) the abstract realm of mathematics must be related to the material world in some manner, since "operations of the physical world are now known to be in accord with elegant mathematical theory to an enormous precision."[36] He recognizes what he calls an "extraordinary concurrence" between the mechanics of nature and sophisticated mathematical theory, and agrees with Einstein that this is not simply a case of manmade descriptions: "It makes no sense to me," he argues, "that this concurrence is merely the result of our trying to fit the observational facts into some organizational scheme that we can comprehend; the concurrence between Nature and sophisticated beautiful mathematics is something that is 'out there' and has been so since times far earlier than the dawn of humanity."[37]

Penrose suggests a triangular relationship in which matter somehow embodies mathematics, mind somehow emerges from matter, and mathematics is somehow related to mind.[38] How else are we to (naturalistically—that is, apart from any theistic explanation) make sense of the mathematical structure of nature, conscious material brains that can grasp it, and the objectivity of mathematics itself (the three-way cosmic resonance)? Penrose schematically situates the three different "worlds" of mathematics, mind, and matter at the points of a triangle, and the adjacent sides of the triangle represent what he refers to as the "deeply mysterious connections" between these three points.[39] Yet he is aware of the possibility that the ultimate explanation lies beyond the scope of modern physics. Particularly where the human mind is concerned, he submits that we may "have to look even farther afield, to an understanding that lies essentially beyond any kind of science whatever, as could be the implication of an essentially religious perspective on these issues."[40]

Physicist and cosmologist Max Tegmark has offered a highly speculative explanation for the mathematics-nature-mind resonance. In a 2008 paper entitled "The Mathematical Universe," he endorsed a radical version of Platonism in which the *universe itself* is a mathematical object of which humans are simply self-aware parts. He explains:

> After Galileo promulgated the mathematical universe idea, additional mathematical regularities beyond his wildest dreams were uncovered, ranging from the motions of planets to the properties of atoms...[Then] the standard model of particle physics revealed new "unreasonable" mathematical order in the microcosm of elementary particles and in the macrocosm of the early universe. I know of no other compelling explanation for this trend than that the physical world really is completely mathematical.[41]

In other words, the rationality of nature is intelligible to human beings because all of reality, including the mental, is one colossal mathematical entity.

Tegmark's Mathematical Universe Hypothesis (MUH), in which mathematical and physical existence are equivalent, suffers from several problems. First, the abstract truths of mathematics are effectually inert, with no inherent power to produce physical manifestation. Thus, the precision with which mathematics maps onto the material world remains unexplained. Second, the MUH does nothing to answer the question of how a mathematical object could give rise to conscious, self-aware minds that can, in turn, analyze the world mathematically. Third, in any version of naturalistic Platonism, such as that required by the MUH, mathematical truths or objects themselves are left with no ontological grounding—they simply *are*, end of story. This separation of mathematics from an originating mind seems unreasonable; as philosopher Alvin Plantinga explains:

> Platonism with respect to these objects is the position that they do exist...in such a way as to be independent of mind; even if there were no minds at all, they would still exist. But there have been very few real Platonists, perhaps none besides Plato and Frege, if indeed Plato and Frege were real Platonists (and even Frege, that alleged arch-Platonist, referred to propositions as *gedanken*, thoughts). It is therefore extremely tempting to think of abstract objects as ontologically dependent upon mental or intellectual activity in such a way that either they just are thoughts, or else at any rate couldn't exist if not thought of.[42]

In other words, the truths of mathematics have an essentially mental quality to them. Plantinga also argues that if an idea is necessarily true, as a mathematical truth seems to be, then it *exists* necessarily, thus eternally.[43] Perhaps the only solution, he suggests, is that mathematical truths are thoughts in the divine mind, a view sometimes referred to as divine conceptualism.[44] A major advantage of situating mathematical truths in the mind of the Creator is how well it explains the applicability of mathematics in the natural sciences and mankind's corresponding rationality. If mathematics, the material realm, and the human mind have the same rational source, existing in Kepler's tripartite harmony, the mystery of their interconnectedness dissolves.

Mathematics, Human Rationality, and the Shortcomings of Naturalism

Some non-theists may, nevertheless, be content to regard objective mathematical truths and their applicability to nature as brute facts, as happy cosmic accidents that need no explanation. However, when it comes to human aptitude for higher mathematics, neurobiology enters the picture, and this necessarily brings up the issue of biological evolution. From a naturalistic perspective, the human brain and all of its capacities are the result of nonteleological processes—natural selection acting upon random genetic variation. This view is confronted with at least two problems where our advanced mathematical aptitude is concerned.

First, the ability to perform the highly complex mathematical operations involved in sciences such as quantum theory and astrophysics is far beyond what could be conceivably required for our ancestors' survival and reproduction. Agnostic physicist Paul Davies has articulated this difficulty well:

> One of the oddities of human intelligence is that its level of advancement seems like a case of overkill. While a modicum of intelligence does have a good survival value, it is far from clear how such qualities as the ability to do advanced mathematics...ever evolved by natural selection. These higher intellectual functions are a world away from survival "in the jungle." Many of them were manifested explicitly only recently, long after man had become the dominant mammal and had secured a stable ecological niche.[45]

Plantinga, too, has noted the difficulty in attributing mathematical abilities to survival of the fittest:

> Current physics with its ubiquitous partial differential equations (not to mention relativity theory with its tensors, quantum mechanics with its non-Abelian group theory, and current set theory with its daunting complexities) involves mathematics of great depth, requiring cognitive powers going enormously beyond what is required for survival and reproduction. Indeed, it is only the occasional assistant professor of mathematics or logic who needs to be able to prove Godel's first incompleteness theorem in order to survive and reproduce.[46]

Assuming that such cognitive capabilities are simply evolutionary "spandrels"—side effects that had no adaptive use at the time they were genetically acquired as neutral accompaniments to genuinely adaptive mental powers—is implausible at best, argues Plantinga.[47] Any naturalistic explanation along this vein is essentially (and permanently) speculative; there is no evidence available (or forthcoming) that could confirm such an account.

Second, the mental deliberation required for even intermediate mathematical operations is directly dependent upon free, goal-directed mental agency. But if the mind is nothing more than the material brain or is at least wholly dependent upon brain states, there is no such thing as free mental agency. Autonomous brain chemicals are in the driver's seat. Yet when presented with a string of mathematical facts from which we set out to draw correct conclusions, we must be able to make free choices along the pathway of reasoning. This requires an agent with the genuine free will that allows him or her to consciously deliberate and direct the reasoning process according to immaterial mathematical content and the external rules of mathematical logic. In other words, authentic rationality exists only if we are able to freely guide our thoughts through what we know are the correct steps of reasoning from one point to another.

Objections to naturalistic theories aren't coming from theists alone. Atheist philosopher Thomas Nagel is a prime example of an atheist thinker who admits the deficiencies of nonteleological explanations for the resonance between the rational structure of nature and the human mind. In his 2012 book *Mind and Cosmos: Why the Neo-Darwinian Conception of Nature Is Almost Certainly False*, Nagel argued, "The intelligibility of the world is no accident. Mind, in this view, is doubly related to the natural order. Nature is such as to give rise to conscious beings with minds; and it is such as to be comprehensible to such beings."[48] Nagel is convinced that the naturalistic, reductive approach to explaining reality is gravely insufficient: "There are things that science as presently conceived does not help us to understand, and which we can see, from the internal features of physical science, that it is not going to explain."[49]

Even so, Nagel rejects theistic explanations in favor of a so-called "natural teleology," some sort of inscrutable cosmic predisposition for the evolution of higher mental faculties that correspond to the mathematical order in nature. Ultimately, he believes that an understanding of why the cosmos is intelligible will involve "a much more radical departure from the familiar forms of naturalistic explanation" if it turns out to even be within the reach of human rationality.[50] In his earlier work *The Last Word*, where he explored many of the same ideas, Nagel admits that his rejection of theistic explanations of the world are his *a priori* philosophy: "I don't want there to be a God; I don't want the universe to be like that."[51]

Paul Davies has also remarked that "there is no logical reason why nature should have a mathematical subtext in the first place, and even if it does, there is no obvious reason why humans should be capable of comprehending it."[52] Davies takes a somewhat similar tack to Nagel's by speculating that there is some as-yet-to-be-discovered, or even undiscoverable, natural principle behind the cosmos:

> Somehow, the universe has engineered, not just its own awareness, but also its own *comprehension*. Mindless, blundering atoms have conspired to make not just life, not just mind, but *understanding*. The evolving cosmos has spawned beings who are able not merely to watch the show, but to unravel the plot.[53]

Davies reaches no final conclusion other than to deem current naturalistic explanations as well as theistic ones "either ridiculous or hopelessly inadequate."[54] Yet his reasons for rejecting theism seem to be, like Nagel's, based exclusively on philosophical and theological preferences.

The Power and Coherence of Kepler's Tripartite Harmony

In naturalistic proposals, we are left without an ultimate explanation for the existence of objective mathematical truths and the inherent rationality and intelligibility of the material cosmos. By contrast, Kepler's tripartite harmony, the view that the material world was created based upon a rational archetype in the divine mind and that man was designed to comprehend it to some extent, has a long and respectable intellectual pedigree in the Western tradition. Scientific progress over the past three centuries has shown the cosmos to be mathematically precise to a degree that Kepler and the other giants of the scientific revolution could never have imagined. Yet naturalism has still come to dominate thinking in many scientific circles. Why is this so? Science does not require it, and it is not an intellectually compelling explanation. In fact, naturalism faces major obstacles on several points, while the theistic view reveals an intended, all-encompassing, and elegant coherence in observed reality.

The existence of an eternal Mind behind all things is a more intellectually satisfying account for the mathematics-matter-mind resonance than simply saying there is no ultimate reason for the incredible reality in which we find ourselves. The mystery of mankind's aptitude for elucidating the mathematical orderliness of nature is solved if man is the free-willed, image-bearing creation of the same source. As Oxford mathematician John Lennox has succinctly put it, "It is…not surprising when the mathematical theories spun by human minds created in the image of God's Mind, find ready application in a universe whose architect was that same creative Mind."[55]

CHAPTER 3

THE STONES CRY GLORY

BR. GUY CONSOLMAGNO SJ

There's this fun experiment I do in my meteorite lab…

I should explain. I study meteorites, those rocks that fall from the sky and give us free samples of the asteroids, and sometimes the Moon or Mars. Once they fall to Earth, some of them are discovered by astute observers; and after those specimens are collected, some of them wind up in museums or university collections, where people like me, in principle, can study them. Of course curators in those places jealously guard the meteorites from anyone else touching them, especially those nasty scientists who want to do terrible experiments on them. But when I arrived at the Vatican Observatory 25 years ago, there was no curator for its collection of meteorite samples. So I stepped into the role and promptly gave myself permission to experiment away.

Our collection was originally assembled in the nineteenth century by a wealthy French amateur scientist, the Marquis de Mauroy. It's a collector's collection, which means it has a little bit of every kind of meteorite. One thing you can do with a collection like this is do a survey across all the different meteorite classes and measure various properties. In my case, I decided to examine the physical properties of these meteorites: their density, porosity, magnetic and thermal characteristics.

One of the properties we measure is a meteorite's heat capacity, which is (as you might guess from the term) the capacity of the rock to hold heat. How much heat does it take to raise the temperature of one gram of a specific rock by one degree—or, if you prefer, how much heat does the rock give off when it drops one degree in temperature?

How do you measure that? There are million-dollar machines that take a tiny slice of sample material and run it up and down the temperature scale, from near absolute zero to room temperature, in a pure vacuum. It takes a while to make these measurements, so you usually let the machine run overnight, and then you spend another night taking calibration data. It's very precise, but it's time consuming. A Jesuit colleague of mine at Boston College, Fr. Cy Opeil SJ, has one of these gizmos, and they're tricky to calibrate and run. Half of the time, the machine needs fixing. But when it does its job, you get truly gorgeous data.

Unfortunately my friend is in Boston, and I'm in Rome. I can't afford to purchase one of those devices for myself. I don't have a million dollars or a full-time technician at the Vatican. Nor do I have enough nights to go through our entire collection rock by rock.

For that matter, measuring just a tiny slice of a meteorite can be misleading. Meteorites are notorious for being wild conglomerations of different kinds of rock stuck together; that's what happens when different kinds of asteroids run into each other in space. That means a slice won't represent the properties of the entire rock. Beyond that, even though I am a scientist who would love to do terrible experiments on these rocks, I am also enough of a curator that I hate the thought of cutting them up.

I was talking about this with a French colleague of mine, Pierre Rochette, when an offhand comment from him led to the idea for the following experiment:

First, take a dewar—an insulated bottle—and fill it with liquid nitrogen. (Industrial-strength refrigerators can make air so cold that the oxygen and nitrogen gases in the air condense into little droplets of liquid. How cold is this stuff? On the Fahrenheit scale, it's more than 300 degrees below zero. We don't use the oxygen, just the nitrogen—there's more of it, and it is less corrosive.)

Next, put the dewar and the liquid nitrogen on a scale, hook the scale up to a computer, and measure, second by second, how the total weight slowly drops as the nitrogen slowly warms up and boils away.

Then drop in the rock sample. At first the weight on the scale will jump up by the weight of the sample. But because the rock is at room temperature, it will immediately heat up the liquid nitrogen so that it starts boiling away like mad—much faster than when the dewar was sitting untouched. The weight of the system plummets as the nitrogen boils off—until finally the rock has been cooled all the way down to liquid nitrogen temperature. Then the boiling stops, and the weight loss just goes back to the same slow decrease that you had before you dropped in the rock.

Line up the *before* trend with the *after* trend, account for the weight of the rock, and the difference in the weights before and after you dropped in the rock is the number of grams of liquid nitrogen that was boiled away due to the rock cooling down. You can look up how much heat it takes to boil off one gram of liquid nitrogen, multiply that by the number of grams of nitrogen that were lost, and that will tell you how much heat was absorbed from the rock.

As it so happens, my training was as a theorist, writing computer models and the like. I never actually spent time in a lab when I was a student. So I've never learned exactly how one is to obtain a dewar. In this case, I went to a local discount store and bought a stainless steel coffee thermos. Likewise, where do you get liquid nitrogen? It happens that our lab at the Vatican is located in the Pope's summer gardens, and the gardens include a working dairy farm, and… have you ever lived on a dairy farm? Cows must have calves in order to give milk. In the old days, farmers would keep a bull around—no jokes about papal bulls, please—but now, like most dairy farms, the dairy farm in the papal gardens keeps bull semen frozen in liquid nitrogen. They have a big tank of the stuff, and we can easily go next door to borrow a cup when we need to brew up a measurement.

In reality, it's not as easy as it sounds. It turns out that all sorts of unexpected little effects happen when you attempt to transport and use liquid nitrogen. For instance, if the cold nitrogen is exposed to the air in the lab, then a thin layer of ice forms on its surface because it's freezing the humidity out of the air. It's a small effect, but the extra weight of the ice is enough to mess up our readings. So we place a little plastic canister over the dewar; it fills up with the nitrogen boiling out of the dewar, driving away the water-rich air. I bought one in a kitchen shop in Italy; it's designed to hold uncooked spaghetti.

There's also the fear that dropping a rock into liquid nitrogen won't be good for the rock. You may have seen demonstrations in which a flower or a banana is placed into liquid nitrogen and then after it freezes, you can pull it out and shatter it. Folks in the meteorite world have all heard that the way to break up one of the hardest materials we deal with, meteorites that are chunks of iron-nickel, is to dunk them in liquid nitrogen. Doesn't my experiment shatter my meteorites? As it turns out, if you want to shatter an iron meteorite, you do dunk it in liquid nitrogen. Then you have to give it a good whack with a sledgehammer. We just have to be careful to keep our sledgehammers out of sight when we do these experiments so as not to give anyone ideas.

Measuring meteorite heat capacity in our lab in Castel Gandolfo. (personal photo)

Over the past several years, my colleague Br. Bob Macke SJ and I have measured hundreds of meteorite samples this way, and we've gotten some interesting results that could fill up this chapter. But what I really want to discuss here is something bigger.

Why do we do these experiments?

Granted, other scientists use our numbers when they make models to explain how asteroids heat up. But why do we—or they—care about asteroids?

It's possible that our numbers may someday help others plan how to mine an asteroid for its mineral wealth, or to deflect it from a path that threatens to destroy all life on Earth. And, seriously, our numbers would be useful for those purposes.

But that's not what gets me up in the morning to spend another day dropping rocks into liquid nitrogen. There's no sense of urgency that says, "Hurry, hurry! If you don't get these measurements done by the end of next Thursday, then five hundred years from now the human race won't know how to deflect an oncoming asteroid and we will all be toast!"

Why do we do it?

There are two parts to that question, both important. What actually motivates me to get up in the morning and go to the lab, and why does society support us to do the science?

To do science requires money, time, and talent. All three of those commodities are precious and are as carefully curated as my meteorites. Science only happens when someone is convinced that the science itself is worth the cost. That's something you can't take for granted. Just talk to congressional funding committees to see what I mean.

Ultimately, the scientific questions that get answered are the ones that someone (or a committee) has decided are worth answering. The way this is done now is a lot of astronomers get together every ten years, take a survey of where they believe their resources should go, and prepare a white paper that guides NASA—and Congress, with luck.

The way it used to be done was astronomers would fight over whose university had the most powerful Congress-critter who could force the passage of an earmark—a request for money—that could be allocated to some project or other.

Remember that probe to Pluto that discovered some pretty heart-shaped thingies on its surface a few years back? That was funded by a billion-dollar earmark pushed through Congress by a senator from Maryland, and the probe was run out of Johns Hopkins University in Baltimore. (No surprise; the base of operations for the Hubble Space Telescope is in Baltimore too.) It was such an outrageous power play that our field finally adopted the once-a-decade survey to stop it from happening again.

The Pluto probe was a long shot. Most of us didn't expect that it would discover very much. Fortunately, it got lucky. On the other hand, the fact that the researchers and developers of this probe got the money means that some other probe to some other destination didn't get funded and never flew. And we don't know what didn't get discovered. Instead of pretty heart-shaped thingies, maybe we would have found life in the oceans of Europa.

But the cost of such ventures is more than just paying for the equipment and the salaries of everyone involved. Every person who is busy doing basic research into planetary astronomy is not busy doing something else that the world might think is more useful or important. Every person who teaches astronomy at a university could be perhaps better employed teaching more practical topics in a business school. Every student who is spending time learning about planets could have stayed back on the farm, raising more crops. For that matter, every drop of liquid nitrogen used in my lab is a drop no longer available to help breed better calves.

Again, one can argue—with validity—that basic research into the sciences, like my research into meteorites and their parent asteroids, might at some future date bring unexpected economic benefits to humankind. A running joke in the field of mathematics is that theoretical mathematicians keep trying to invent gloriously useless mathematics, only to find out a generation later that the useless is actually quite useful to some scientist or engineer. (Non-Euclidean geometries and group theory are two examples that come to mind.) But I think that argument misses a bigger and more important difference.

There is a temptation to divide human experience into that which is useful versus that which is useless—say, comparing growing food versus writing poetry. That parallels the temptation to divide our human experience into separate categories, such as emotions versus logic, like those wonderful Star Trek characters Kirk and Spock. But it's a false division. Real people are not just Kirk or just Spock. Heck, even Kirk and Spock were not entirely Kirk or Spock. No experience is purely utilitarian or completely useless.

I would say this sort of false dichotomy is the same as the temptation to divide our lives into airtight compartments of faith versus science. As a scientist at the Vatican, I get asked about science and religion all the time. And it was one such conversation that gave me an interesting insight into the topic at hand—why we do science. Oddly enough, that conversation was with Captain Kirk.

How I wound up talking to William Shatner, the actor who played Captain Kirk in the original *Star Trek* series…well, it's a long story—too long to go into here. But when I described myself as a Jesuit scientist, he was flabbergasted. "Wait a minute, wait a minute!" he said. And as we talked, it suddenly became clear to me what was so obvious to him but that I had never grasped. He saw religion and science as two separate and competing sets of truths. Two separate books of facts. And what should happen if the facts in one book contradicted the facts in the other?

Of course. If you think of science as a big book of facts, then you could imagine that kind of conflict. But I know that science is not a big book of facts.

Consider this: The orbits of the planets are facts. Now, you can describe them by referring to Ptolemy's epicycles, or circles within circles encircling Earth. Or you can describe them as Kepler did—elliptical orbits around the Sun. Ptolemy's epicycles are more precise. With an infinite number of circles you can match perfectly the orbits of any body, whereas Kepler's ellipses are only approximately true because they don't account for how one planet pulls on the orbit of another.

But only Kepler's ellipses can help put us on the path to Newton's discovery of the law of gravity.

Science is not the facts of the orbits; it is what you do with those facts. It is the search for insights that come from facts. And it is also being open to the realization that Newton's insights, Newton's laws, are not the last word. Not even Einstein's theory of general relativity, the modern replacement for Newton, is the last word. I suspect that in the year 3000, science will look very different from what we're teaching today.

Incidentally, our faith is not based on rigid certainties either. I shared with William Shatner the phrase that Anne Lamott famously used to describe faith: "The opposite of faith is not doubt, but certainty." (Anne was quoting a famous theologian, Paul Tillich, who used a lot more words to make the same point.) That was completely the opposite of what Shatner thought faith was about. He had heard the phrase *blind faith* and thought that faith meant accepting something as certain without confirming it, or worse, closing your eyes to the facts and proceeding on emotion. But that's not faith at all.

Blind faith is not walking with a blindfold or blinding ourselves to truth. It's proceeding after we've done everything we can to see, yet still can't see everything. Because even when we are still somewhat blind, when we don't have total and complete knowledge of the truth, we still have to proceed.

But we never have all the facts. And so faith is how we deal with the fact that we have to keep moving forward anyway—that is, make choices about where we'll go to school, what career we'll pursue, where we'll live, whom we'll marry.

Or what science we'll do.

All of life is about making crucial decisions on the basis of varying amounts of inadequate information. It's a leap of faith to choose a field of research, to start a new project, to choose to put some experiments on your spacecraft and not others.

The decisions that change our lives are made not only on the basis of inadequate and often incorrect information; sometimes the most important decisions are made by ignorant, stubborn, and inexperienced teenagers. We were all once-goofy teens who made decisions that determined the shape of our immediate and even distant future.

Which returns us to the question: Why does anyone become something as useless as a professional meteoriticist?

Why did I decide to study planetary sciences? I started as a history major at Boston College. My best friend from high school was up the road at the Massachusetts Institute of Technology (MIT), and I used to hang out there with him every weekend. They had weekend movies, and you could explore basement tunnels that connected the buildings, and in the student center was the world's largest library of science fiction. It was truly the home of nerds and geeks—people like me. I wanted to be a fellow nerd; why not go to a nerd school?

When I applied to transfer, MIT wanted me to declare a major. I figured I was too incompetent to build things like an engineer, and I was afraid of trying to hold my own against physics majors who had been studying the stuff all through high school. I had spent my high school years doing Latin and Greek. When I discovered MIT had an Earth and Planetary Sciences department, I thought, *Planets! That's where people have adventures!*

MIT accepted me. And when I got there, I discovered to my horror that I was joining the *geology* department. Geology? What could be more boring than studying rocks?

Still, I was ecstatically happy just to be there, happy in a way I didn't think could ever be possible. Being a nerd was what I was good at, and more important, this was where I belonged—even if it meant staring at a bunch of rocks.

And then I took a course on meteorites. Rocks that fall from the sky. Pieces of outer space that you can actually hold in your hands! I was hooked. In order to get closer to these wonderful bits of science fiction, I threw myself into understanding the physics and chemistry of how rocks were formed.

Ultimately, I fell in love with this line of study. I had finally found my passion. It wasn't the science fiction; it was the science. It wasn't the tunnels; it was the exploration. It wasn't the movies; it was the imagination.

More to the point, it wasn't just the work. It was being part of a community of fellow nerds. I would venture to say that for every Harry Potter fan who wishes he or she could do magic, there are a dozen who would be happy just to live at Hogwarts. One of the longings I had as I read *Lord of the Rings* was to be a part of a fellowship. Science is sharing stories with a community, stories about what we've learned of the natural world.

The Allende meteorite, which fell in northern Mexico in 1969. Some of the white bits have been known to contain grains of dust from other stellar systems. (personal photo)

This meteorite, which fell near Nakhla, Egypt, in 1911, has been identified chemically as coming from the crust of Mars. (personal photo)

To share stories, you have to have a community. And without a community interested in hearing your story, you won't have anyone to talk with. Eventually, if no one wants to listen to your stories about your adventures in the lab, you'll stop having those adventures. If you don't have the support of a community, it isn't going to happen. Science can't happen apart from such support. Furthermore, without a community, the things you share can't be passed on to the next generation. And that's why it makes a difference what your fellow participants think about the things you choose to do.

Society also means our community of fellow scientists. It turns out that there is a small but dedicated group of scientists the world round who specialize in the study of meteorites; we call ourselves the Meteoritical Society. And the work we do in this field is strongly influenced by what the other members of our field will support. That doesn't just mean whether or not we'll get grant money to do a particular bit of research. It also means whether we'll get an audience to listen to us when we present our work at the annual Meteoritical Society meeting.

I remember the "MetSoc" meeting in Berlin in 1996, when I presented for the first time the data I was beginning to take on the physical properties of meteorites. One of the grand old men of the field came up to me and said, "Guy, why are you measuring meteorite densities? Nobody does that." He was right. It was a new field. It took courage—or foolishness—to do something where I couldn't be sure whether there was an audience for my results.

In fact, the first audience was me alone. I knew from my computer modeling experience that such models work best when you can input real data, not just guesses, for how the material inside a body holds mass or heat. And because the Specola Vaticana was willing to support me and my modest equipment needs, I did not have to worry about getting a grant to fund my work (or my salary). I didn't even have to worry about having a successful outcome within six years in order to have something to show at a tenure review and thus keep my job, or get a better position at some other institution. This freedom allowed me to concentrate my efforts on a branch of science that I found personally appealing without a host of other worries.

As it happened, two completely independent developments in asteroid science during the 1990s made our data quite significant. At that time, spacecraft missions were beginning to be targeted toward asteroids and comets (including missions like the spacecraft Galileo, which was directed to fly past an asteroid en route to its final destination, Jupiter). Meanwhile, improved adaptive optics on Earth-based telescopes led to the discovery of a number of asteroids with small Moons. Why did that matter? Measuring how our asteroids perturbed the orbits of spacecraft or small moonlets gave us, for the first time, an accurate measure of an asteroid's mass; meanwhile, these improved images also told us the asteroids' sizes and shapes. Mass divided by volume is density. For the first time, we were given accurate measurements for asteroid densities.

What happens when you compare the densities of asteroids to the densities of the meteorites whose spectra match the asteroids? If the asteroids and meteorites have the same spectral colors, they should be related; those asteroids were presumably the places where those meteorites had resided before they were chipped off the asteroid's surface and sent on an orbit toward Earth. But we found out that the meteorites were roughly twice as dense as their parent bodies!

This tells us that the asteroids we see in space are not solid rocks, but loose piles of rubble. In other words, the asteroids in the asteroid belt today are made of stuff that has been constantly shattered and then fallen back together. That gives us a whole new window into the processes going on in that part of the solar system.

At the same time, theorists had been working on idea of how the heating of an asteroid's surface can cause it to drift about in its orbit (and even change how fast it spins), an important step toward understanding why these asteroids would gradually move into crossing orbits—where they can run into each other and produce that rubble (or hit Earth). Our heat capacity measurements are essential to modeling just how quickly this effect can move the asteroids about.

So these days, our physical properties data are used all the time. Yet back when I started playing with my meteorites, I had no idea how the data would be used. In fact, I couldn't have known what the data would mean until I had them in hand. I am still coming up with new ideas that my data can test.

It's funny—in grade school, we were taught that a scientist invents an experiment to test a theory. My experience has been the opposite. I make the experiments on a completely intuitive hunch—in some cases, simply because it seems like a fun thing to do. It's only after I see the results do the possible theories (and tests) come to mind.

That's why we can't separate out "useful" from "useless" activities. We can't know ahead of time what results are going to be useful or not. After all, Kepler had no idea that his ellipses would turn out to be so important; he was long dead by the time Newton used them to demonstrate the law of gravity.

If we did not have human motivations to do the work we do, we wouldn't do the work. If we didn't have human, nonrational ideas about what to do, we wouldn't know where to begin in order to make progress. And if we didn't believe in a universe whose meaning goes beyond economic measures of value, we wouldn't know how to value (much less evaluate) the work. And that means that we would not be fully alive.

Ignatian spirituality, which forms the spiritual atmosphere of my religious order, the Society of Jesus, emphasizes engagement with the world and "finding God in all things." This aligns exactly with the work of a scientist. But even more than that, it provides a motivation for doing science independent of a yearning for glory or a desire for wealth or power.

To be sure, there is not much wealth, power, or glory to be found in meteoritics! But I have encountered fellow scientists who seem to be more interested in showing up their perceived rivals than in coming closer to the truth. Or, more commonly, those who have forgotten why they went into science in the first place and now do the work only because it is the one job they are qualified for.

I speak from experience. I did not join the Jesuits until I was nearly 40 years old. At that time, I was already established as an astronomer. During my years before I entered the Society of Jesus, I often found myself drifting toward doing my job only because it was necessary to.

> If you believe that God created the cosmos...then science becomes an act of growing closer to the Creator.

Now that I am a Jesuit (and with the very practical advantage that I don't have to worry about supporting a family), I find that my attitude toward my work has changed completely. I do it out of joy—both the joy of discovery as well as the simple joy of becoming more intimate with this physical universe. If you believe that God created the cosmos, and if you believe that God so loved the world that he sent his Son to become a part of it, then science becomes an act of growing closer to the Creator. In that way, it becomes an act of prayer.

And what is prayer? I end with one final story from the days when I was a child spending summers on the shores of Lake Huron. (The Michigan shoreline and lake bottom were covered with rocks; I should have known they would figure into my future.) I recall a rainy Sunday afternoon when I couldn't go out and play on the rocks. Instead, my mom pulled out a deck of cards and dealt a hand of Rummy, a game even I could play at the age of ten. But then I had one of those insights that come at odd times when you're a child. Why was my mom playing cards with me? She was a grown-up, she could win far more easily than I could. What was she getting out of the game?

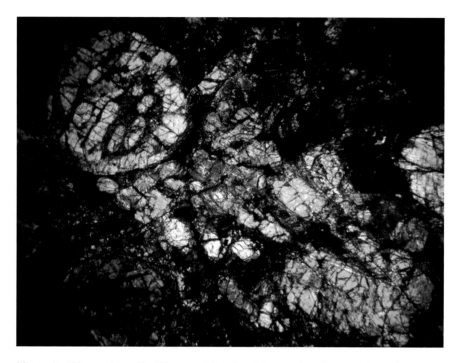

Meteorite thin sections, like this one of the Knyahinya meteorite, are slices about one-hundredth of a millimeter thin, which allows the individual grains to be examined by a microscope illuminated by light that passes through the slice. Often, as here, the thin slice is placed between two crossed polarizing filters; the colors that pass through both polarizers indicate the chemical composition of the different crystals. This image represents a magnified area only a few millimeters wide. (personal photo)

It was her way of spending time with me. It was her way of showing that she loved me—something that can be hard to tell a ten-year-old boy.

When I am in the lab now, I feel that I am playing a wonderful game with the universe, puzzling out its hidden secrets. And the one sitting opposite of me at the table, setting out the puzzles pieces for me, is the Creator. This is his way of talking to me, of telling me how much he loves me. Every jolt of joy I get when I suddenly understand something is a mirror of the Joy who surprises us in prayer.

In Luke's Gospel, Jesus's disciples cried out in praise, "Blessed is the King who comes in the name of the Lord! Peace in heaven and glory in the highest!" (Luke 19:38 ESV). When the Pharisees asked Jesus to rebuke his disciples for their adoration, Jesus replied, "I tell you, if these were silent, the very stones would cry out" (verse 40 ESV). My meteorites are indeed crying out "Glory!" and beckoning our silent planet to awaken and sing to the Lord once more.

I do experiments in my lab just because I love doing the work. I mean, meteorites! And liquid nitrogen! What's not to love?

I know now that the love I experience is derived ultimately from the Creator of the rocks I experiment with, who is also the Father of Love.

Or, to put it another way: I have this fun experiment that I get to do in my lab…

CHAPTER 4

ESCHATOLOGY OF HABITABLE ZONES

GUILLERMO GONZALEZ

The Lord sure makes some beautiful worlds.

THE FORBIDDEN PLANET (MOVIE, 1956)

We are truly living in a golden age of scientific discovery. It is easy for me to choose the most important discovery made during my career: planets orbiting other stars (exoplanets). I can still remember that day in October 1995 when I heard the announcement on BBC radio of the discovery of a planet orbiting the naked-eye star 51 Pegasi (51 Peg). I was visiting collaborators in Bangalore, India. I had timed my trip such that I could also join a scientific expedition from the Indian Institute of Astrophysics to observe the total solar eclipse that would take place on October 24.

On Exoplanets and Habitable Zones

Since then, thousands more such planets have been discovered. Their variety seems almost as great as their number. Already with 51 Peg it was clear that exoplanetary systems are not just carbon copies of our solar system, as astronomers had initially expected. Its planet completes an orbit every 4.2 days. Termed a "hot Jupiter," it is similar in mass to Jupiter, yet it is much hotter. There is nothing like it in our solar system. Mercury, the closest planet to the Sun, takes a leisurely 88 days to complete one orbit.

Within a few years, surveys of nearby stars revealed many planets with somewhat larger, less circular orbits. Again, these are unlike the orbits of the planets in our solar system, which tend to have nearly circular orbits. Discoveries with NASA's Kepler space telescope have shown that planets in our region of the Milky Way Galaxy are common. As of summer 2018, there were nearly 4,000 confirmed exoplanets.[1] About 30% of nearby Sun-like stars have at least one planet at least as large as Earth with an orbital period of less than 400 days.[2]

We are living in the "age of astronomical surveys." The ongoing Gaia space observatory mission is expected to yield about 20,000 giant planet discoveries by the time its nominal five-year mission is completed in 2019.[3] The Transiting Exoplanet Survey Satellite (launched in April 2018) is expected to discover more than 20,000 planets.[4]

The three basic types of planets in our solar system are gas giants like Jupiter and Saturn, ice giants like Neptune and Uranus, and terrestrial planets like Earth and Venus. All three types are also found among exoplanets, but there is also a fourth type, super-Earths. Super-Earth planets are larger than Earth and can resemble terrestrial or gas giant planets.

Every few months a science writer breathlessly reports on the discovery of yet another "Earth-like" planet. This is misleading. What he really means is merely that a planet is "Earth-size." To state that a planet is Earth-like is to imply that you can, say, grow tomatoes and raise bunnies there. The Earth-like bar is a rather high one, though, and it is not at all clear that we have yet discovered even one truly Earth-like planet. To understand why this is so, we need to consider some background information.

When it comes to supposedly Earth-like planets, more accurately, astrobiologists want to know if there are any exoplanets that are habitable. A habitable planet is one that, while not necessarily inhabited, at least possesses all the requirements for life. Mars is the most Earth-like planet we know of. It is not a habitable planet, even though it resides within a habitable planetary system and was likely inoculated by Earth life early on.[5] So what exactly makes a planet habitable?

If we are talking about life based on the periodic table of the elements (seems like a good choice), then our options would appear to be rather limited. Carbon-based chemistry in a liquid water medium really does seem to be a nonnegotiable starting point.[6] A bunch of other elements in the right relative abundances and chemical forms are also needed, as well as a dynamic environment with stabilizing feedbacks to cycle them in the right ways. A fine balance between dynamism and stability is required on multiple scales.

While some astrobiologists would be satisfied to learn whether rudimentary single-celled life exists on other planets, most are after the big prize—complex and even intelligent life. Still, finding evidence of past or present life of any sort on another planet would show, once and for all, that getting life from nonlife is not so difficult and can happen naturally, right? Not so fast. The simplest explanation would seem to be that whatever was the cause of life on Earth would also be responsible for life on other worlds. The best science today does not support a natural origin for life on Earth.[7]

Astrobiologists employ a unifying concept called the *circumstellar habitable zone* (CHZ). In its most basic form, the CHZ tells us where around a star a planet needs to be to maintain liquid water on its surface for a geologically significant period. Thus, the CHZ restricts the range of distances a planet must reside from its host star to be considered habitable. The CHZ gives us a necessary but insufficient condition for habitability. For example, the CHZ by itself doesn't tell us whether the planet has any water; this must be assumed, determined from planet formation simulations, or observed. Early treatments of the CHZ concept simply took the present Earth and moved it closer to or farther from the Sun.

Motivated in part by a desire to explore the habitability of known exoplanetary systems, astrobiologists are beginning to offer a more complete treatment of the CHZ, taking into account many other factors. These include the mass and the variations in the energy output of the host star, the planet's rotational and orbital properties, and details of the system's formative stages and long-term dynamical stability.[8] Taken together, these many factors greatly reduce the probability of a given planet's habitability. For this reason, they are often called "Rare Earth" factors, after the eponymous book.[9]

Astrobiologists have learned that the properties of exoplanet systems span a wide range. Some orbit short-lived stars more massive than the Sun as well as small but temperamental long-lived red dwarfs.[10] Some reside less than a tenth of the Earth-Sun distance from their host stars, while others have been found at hundreds of times the Earth-Sun distance. Most planets belong to single stars, but some are members of binary systems. A few have even been found in star clusters.

The presence of an Earth-size planet in the CHZ of the nearest star to the Sun, Proxima Centauri, has inspired some astronomers to propose sending an interstellar probe there.[11] Estimated travel times are less than a century. However, the star's frequent and intense flares have dampened enthusiasm for finding life there.[12]

Life on Earth does not just depend on the goings-on within the solar system. Surprisingly, it also depends on what happens (and has happened) in the broader universe. Nearby passing stars and interstellar clouds can perturb the orbits of the Oort cloud comets, threatening the planets with comet showers. The Oort cloud is a vast reservoir of some trillion icy bodies surrounding the Sun that accounts for the observed long-period comets. Nearby supernovae and gamma ray bursts pose dangers from their intense radiation. These threats depend on our location within the Milky Way Galaxy; the farther we are from the galactic center, the safer. There are likely additional Rare Earth factors on cosmic scales beyond the Milky Way Galaxy.

Cosmology is the study of the structure and dynamics of the cosmos. A century ago, astronomers believed the universe was eternal and static, with no beginning and no end. We now know that it had a beginning[13] and has changed dramatically since its origin. Over the last century cosmology has developed into a full-fledged science. Over this brief period we have been able to measure the properties of the cosmos with a high degree of confidence. What astonishes me is how quickly we have managed to do this and how easy it has been.

Why All This?

I still remember as a young boy watching the Apollo Moon landings and the first episodes of the original *Star Trek* TV series. Over my lifetime I've been captivated by the detailed images returned by space probes sent to every planet in the solar system, including Pluto, the now nonplanet. And I'm not alone. The public's enduring appetite for all things space is evidenced by the seemingly endless stream of new Star Wars movies and *Star Trek* spinoffs.

There is something about seeing the stars on a clear dark night away from city lights that evokes in us a deep sense of awe, wonder, and the divine. Psalm 19:1 was the earliest written expression of this divine sense. Cicero quotes Aristotle writing something very similar:

> Let us assume that there were human beings who had lived always beneath the ground…And suppose, then, that at some time the jaws of earth would open and they would be able to escape from these hidden abodes and make their way into the regions which we inhabit. When thus they suddenly would gain sight of the earth, seas, and the sky…and, again, when night had darkened the lands and they should behold the whole of the sky spangled and adorned

with stars…when they should behold all these things, most certainly
they would have judged both that there exist gods and all these marvelous works are the handiworks of these gods.[14]

Even agnostics and atheists sometimes admit to feeling a deep sense of wonder and awe when viewing the starry heavens. Carl Sagan wrote, "Hidden
within every astronomical investigation, sometimes so deeply buried that the
researcher himself is unaware of its presence, lies a kernel of awe."[15]

Likewise, as a young boy I was deeply moved by my observations of celestial
objects with my first (toy) telescope. I came to believe that there must be a Mind
behind it all. This, and to a lesser degree, the Apollo landings and *Star Trek*, led
me to dedicate myself to study astronomy—first as an amateur, and then as a
professional. I know my story is not unique. I have heard and read accounts from
others who were motivated to study science as a result of similar experiences.[16]

The desire among early modern scientists to "think God's thoughts after
Him," to learn about God by studying his creation, was arguably the major
inducement to birth science.[17] Today, Christians should embrace science as the
God-given gift that it is and reject the distorted history of science presented by
the new atheists. When I read some of the original writings of Kepler, Newton,
Boyle, Faraday, and others, I feel a close affinity to them. Maxwell "believed that
God made the universe, that the laws of physics were God's laws, and that every
discovery was a further revelation of God's great design. At the same time, as a
devout Christian, he believed that the true nature of God was to be found in the
Holy Bible, which he knew as well as any scholar of divinity."[18] The materialist
philosophy that seems to underlie so much scientific discourse today, in contrast, is like foreign invaders intent on displacing the original occupants of a land.

About 20 years ago I began to ponder a number of "What if…?" type of
questions regarding our earthly existence. One of them was "Why can we see
the stars?" This is the kind of question that a scientist working within a materialist framework is unlikely to ask. We can try to answer this question at two levels: the scientific and the theological. First, the scientific.

It should not be a given that our home planet would permit us clear views
of the distant universe and that with our unaided vision we would be able to
see anything apart from our host star. Much has to come together just right for
us to get the celestial views we enjoy. We need a planet with an atmosphere thin
enough and made up of the right kinds of gases that give us clear views in the
visual part of the spectrum. And it can't be completely cloud-covered, like Venus
or Titan. We need a planet that rotates on its axis fast enough such that it is not

"rotationally synchronized" with its orbit, allowing for a day/night cycle. It's best to have only one host star as opposed to two or three or more, allowing for darker night skies. On the other hand, there should be abundant stars close enough to us that we can see them easily.

The Andromeda Galaxy, the closest large galaxy to the Milky Way, visible to the unaided eye. (personal photo)

Galaxy NGC 891, a spiral galaxy viewed edge-on. (personal photo)

For us to survive, we need to live on a planet with an atmosphere. For this reason, we should not be at all surprised to find ourselves living in such a place. We should be surprised, however, that this atmosphere we need to survive does not prevent us from seeing the stars—or as Hans Blumenberg put it so eloquently:

> The combined circumstance that we live on Earth and are able to see stars—that the conditions necessary for life do not exclude those necessary for vision, and vice versa—is a remarkably improbable one. This is because the medium in which we live is, on the one hand, just thick enough to enable us to breathe and to prevent us from being burned up by cosmic rays, while, on the other hand, it is not so opaque as to absorb entirely the light of the stars and block any view of the universe. What a fragile balance between the indispensable and the sublime.[19]

As I discussed in the book *The Privileged Planet: How Our Place in the Cosmos Is Designed for Discovery*,[20] the requirements for a habitable planet and the conditions needed for clear views of the stars can be traced to fundamental physical principles. When the requirements for habitability (for observers) are satisfied, so are the conditions for the visibility of the stars. In other words, the universe is set up in such a way that when you have a planet habitable to beings like us, then the planet will also permit clear views of the stars. The universe seems to be extravagant in this way (and in other ways). I believe this constitutes strong evidence for design.

Astronomers have learned a great deal about the universe from their ground-based observations, but being able to put telescopes into space has also been beneficial to them. The possibility of space travel shouldn't be taken for granted either. Both the construction and the launch of rockets that can go beyond Earth's atmosphere depend on a number of planetary factors. First, you need abundant, cheap, and reliable energy sources that can power industry. Fossil fuels have been indispensable in powering modern society, with nuclear power coming second. Neither are the raw materials needed to build rockets and other modern devices to be taken for granted.[21] The availability of these fuels and raw building materials depends on the habitability of a planet.[22] In other words, the same conditions that result in a habitable planet like ours also provide abundant and accessible raw materials and fuels needed for advanced technology.

Also, let's not overlook the fact that without a clear view of the starry heavens, we wouldn't have much motivation to launch rockets! Even better is the combination of clear views with close celestial neighbors. People have been dreaming of visiting the Moon since the dawn of civilization, finally accomplishing it in 1969. Within a mere 20 years of that milestone we sent probes to every planet in the solar system.[23] That seems too easy! Now we are preparing for manned missions to Mars.

Getting a rocket based on chemical fuels (the rockets in use today) off the ground is not easy. Tremendous amounts of chemical energy must be harnessed in a safe way. The main hurdle to overcome is the strong gravity of the planet, which constantly pulls back on a rocket. It becomes exponentially more difficult to launch a rocket into space from planets only modestly larger than Earth.[24] And if you want to engage in interstellar travel, our solar system seems well suited for that task too. It is worthwhile quoting astrophysicist Abraham Loeb on this topic at some length:

> By a fortunate coincidence, the escape speed from the surface of the Earth, 11 kilometers per second, and the escape speed from the location of the Earth around the Sun, 42 kilometers per second, are just around the speed limit attainable by chemical propulsion. This miracle allowed our civilization to design missions, such as *Voyager 1* and *2* or *New Horizons*, that will escape from the solar system into interstellar space. But is this fortune shared by other civilizations on habitable planets outside the solar system?…Paradoxically, the gravitational potential well is deeper in the habitable zone around lower mass stars. A civilization born near a dwarf star would need to launch rockets at a higher speed than we do in order to escape the gravitational pull of its star, even though the star is lighter than the Sun…Nevertheless, this global perspective should make us feel fortunate that we live in the habitable zone of a rare star as bright as the Sun. Not only that we have liquid water and a comfortable climate to maintain a good quality of life, but we also inhabit a platform from which we can escape at ease into interstellar space. We should take advantage of this fortune to find real estate on extrasolar planets in anticipation of a future time when life on our own planet will become impossible.[25]

One should take note of "coincidences" like these. Are we beginning to see a pattern here? We have a clear atmosphere that permits us to see the Moon, planets and stars, beckoning us from near and afar. We are provided with the resources to develop advanced technology to take us away from Earth. And

Earth is just small enough and at the right distance from the right kind of star to make leaving the solar system a relatively easy task with our technology.

There's more. Liquid hydrogen is the best propellant for chemical rockets in the sense that it gives the most push for the weight of propellant used. And oxygen, second only to nitrogen in abundance in the atmosphere, is one of the best oxidizers. The exhaust from a rocket that uses this potent chemical cocktail is plain water. Hydrogen and oxygen can be extracted from water by the simple process of electrolysis. We'll never have to worry about running out of rocket fuel on Earth!

It is no accident that we find ourselves living on a planet with abundant water. Water possesses a number of anomalous properties that make it exceptionally well suited for life.[26] It has also been an important player in concentrating mineral ores in the crust. Water, then, not only makes Earth a habitable planet, it permits its intelligent inhabitants to develop the high technology needed to leave their nest.

Processes in the early solar system required fine-tuning to deliver the right amount of water to Earth. Today, astronomers believe that most of our water came from water-rich bodies in the asteroid belt region.[27] It contains more than 100 million asteroids more than 100 meters across. Efforts are underway to begin mining them within the next decade.[28] Asteroids are a great resource for raw materials for several reasons. The surface area to volume ratio is very large compared to the same amount of material in a single body. This means that most of the material is within a short distance of a surface. Asteroids vary in their composition. Some are pure metal, others are rocky, and some contain abundant water.

> The cosmos is not only designed for scientific discovery from Earth, but it is also designed for us to leave Earth and explore it.

Industrial technology continues to advance, and highly automated mining and manufacturing equipment are just the technologies needed to mine asteroids and build large structures cheaply, quickly, and safely. In particular, once it is possible to build mining and manufacturing robots that can build mining and manufacturing robots, it will be possible to build large interstellar ships.[29]

No need to live our lives like the dwarves of Middle-earth. Once built among the asteroids, an interstellar ship can depart on its long journey.[30] Building an interstellar ship without access to an asteroid belt would be an enormously more expensive endeavor. I don't know how close we are to beginning such a project, but I would not put it beyond 50 years.

It appears, then, that the cosmos is not only designed for scientific discovery from Earth, but it is also designed for us to leave Earth and explore it. And what will we explore? Exoplanets, of course! I don't doubt that within the next 10 years we will have discovered all the exoplanets worth visiting within the nearest 10 to 20 light-years from us. We will know all sorts of details about these planetary systems, including their ages, the planets' orbits, their masses, and the types of atmospheres they have. We will be able to choose the most interesting targets and send ships to them.

Scientists sometimes need to decide whether something found in nature is designed. Archeologists often have to decide whether unusually shaped stones are the products of natural geologic processes or of human artisans. Sometimes it may be obvious that something is designed, but the purpose remains elusive. When we are able to determine what something was designed for, then we have greater confidence that it was indeed designed. An archeologist who concludes that the stone he just dug up was an axe used for chopping wood can be confident he has found an artifact.

Evidence of design is ubiquitous, from fundamental particles to living things to the solar system to the cosmos as a whole. The most obvious purpose of this design is for the existence of life. Another purpose is for some of that life to discover truths about the cosmos through science. And, I am arguing here, for the first time, that interplanetary and even interstellar travel were also purposed from the beginning. We can see the stars so that we can learn about the cosmos and *so we can visit them*.

Notice that the inference to interstellar travel as a purpose stands in a different category from anything else we have done up till now. While we have achieved interplanetary travel, interstellar travel has yet to be developed. This purpose is strictly predictive!

I said earlier that I would give scientific and theological answers to the question "Why can we see the stars?" I've given some scientific answers, and, yes, I do consider my inferences to design and purpose to be in the category of science and not theology. Warning to the reader: The next section includes some speculative theology.

The crew of Apollo 10, Thomas Stafford, John Young, and Gene Cernan head for the moon on May 18, 1969 as a dress rehearsal for the moon landing that would come a couple months later with the crew of Apollo 11. (Courtesy of NASA)

On July 20, 1969, Neil Armstrong and Edwin "Buzz" Aldrin safely landed the Eagle on the lunar surface and became the first two human beings to set foot on another world, while Michael Collins orbited high above them in the return vehicle Columbia. (Courtesy of NASA)

A New Heaven and a New Earth

A rainbow, a mountain vista, a tall waterfall, a Pacific atoll—these are sights everyone would call beautiful. They evoke awe and wonder in us. The sight of the stars on a dark, clear night, however, seems to touch something even deeper within us. I believe there may be a theological reason for this.

What and where is heaven, and what is its relation to our present existence? Popular answers to these questions include the idea that heaven is a very different place than our earthly existence. Heaven is not of this world; it is on a purely spiritual plane. And there are some who believe that when Christians die, their souls leave their bodies behind and they join Jesus in heaven as angelic beings. But these popular perspectives are not what Scripture teaches.[31] The confusion no doubt arises from some biblical passages that seem to be talking about a spiritual existence, while others speak about a physical existence after death.

The book of Revelation gives us the clearest description of our future relationship with God and heaven. The apostle John wrote,

> I saw a new heaven and a new earth…I saw the Holy City, the new
> Jerusalem, coming down out of heaven from God…And I heard a
> loud voice from the throne saying, "Look! God's dwelling place is
> now among the people, and he will dwell with them. They will be
> his people, and God himself will be with them and be their God"
> (Revelation 21:1-3).[32]

God granted John a vision of a future time when his special dwelling place,
heaven, will come to a redeemed and resurrected people and to Earth, the New
Earth. The present (preresurrection) heaven is a different place than our present home because God's special dwelling place is not here.

We don't know for certain what the New Heaven and New Earth will be
like, but the Scriptures do give us clues. Jesus's postresurrection appearances
are a glimpse of our future resurrected physical bodies (Philippians 3:21). The
Lord interacted with his disciples—talking, walking, and even eating with them.
They recognized him. Jesus showed them his stigmata (Luke 24:39-43; John
20:27). These events show the continuity between the body that was nailed to
the cross and the body that walked out of the tomb.

But there was also discontinuity.[33] Jesus was not merely resuscitated with
the same old body. He was resurrected with a radically transformed body. Jesus
appeared and disappeared in inexplicable ways (Luke 24:30-31; John 20:19).

Just how discontinuous will this change be? The analogy between the conversion of the believer and the redemption of the cosmos implies that there will
be more continuity than discontinuity. The New Testament seems to teach the
transformation of the physical cosmos rather than its annihilation followed by
replacement.[34] If this is so, then there should be aspects of the new that appear
very similar to the old.

The New Testament is clear that the final redemption will not be limited
merely to Earth and its inhabitants. It will be cosmic in scope. In Matthew 19:28
Jesus proclaimed the coming "renewal of *all* things." Similarly, Peter spoke of
the "restoration of *all* things" in Acts 3:21 (NLT). The phrase "a new heaven and
a new earth" from Revelation parallels Genesis 1:1, "the heavens and the earth,"
which encompasses all of creation.

In Romans 1, Paul reminded his readers that aspects of the Creator can be
known from the creation. Paul no doubt was familiar with Psalm 19:1: "The
heavens declare the glory of God; the skies proclaim the work of his hands." The
starry heavens are singled out by the psalmist as being particularly informative
about God. I suggest that those aspects of the physical cosmos that point most

directly to God will appear most similar in the redeemed (new) creation. This has profound implications.

First, when we look up at the starry skies, we are seeing heaven! It is not the present heaven, but it gives us a glimpse of the future heaven/new creation. Second, we can make educated guesses about some of the activities we will be doing in the new creation. No doubt, some activities will be like those we do now: worshiping God, interacting with others, building things, traveling on Earth and in space, etc. We will be walking with God in the gardens like Adam did, but this time he will not merely be visiting us. He will be living with us!

Thus, the deep feelings we experience when we gaze at the stars, and also at earthly wonders, come from our God-given desire for our final destination. They are reminders of our pre-Fall Edenic state and pointers to our promised future. Our fascination with space travel in movies and in reality foreshadows our future condition. We won't be strumming harps in the clouds for eternity. We will be visiting exoplanetary systems in this galaxy and others. And because we will live forever, long travel times will not be an issue.

Many questions come to mind at this point. About all I can do this side of the new creation is voice them and offer a few speculative pointers. For instance, are there intelligent beings like us on other planets? Some materialists believe we are very likely alone in the cosmos; we are the lucky lottery winners. Other materialists believe that we cannot—or rather, *must not*—be alone. Why? Because we can't be special, or something.

Christians have also been on both sides of this issue. Perhaps the majority view is that there can't be extraterrestrial human-like beings because Christ would have suffered and died countless times across the cosmos to save them. The "plurality of inhabited worlds" view was even considered heresy by the Roman Catholic Church.[35] C.S. Lewis thought otherwise:

> We know that God has visited and redeemed His people, and that tells us just as much about the general character of the creation as a dose given to one sick hen on a big farm tells us about the general character of farming in England…It is, of course, the essence of Christianity that God loves man and for his sake became man and died. But that does not prove that man is the sole end of nature. In the parable, it was one lost sheep that the shepherd went in search of: it was not the only sheep in the flock, and we are not told that it was the most valuable—save insofar as the most desperately in need has, while the need lasts, a peculiar value in the eyes of Love. The

doctrine of the Incarnation would conflict with what we know of this vast universe only if we knew also there were other rational species in it who had, like us, fallen, and who needed redemption in the same mode, and they had not been vouchsafed it. But we know of none of these things.[36]

Perhaps, as Lewis wrote about in his science fiction trilogy, there are beings on other worlds who are not fallen like us; once we are redeemed, we could have relations with them. I believe the Christian is free to hold to either position regarding extraterrestrial beings. We don't know enough about God's purposes to say one way or the other.

Cosmology has something to say about the past, present, and future of the physical cosmos. The most significant recent development in cosmology occurred in 1997 when it was discovered that the cosmos is accelerating in its expansion. If the cosmological parameters remain unchanged in the new creation, then we can expect the galaxies to continue to move apart with ever-increasing speed. Eventually the Milky Way will be torn apart, followed by planetary systems, and even planets.[37]

At the same time, the rate of star formation has been declining and will continue to do so into the indefinite future. Hundreds of billions of years from now, the primary light sources will be dim red dwarfs, like the red embers of a dying fire. The future universe, as predicted by modern cosmology, will be a cold, dim place. Long before we reach that dismal era, Earth's Sun will have ceased to shine, and before that, Earth will have been engulfed by the swelling Sun, and before that, Earth will have been hit by multiple asteroids and comets and exposed to multiple nearby supernovae.

If we are to live eternally in the new creation, then clearly something has to change in the physical cosmos between now and then. God is creator and sustainer of the present cosmos. And he will sustain the new creation in a different manner. I look forward to the surprises he has in store for us.

CHAPTER 5

THE GLORIOUS DANCE OF BINARY STARS

DAVID BRADSTREET

O n the night of November 12, 1782, a rapid decline in the brightness of a well-known star in the constellation of Perseus astonished the 19-year-old deaf-from-birth English astronomer John Goodricke. The Arabs had named the star Algol, which translates to "the Demon Star" or "the Ghoul." It has since been attributed to be the eye of the monster Medusa, whose face could turn to stone anyone who gazed upon it.

The star's name seems to indicate that even in early times observers noted that this distant body was *very* peculiar. Its variability had been noted by others, but Goodricke was an especially careful observer, and he noticed that it changed from second to fourth magnitude (a factor of more than six times in brightness!) in only seven hours. It repeated this drastic dip in brightness every two days and roughly 21 hours. In Goodricke's time, such a radical change in brightness over such a short span of time was unheard of. Variable stars more typically had been observed to slowly change in brightness over a period of several months, like the star Mira (Arabic for "Wonderful"), which goes from easily seen to invisible over a span of approximately 330 days.

While growing up, Goodricke had overcome nearly insurmountable cultural prejudices against the deaf—prejudices that were common during the eighteenth century. Most people equated those born deaf to being hopeless idiots. Goodricke, thanks to dedicated parents who sent him to a unique and innovative school for the deaf in Edinburgh, Scotland, developed into a well-respected young scholar. His brilliant mind and heightened other senses allowed him to make accurate visual observations.

Within two days of his Algol observations, Goodricke had postulated that the only way for such a significant and rapid loss of light to occur with an equally rapid return to its original brightness would be for another body to pass in front of the star, causing an eclipse. His and others' subsequent observations and confirmation of the details of the light variation soon earned Goodricke the coveted Copley medal, the highest honor awarded to an English subject for the most important scientific discovery of the year. And this at the ripe age of 19! How unfortunate that his budding career ended just two years later, due to his untimely death as a result of a sickness at 21.

It seems astounding that such a momentous discovery came about via the naked-eye observations of such a young man. The existence of variable stars was thought to be an exception to the general rule held then that stars were constant in their energy output. This was reflected in the peculiar nomenclature (astronomers have real issues naming things in a logical way) that limited variable star names to letters of the alphabet coupled with the abbreviation of the constellation in which they were located. We have since learned that there are countless variable stars, and that variability is an inherent stage in the life of all stars.

What we will concentrate on in this chapter are binary stars—stars whose gravitational attraction to each other keep them locked together in a perpetual orbit around each other. What were once thought to be rare have been discovered to be estimated at 60% of all the stars that we see in the sky! Our Sun, so often touted as an average star, is in the minority when it comes to being single and not part of a multiple system. Stars typically have companions, and how apropos that the word *companion* means "sharing bread." This communion between stars will allow us, through their dance about each other, to determine a vast number of their fundamental characteristics—which otherwise would be undiscernible.

Their celestial dances are reminiscent of the dances for joy and celebration we often see in Scripture as natural reactions of joy to the glory of God (for example, King David dancing with all his might in 2 Samuel 6:14, and the injunction to "praise His name with dancing" in Psalm 149:3). Indeed, as you will see, the dances of binary stars bring me great joy and fulfillment as an astronomer who loves to interpret and understand God's creation.

What Good Are They?

Of what use are binary or double stars? Are they just an accident of nature that are interesting but serve no useful purpose other than as a curiosity of creation? As is so often the case in God's universe, the answer to this is a resounding no! As we will see in the following pages, the existence of binary systems is a crucial and necessary boon to our understanding of all stars in general, for it is only through the careful analysis of the interactions of these systems that we can accurately and directly measure the fundamental characteristics of stars other than our Sun.

Why So Many?

First, let's address a possible reason why such vast multitudes of binary systems exist. Stars form from huge clouds of gas and dust within the spiral arms of galaxies. Like herding cats, you can imagine that convincing atoms of gas and dust to collect in one spot is not an easy endeavor! There are mitigating factors fighting such a condensation. If you attempt to compress a gas, its temperature rises because the atoms begin to collide and move faster and faster. Faster-moving particles are more difficult to constrain because they want to race away in all directions. In addition to increasing temperatures, if there are any magnetic fields present within the cloud, these forces will also resist collapse into a smaller volume. Finally, in the same way that ice skaters bring their arms closer to their bodies as they begin to spin, as moving particles move in closer to the axis of rotation, the rate at which they spin will accelerate, thus propelling the bodies away from each other. This increase in orbital speed is due to the conservation of angular momentum—that is, as a rotating mass moves in toward the rotational axis, its orbital speed will increase. All of this tells us that the odds seem stacked against gas clouds collapsing into stars.

Surmounting the Odds

In order to overcome these three formidable obstacles, there must be an overarching gravitational field, which is always caused by the presence of mass. Thus, only large clouds of gas and dust that contain nearly unthinkable amounts of mass are able to collapse upon themselves to eventually overcome the impediments to condensing. But you cannot merely do away with angular momentum.

It has to be redistributed somehow, and apparently nature solves this problem in the following way. Because you need large masses of gas to initiate the collapse, far more mass than you can use to create a single star, these massive clouds of gas and dust subfragment into smaller clouds. As they condense, they can further subfragment into even smaller clouds from which individual stars can be formed.

This is why there are so many *clusters* of stars—stars are born in large groups because they initially need large amounts of mass just to begin to collapse. When stars form together in clusters we say that they are *coeval*, which is a term used to indicate that they're all born at the same time from the same cloud of gas. But we still have the angular momentum problem! If a star collapses into a single star rotating too rapidly, it will break apart. So it seems that God has created a process whereby these clouds most often split into two stars, dividing up the angular momentum and allowing two (or more) stars to form. In the sharing of the angular momentum these two stars can form normally and not break apart from spinning too rapidly, as well as keeping angular momentum in the form of their orbits around each other.

> God leaves nothing to chance and has a
> purpose for everything in his creation.

This is why we believe that there are so many binary star systems in the universe. Single stars probably exist when the original collapsing cloud does not contain as much initial spin and hence not too much angular momentum for it to be distributed into a single star. Again and again I am reminded of David's praise to God in Psalms 8:3, where he said that the stars are the work of God's fingers. God leaves nothing to chance and has a purpose for everything in his creation.

Are Two Better Than One?

We see that the creation of double stars appears to be God's solution to redistributing angular momentum in such a way as to allow stars to form. But again, so what? As long as *some* single stars can form, who cares about the existence of binaries?

Let's investigate what we can learn from studying the interactions of two stars that are relatively close to each other and are gravitationally bound so as to orbit each other. One of the most important tenets in astrophysics is the Russell-Vogt theorem. This theorem states that all of a star's characteristics and future evolution (birth, growth, and death) are determined solely from its initial mass and chemical composition. In other words, if you tell astrophysicists what elements a star is formed from and exactly how much material composes the star, they can create computer models that will accurately predict its entire lifetime. Chemical compositions of stars can be determined from spectroscopy, the science of spreading out the light of stars and examining it in minute detail. Each element emits different colors or wavelengths of light, and these can be measured very accurately from the light collected from stars.

Double Stars for the Masses

But, what about mass? How can we measure the mass of a star? Bathroom scales seem out of the question. So where does that leave us? As silly as that statement about bathroom scales seems, it does belie a critical point about how we measure mass. When you step on a bathroom scale, what exactly is being measured? It is the force of gravity between you and Earth, a force that we have named *weight*. Weight is not mass, but rather, the force of gravity from Earth acting on a mass that causes it to accelerate. If you are out in space, far from any other mass, then you have no weight, but your mass remains the same. The bathroom scales are measuring how hard Earth is pulling on you, and conversely, how hard your mass is pulling on Earth. Those pulls are exactly the same but in opposite directions, yet the actual acceleration of the two bodies (you and Earth) are different in exactly the same ratio as the ratio of your mass compared to Earth. That's why when you jump off a chair you appear to do all the falling, but in reality, Earth is rising up to meet you (although an incredibly small amount!).

But the principle is the same. We can measure mass by its gravitational interaction and subsequent motion due to another mass. This is exactly why binary stars are so critically important. By measuring how far apart the stars are and the rate at which they fall around each other (we call this an orbit), we can measure the exact sum of their masses. And if (by some means that we'll investigate shortly) we could determine the ratio of the masses of the two stars, then we can mathematically combine these two pieces of information (sum of the masses and the ratio of the masses) to determine their individual masses. This is the *only* way that we can directly measure the masses of stars.

But how? Like Algol, the time it takes for the two stars to orbit each other can be relatively easily measured by timing the length of similar eclipses. But how do we determine the mass ratio of these binary stars, not to mention the distances separating them? Or, for that matter, anything else about them? In this chapter I will limit my discussion to the types of binaries whose orbital planes lie close to Earth's line of sight—that is, when these stars orbit each other they block each other twice in their orbits as seen from Earth. These are called *eclipsing binaries*. Figure 5.1 shows a typical binary system with their respective orbits at varying degrees of tilt relative to Earth's line of sight to it. Zero degrees means that we see a top-down view of the stars, so of course we would never see them block each other as they orbit. This system would just begin to show eclipses at 75 degrees, and if the tilt were greater the eclipses would become more and more extreme, reaching its maximum when the orbital plane is exactly in Earth's line of sight (90 degrees—edge-on view).

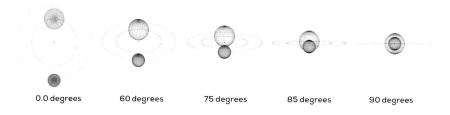

0.0 degrees   60 degrees   75 degrees   85 degrees   90 degrees

Figure 5.1–*A binary system at varying degrees of tilt (inclination) relative to Earth's line of sight*

Principles of Stellar Aging (Evolution)

Before we delve into the details of eclipsing binaries, we must set down a few crucial statements that we'll need in order to understand the significance of our findings from binary systems. Single stars are born when a cloud of gas, mostly hydrogen and helium, condense by their own gravity into a com-pressed-enough object that allows nuclear fusion (think hydrogen bombs) to occur at their dense and hot cores. After searching for a happy state (called hydrostatic equilibrium), the stars merrily fuse hydrogen into helium for mil-lions to billions of years in a stage of their lives called the *main sequence*. This is the longest stage of most stars' lives because they have lots of hydrogen to fuse. Our Sun is a main sequence star that has spent about 4.5 billion years turning hydrogen into helium at its core. But the more massive a star is when it begins fusing, the shorter is its time as a main sequence star because it burns its fuel so voraciously.

When a star runs out of hydrogen at its core, the helium ash being produced begins to contract and heat up, which accelerates the rate of hydrogen fusion in the upper layers of the core. This increased rate of fusion causes the star to expand and begin to become a red giant, a star whose size can ultimately be larger than the *orbit* of Jupiter around the Sun! Thus, it is no longer a main sequence star, but on its way to becoming a red giant, also known as a subgiant star.

That's all the stellar evolution that we need for our discussions. (Single-star evolution is a topic that deserves several books of its own.) Just remember that when stars are single, the more massive the star, the more furiously it fuses hydrogen into helium, and the less time it spends as a main sequence star. High-mass stars evolve (age) much more rapidly than low-mass stars. This fact will rear its ugly head shortly when we get into binary star evolution.

Forming Binary Star Systems— Gravitational Tugs of War

Let's investigate a little more deeply some of the characteristics of the light coming from typical eclipsing binary stars. As we do (we'll attempt to do this without the foreboding mathematics), you will start to see that by beginning with "simple" binary systems and then proceeding to slightly more complex systems, you will gain an intuitive sense for exactly what is going on.

A single star, if it's not rotating too fast, will gravitationally form itself into a sphere. A sphere is a surface where the gravitational force is identical on all parts of it. In other words, neglecting Earth's rotation, if Earth were a perfect sphere, you would weigh the same on all parts of its surface. This is such a take-it-for-granted idea that we forget the significance of the fact that in order for this to happen the planet's surface must be a sphere!

But, what if we place *another* strong gravitational mass in the vicinity? What if two stars form in proximity to each other? Then we will have the gravity of the star itself attempting to form its surface into a sphere, but also the tugging (tidal) influence of an external gravitational source. Without getting bogged down into the mathematics of this, the result is what are called *Lagrangian surfaces*, and they are amazingly complex. Their bizarre shapes depend upon the ratio of the masses of the two stars and how close the stars' surfaces are to each other. Consider the diagram below (Figure 5.2):

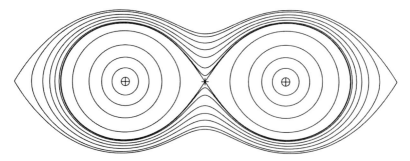

Figure 5.2–Lagrangian surfaces for a binary system with mass ratio of 1.00

Figure 5.2 shows multiple Lagrangian surfaces for two stars with equal masses (so their mass ratio is 1.00). The centers of the two stars are located at the two plus signs at the centers of the two sets of curves. The plus sign midway between them is the center of mass or balance point of the two stars.

The many strangely shaped curves represent surfaces of constant magnitude gravitational force, although each separate curve is a different magnitude from the ones above and below it. Look at the curves closest to the two outermost plus signs. These are nearly perfectly spherical. They represent the possibility of stars forming into spheres—that is, if the stars' surfaces are widely separated from each other, then they can be spherical. But as you progress outward from the plus signs, the surfaces begin to vary more and more from spherical shapes into odd teardrop shapes. Especially note the surface that crosses over into a figure-eight. This special curve is called the *inner Lagrangian surface*, and the crossover point is particularly significant. It marks the spot in space where the gravity of one star exactly balances the gravity of the other. If you placed a gas molecule at this point between the two stars, it wouldn't know which way to go. It would feel exactly the same gravitational force from each star. However, any tiny nudge in either direction would send it careening toward the star in whose direction the nudge pushed it.

Figure 5.3 depicts the Lagrangian surfaces for two stars whose mass ratio is 0.40—that is, the less massive star on the left is only 40% the mass of the larger star.

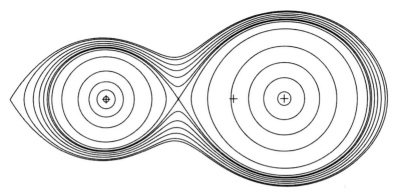

Figure 5.3—*Lagrangian surfaces for a binary system with mass ratio of 0.40*

The plus sign between them is still the center of mass or balance point of the two stars. Think of two unequally weighted people on a seesaw. If they both sit on the ends of the seesaw, the balance point would not be in the middle of the board, but off in the direction of the more massive person.

The important idea to take from Figures 5.2 and 5.3 is this: Two stars of a particular mass ratio can take on the shape of *any* of these curves. Small stars (compared to their separation distance) can be mostly spherical; larger stars will begin to distort into teardrop shapes. And if both stars' surfaces are large, they can even form into stars whose shapes extend beyond the inner Lagrangian point. These binaries would literally be in contact with one another! Wait— stars that actually touch each other? Do they exist? Let's find out…

Real-Life Examples

1. *GZ CMa*

Consider the eclipsing binary system GZ CMa. (Remember the means of "naming" variable stars? The letters GZ are letter identifiers, and CMa is the official abbreviation for Canis Major, or the Big Dog, the constellation in which this binary resides.) These two stars are drawn below to scale in Figure 5.4, and the small circle centered on the center-of-mass plus sign represents the size of the Sun compared to them.

Figure 5.4–*GZ CMa system to scale: The circle represents the size of our Sun, positioned on the center of mass of the binary*

The stars are spherical, and as such, when they orbit each other around their common center of mass (the balance point between them, also called the *barycenter*), there will be almost no light variation outside of the eclipses because a spherical star gives off the same brightness no matter what side of it you see. If we plot the light coming from the two stars as seen from Earth as a function of time it's called a *light curve*, shown in Figure 5.5.

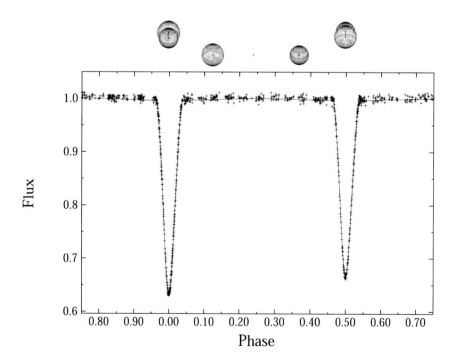

Figure 5.5–*The light curve and models of GZ CMa*

The horizontal axis in Figure 5.5 contains the time or phase which is a normalized time such that the interval from 0 to 1 equals the period of time for the stars to orbit each other (the orbital period of the binary). The vertical axis plots the brightness (flux) of the system, with brighter values toward the top of the axis, and fainter values toward the bottom. The deeper eclipse is situated at phase 0.00, and the other shallower eclipse occurs naturally halfway through the orbit at phase 0.50 for circular orbits.

The tiny plus signs in the light curve denote actual telescopic observations of the light level of the binary at different times (phases) of its orbit. The solid curve through the data points is the theoretical output from the models shown above the light curve. Each set of models at the top of the diagram corresponds to that phase in the light curve. Starting from the left, we have phase 0.00 (the time of deepest eclipse), phase 0.25 (where you can best see both stars and hence this is the brightest part of the light curve), and phase 0.50 (the time of the less-deep eclipse). We can reliably determine the stars' characteristics—such as size, shape, temperature, etc.—by trial-and-error modeling until the theoretical light curve matches the observed data.

When the larger and hotter star is blocked by its cooler, smaller companion at phase 0.00, we see that there is a loss of light, or an eclipse, and a dip in the light curve. When the larger star blocks its cooler companion halfway through its period (phase 0.50), we lose light from that smaller star, resulting in another eclipse and a second, less-extreme dip in the light curve. An interesting phenomenon happens with regard to circular-orbit eclipsing binaries (as opposed to eccentric orbit systems). At both eclipses, the exact same amount of stellar surface area is blocked. Figure 5.6 demonstrates this.

In other words, when the small star blocks off the larger one, the area it blocks is a function of its size. This means that if one eclipse is deeper than the other, that one star's surface must be brighter and therefore hotter than the other, since equal areas are eclipsed. For GZ CMa (Figure 5.5), this infers that the larger star's deeper eclipse at phase 0.00 tells us that it must have a slightly higher temperature than the smaller star. Likewise, because the smaller star's eclipse at phase 0.50 is shallower, this means that the smaller star's surface brightness is less than the larger star's and hence its temperature must be less as well. In fact, with the help of careful measurements we can determine quite precisely what that temperature difference must be. Think of it this way: If both stars had the exact same surface brightness and therefore identical temperatures, then we would lose exactly the same amount of light at each eclipse because the areas covered by each eclipse are identical. We can see from the nearly identical depths of the eclipses that the temperatures of the two stars of GZ CMa must be *almost* the same, and they are!

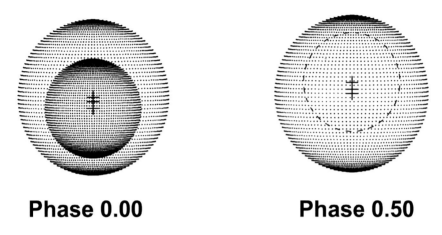

Phase 0.00   Phase 0.50

Figure 5.6—The stellar surface areas blocked at each eclipse are identical for circular orbit binaries

2. EE Peg

Let's look at another system, EE Peg, shown in Figure 5.7.

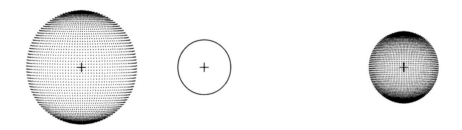

Figure 5.7—Scale model of EE Peg with Sun to scale at center of mass

Again, we have almost spherical stars, but their proximity to each other distorts them from spheres, with slightly elongated portions pointing toward each other due to gravitational tidal effects. (More on this soon.) Think of a spinning football. If it were giving off light, because its shape is asymmetrical, as it rotated we would see more light from it when its longer cross section, or the side of the football, faced us. When the pointy end faces us, we see its smallest surface area and thus less light. Stars will do the same thing if they're not spherical, and typically close binary stars are *not* spherical but take on those strange Lagrangian shapes we saw in Figures 5.2 and 5.3. You will see in Figure 5.8 that when the stars are not eclipsing, the light level is not as constant (that is, the curve is not as flat) as it was for GZ CMa, which means that one or both of the stars are nonspherical.

Look at the eclipses in Figure 5.8.

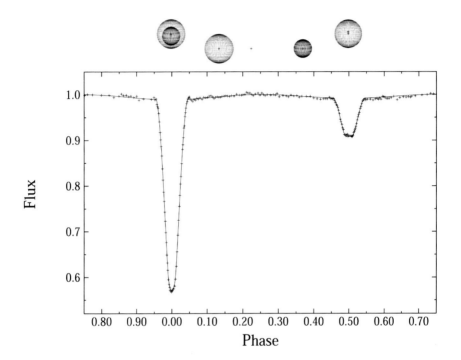

Figure 5.8—*The light curve and models of EE Peg*

One eclipse is much deeper than the other. This means that one of the stars is much hotter than the other. Also, look at the strange flat bottom of the shallower eclipse at phase 0.50. Here the light is almost constant for a brief time. What could that mean? It's as though we see only one star for a short period of time—and that's exactly what it means. The smaller star is completely hidden behind its larger companion, so during this "total" eclipse we see the light from only one star for the amount of time represented by the flat bottom of that eclipse.

In summary, looking at the light curve of EE Peg, we see small out-of-eclipse light variations (meaning slightly asymmetrical star or stars) as well as very disparate eclipse depths (very different temperature stars) and a flat-bottomed eclipse (the cooler star is completely blocked by the larger, hotter companion). I hope you're beginning to see the tricks of this trade!

3. Bizarre Algol, the Demon Star

Let's check out another light curve in Figure 5.9. This is for Algol, the Demon star, mentioned at the beginning of this chapter. Inspect its light curve and see if you can infer anything about the two stars.

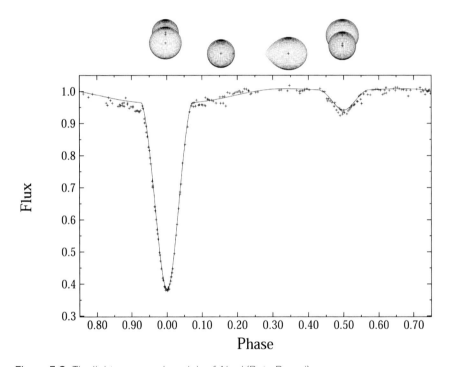

Figure 5.9–The light curve and models of Algol (Beta Persei)

Notice the huge disparity in eclipse depths. This must mean that the two stars are vastly different in temperature. The light curve is never flat (constant brightness), so there are no total eclipses, and one or both stars are nonspherical because the light variation is never constant, even out of eclipse. Algol turns out to be an extremely interesting binary, as shown close-up in Figure 5.10.

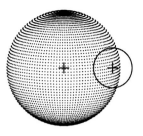 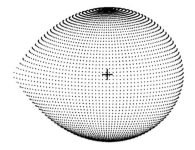

Figure 5.10—Algol to scale with the Sun shown as a circle around the center of mass

Algol consists of a hot (12,500 °K) main sequence star and a cooler (5,000 °K) subgiant star attempting to become a red giant, with the less massive and cooler star filling its inner Lagrangian surface and the much hotter and more massive star still a happy main sequence star. In other words, the smaller star is giving up its mass to the larger star. How awesome is that? In fact, this is a seemingly impossible situation! The more massive star is the less evolved star. The less massive star is a subgiant, having left the main sequence before its significantly more massive companion. This should not happen in a system that is coeval (stars born at the same time)! This seeming contradiction is known as the *Algol paradox*. And there are many systems just like Algol, so it's not a fluke. What in the world causes these bizarre binaries?

It turns out that Algol-type binaries are systems that have evolved as the massive stars have aged, as discussed earlier. But, unlike single stars that go their merry way through their lives, having a close neighbor with its accompanying gravitational influence changes everything. We believe that Algol's original state had the now less massive star originally as the more massive star. Because of its greater mass, it evolved faster than its less massive companion, and as it expanded with age its surface bumped into its inner Lagrangian surface. Remember that the crossover point in that convoluted surface is the point at which the gravity between the two stars is exactly balanced. Any gas at that position feels exactly the same gravitational pull on both sides, and it doesn't know where to go next. However, the pressure from the expanding star gives that gas the additional nudge it needs to push it into the gravitational pull of the less massive companion, and that gas will eventually spiral onto the less massive star. You can see where this is going. Like air exiting the nozzle of a balloon, the expanding star exchanges much of its mass to its smaller companion until *that* star eventually becomes the more massive star.

This scenario is accelerated as the once less massive star's inner Lagrangian surface expands to adjust to its increasing mass and conversely the once more massive star's inner Lagrangian surface begins to shrink, forcing even more gas through the inner Lagrangian point. Once the expanding star has shed itself of enough mass onto its companion, it settles down to a much less turbulent mass exchange, which is the state of Algol at present. Meanwhile, the now more massive hot blue star will begin to evolve like the massive star that it now is, but that takes millions of years to occur. So we see that the Algol paradox is explained through mass exchange such that the now more massive star has only been a hot blue main sequence star for a relatively short period of time, and the now less massive, cooler component is the more evolved star (subgiant), even though it now has a smaller mass than its presently more massive companion.

4. *V1010 Oph—Curiouser and Curiouser*

Ready for more strange members of the binary zoo? Let's consider the light curve of V1010 Oph shown in Figure 5.11.

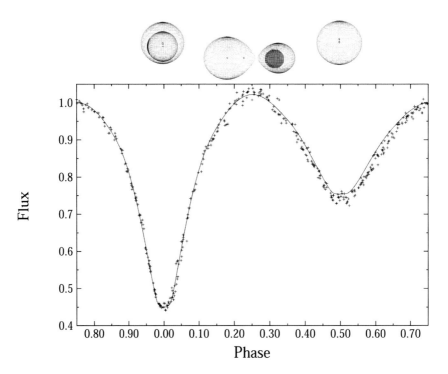

Figure 5.11—*The light curve and models of V1010 Oph*

V1010 Oph demonstrates light variability throughout its light curve, but even more extremely than does Algol. This means that both stars must be misshapen spheroids. The eclipse depths are also different, so the temperatures of the stars are also disparate (see Figure 5.12).

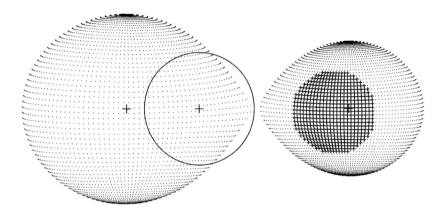

Figure 5.12–*The model of V1010 Oph with the Sun drawn to scale as a circle around the center of mass*

The excessively hot region on the smaller star as indicated by the crosshatches confirms these ideas, and to accurately model this light curve you must place a hot region on one of the stars (in this case, the smaller one). This is because part of the light curve that should be symmetrical is higher than expected, indicating a hotter region on one of the stars. Our Sun exhibits cooler spots (sunspots), and through examining light curves, we have determined that other stars have similar inhomogeneities (hot or cool spots) on their surfaces as well. You will also perhaps be surprised at how close the two stars are to each other. They appear to be almost touching. Could binary stars get so close that they could orbit each other while in contact with one another? Let's take a look.

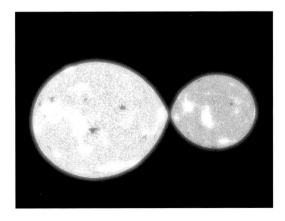

5. *AB And—An Overcontact System*

Examine the light curve of AB And in Figure 5.13.

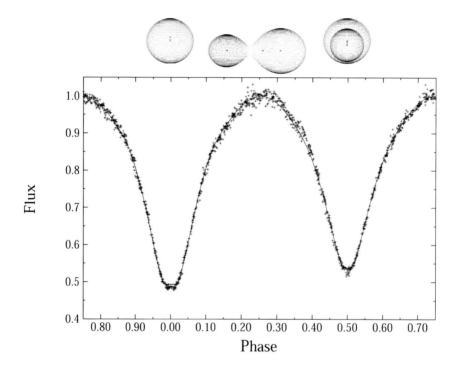

Figure 5.13–The light curve and models of AB And

What can you determine from the light curve? The eclipse depths are nearly equal, so the temperatures of the two stars must be almost the same. The eclipse at phase 0 appears to be slightly deeper as well as flat, so the eclipse is total, and the hotter star must be the smaller star (or it couldn't be totally hidden from view to allow the constant light level). The light levels are continually changing outside of eclipse, so both stars must be very nonspherical. Indeed, if you examine the model (see Figure 5.14), we find that AB And is a typical overcontact system—that is, two stars that are so close to each other that they are literally touching and sharing energy. This explains why the smaller star is hotter than the larger star (the larger star *should* be the hotter one). The smaller star is siphoning energy from the larger as the system attempts to reach some kind of thermal equilibrium.

Are these overcontact systems rare? Not at all—they are very numerous as binary systems go.

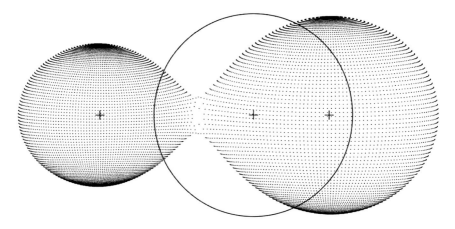

Figure 5.14–*The model of AB And with the Sun drawn to scale as a circle around the center of mass*

We've seen a progression of binary systems in this chapter—from stars that are distant enough from each other to not perturb their spherical shapes to systems that look like dumbbells! Could there be even more extreme systems?

6. *Last But Not Least–AW UMa*

Yes! Let's look at one more—AW UMa. Its light curve (see Figure 5.15) indicates it consists of two stars with nearly identical temperatures, and one of the stars is totally eclipsed as seen from the flat-bottomed eclipse at phase 0.5. When the system is modeled, we find the overcontact binary as shown in Figure 5.16. Here we have a massive star with a tiny star attached, nearly 13 times less massive than its companion. It looks as though it is being consumed by its larger neighbor—and that's exactly what most astronomers now believe is occurring. As these overcontact binaries orbit each other, fighting and twisting in their orbits, they are losing angular momentum to their surroundings. And as they do so, they will eventually coalesce into a single star. The process must take millions of years, but this scenario has become the widely accepted paradigm for the end stage of low-mass close binaries.

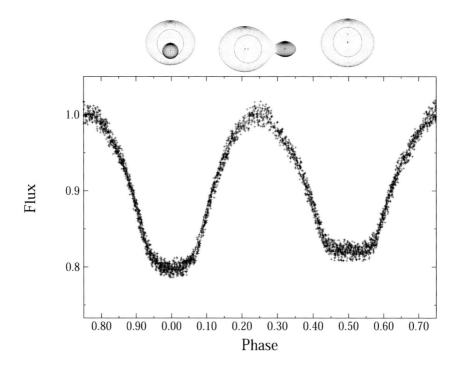

Figure 5.15–The light curve and models of AW Uma

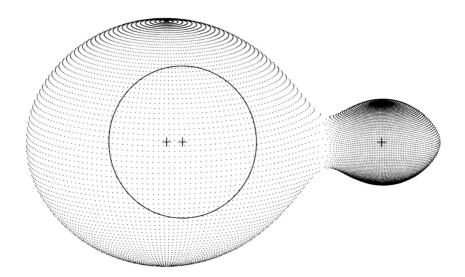

Figure 5.16–The model of AW UMa with the Sun drawn as a circle about the center of mass

This sounds outlandish! Are there any stars that exhibit strange characteristics that could be explained by binary coalescence? Yes, there are. In large star clusters, especially older clusters called *globular clusters*, there are stars that are still on the main sequence, whereas most of the stars of their mass have long ago raced away toward the red giant phase. These so-called "blue stragglers" (they are among the bluest, hottest stars in the cluster when there shouldn't be any) are best explained as binaries that have only relatively recently coalesced and formed massive stars, and as such have not evolved as they would have had they been born with their present mass. These recently coalesced massive stars stick out amongst the cluster because their similarly massed single-star neighbors are long gone by becoming red giants. It's the simplest and best explanation for these stars.

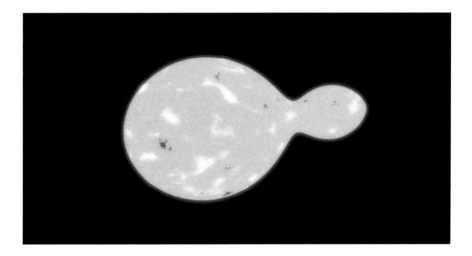

May All of This Coalesce in My Mind!

If you've managed to stay with me thus far, your mind must be reeling! My students routinely exclaim, "I had no idea that any of these systems even existed. What a fascinating universe God has created!" My point in relating some of the details of binary star analysis and rudimentary binary star evolution is to drive home the idea that God has carefully laid out clues that he invites us to discover. Psalms 111:2 tells us, "Great are the works of the LORD; they are studied by all who delight in them" (NASB).

Using telescopes, careful data-gathering techniques, and powerful mathematical methods and modeling, we have come a long way toward understanding stars and the ways that they behave, as both single stars and multiple star systems. In this chapter I've only begun to lay out the wonders of what can be deduced from studying binary stars, and I hope it's been enough to amaze you and help you to understand a bit more about how astronomers know what they state about their discoveries.

Exciting Recent Developments

Let me conclude by briefly discussing some relatively new results from studying more exotic binary systems. You may have heard about the discovery of gravity waves washing over Earth—waves that are detected by ultra-sensitive devices like the LIGO (Laser Interferometer Gravitational-Wave Observatory). These gravity waves (like ripples on the surface of the ocean, except that these are literally ripples on the fabric of space itself!) are postulated to have been propagated when two orbiting neutron stars (tiny stars, each two to three times more massive than our Sun yet incredibly dense and roughly ten miles in diameter) finally coalesced as their orbits spiraled together. This results in a cataclysmic release of gravitational energy and electromagnetic radiation—that is, a measurable gravity wave along with a flash of light. This fantastic measurement is yet another vindication of the work of Einstein's general theory of relativity. He predicted that such waves should exist! Through precise measurements of the light and gravitational waves emitted from such a coalescence, astronomers can measure the value of the Hubble constant, which is a number describing the expansion rate of the universe. Knowing this number precisely, a central goal of cosmology, can tell us the age of the universe as well as whether it's infinite or finite in size.

Even more fantastic is the prediction of what might occur if a binary pair consisting of a black hole and a neutron star coalesce. Because of the nature of black holes, as opposed to neutron star pairs, the merging of a black hole with its companion neutron star can theoretically resolve much of the uncertainty in measurements inherent in neutron star mergers. This promises to yield more accurate and reliable results, but the problem is that black hole-neutron star binaries are thought to be rarer than neutron-neutron star binaries. However, the LIGO is being enhanced to be even more sensitive and able to measure out to far greater distances than before, so beginning in 2019 we will have a much better chance of observing these mergers. We may soon have a more secure value of the Hubble constant and the implications that its value will connote. We live in exciting times for binary star research—that's for certain!

God, the Gracious Mind-Blower

Is it not mind-blowing what an incredibly diverse and imaginative God we serve? God declares in Isaiah 45:12, "It is I who made the earth, and created man upon it. I stretched out the heavens with My hands, and I ordained all their host" (NASB). And it is Jesus, according to Hebrews 1:2-3, who has not only created but sustains every part of the universe. The many varieties of stars exist both to bring him glory and also to instruct us toward understanding some of the mysteries of his creation. Though we are far from understanding all of God's laws (ordinances, as he challenges Job in Job 38:33), through his grace we can begin to catch a glimpse of the magnificence of them.

Like the fantastic diversity of life on Earth, we also see an incredible panoply of stars and combinations of stars which, in and of themselves, are wonderful. But the very fact that they exist allows us to study and understand them even more clearly than we could ever have done if they didn't exist! This speaks to us of another aspect of grace, that undeserved favor where God gives us enough clues to unravel great mysteries. I would like to emphasize that as we reach new heights of knowledge about our universe, we should give to *him* praise, honor, and worship, and not to ourselves. He has provided the means for us to understand him better, and certainly he could have designed the universe to be totally incomprehensible. For me, studying the glorious dance of the binary stars is indeed a marvelous exercise in worship as well as scientific inquiry. I hope that you have experienced some of that joy and wonder as you worked your way through this chapter.

CHAPTER 6

GOD, BLACK HOLES, AND THE END OF THE UNIVERSE

DR. SARAH SALVIANDER

The end of the universe is not a time, but a place. With this knowledge, some people imagine that if the universe were finite and had a boundary, it must be unimaginably and comfortably far away. The truth is that the end of the universe is only 26,000 light-years from Earth. It exists in our Milky Way Galaxy and lies in the direction of the constellation Sagittarius. But if you look there, you won't see the end of the universe—it is invisible.

The end of the universe is not metaphorical; it's physical, it's real—a fact that suggests the possibility of voyaging there someday. Though 26,000 light-years is a relatively short distance in our vast universe, the swiftest spacecraft we have wouldn't reach the end of the universe for an impractical 100 million years or more.

Remarkably, our inability to see, touch, or travel to the end of the universe is not an insurmountable hindrance to our understanding it. Natural philosophers knew about atoms and scientists knew about the planet Neptune long before they could see them. How did they know these once-unseen things existed before they were seen? Why did they have the ability to believe in unseen things? It was strong mathematical arguments, the behavior of what can be seen that reveals the unseen, and a deep faith that made such belief possible.

Scientists and Christian theologians both use what is visible to help people understand the great, often invisible, and seemingly incomprehensible forces that shape our reality. Much of the natural world is only temporarily hidden from us because technology isn't yet up to the task of revealing it. However, in the case of God and some of his greatest natural works, invisibility is a quality inherent to what scientists and theologians are looking for. That's certainly true of what lurks at the center of our galaxy.

For decades, astronomers tracked the strange orbits of visible stars whipping around a tiny, empty point in space at the center of our Milky Way. Stars don't normally orbit empty regions of space, and no known theory could explain such behavior. Astronomers believed that the stars must be orbiting an enormous mass of some kind, even though none could be seen. They peered at the region with telescopes that could see beyond the limits of visible light into the realms of radio, infrared, ultraviolet, and X-rays. Wisps of energetic emission were observed emanating from the region, but still no hint of the hulking mass itself could be seen. But their faith in a rational universe with a cause for everything gave them the determination and confidence to pursue the elusive answer.

Few things stir the imagination like black holes, where the flexible fabric of space and time becomes so warped that nothing—not particles, not light, not even time—can escape their relentless gravity. Stars and other bodies can orbit black holes at a cautious distance, but anything that wanders too close to the "boundary" of a black hole—the infamous event horizon—will be inexorably drawn in and lost to the universe forever. For that reason, the horizon of a black hole is effectively a place where the universe ends.

Once thought to be extraordinarily rare, the universe abounds with black holes. Hundreds of billions—perhaps even quintillions—of black holes inhabit our observable universe, and each is a gateway to oblivion. We have evidence for the existence of modest star-massed black holes—as many as a billion of these inhabit our own Milky Way—as well as evidence of gargantuan black holes that lie at the centers of most of the hundreds of billions of galaxies in the observable universe.

Strange, fantastic, and invisible though they are, the existence of black holes is considered almost commonsense in the twenty-first century. It was not long ago, however, that black holes were regarded as absurd—even outrageous—by the best scientific minds struggling to comprehend the invisible.

Black Holes: A Scientific Epic in Three Parts

Part 1: The White Dwarf Controversy

Located in the constellation Canis Major is the burned-out core of a star that died long ago. Sirius B was once a bright blue-white star about five times the mass—the total amount of material—of the Sun in our solar system. In the final phase of its life, Sirius B swelled to become a red giant. Then it puffed off its outer layers, exposing an extremely hot but inert core. Astronomers call these cores white dwarfs. Sirius B lost most of its mass to outer space in its red giant phase. As a white dwarf, it retained approximately the mass of the Sun, though it shrunk down to about the size of Earth, making Sirius B extraordinarily dense.

In the early twentieth century, white dwarfs spawned a crisis in astronomy. Astronomers' first attempts to estimate the density of Sirius B produced a number that was absurdly high—about 61,000 times the density of the Sun. That meant just one teaspoon of white dwarf matter would weigh 670 pounds on Earth.[1] At this density, astronomers had no idea how a white dwarf could possibly support itself against the crush of its own gravity.

A star like the Sun that is in the main phase of its life supports itself against the inward squeezing of gravity through the outward push of thermal pressure—the pressure produced by the random motions of particles heated up by nuclear reactions in a star's core. But what happens when a star exhausts its fuel and eventually radiates away all of its heat?

At first astronomers thought that the core of a dying star would shrink under the compression of gravity until it was able to support itself with the sort of pressure that holds together ordinary solid objects, like rocks. But this sort of pressure is no match for the gravity of a white dwarf. Classical physics—the theories of physics that predate quantum mechanics—predicted that a white dwarf should collapse infinitely under its own gravity, leaving behind a hole in space—something that scientists found unthinkable.

The story of black holes really begins with two of the greatest scientists of the twentieth century: Subrahmanyan Chandrasekhar (Chandra), then a young student from India, and Sir Arthur Eddington, Chandra's mentor and the most renowned astrophysicist at the time. The story of their relationship and the role it played in the pursuit of knowledge about black holes reveals the never-ending struggle between the faith that propels mankind to greater understanding and the inherent human failings that hinder the search for truth.

Chandra had become enchanted with white dwarfs after reading a book by physicist R.H. Fowler. Invoking the revolutionary new physics of quantum mechanics, Fowler proposed that it was the motions of electrons—tiny negatively charged particles—in a white dwarf that supported it against the crush of gravity. According to one of the basic results of quantum mechanics, known as Heisenberg's uncertainty principle, as electrons are compressed by gravity, they begin to move rapidly, producing a very strong outward pressure. Chandra thought the idea had great promise and traveled all the way to England to pursue white dwarf physics under the guidance of some of the greatest scientists of the time, particularly his sponsor Eddington.

Chandra gave life to Fowler's idea by working out some very difficult mathematics. Going through the mathematical calculations is a necessary step in science. If a theory doesn't have equations and doesn't produce accurate mathematical results, it's not really a physical theory, it's just conjecture.

Coming up with the right equation for white dwarfs was no small feat. Chandra realized that the white dwarf electrons would be so immensely squeezed by gravity that their speeds would reach the point where Einstein's special theory of relativity had to be considered. No one had ever tried to combine quantum mechanics and relativity before, but Chandra figured out the mathematics that explained how white dwarfs could resist infinite gravitational collapse—up to a point. Chandra calculated that any white dwarf star weighing less than 1.4 times the mass of the Sun was safe from a catastrophic fate. It was Chandra's faith that there must be an answer that drove him to succeed at such an arduous effort.

Eddington was impressed with Chandra's work, but he was also profoundly disturbed by its implications. Eddington abhorred the idea that a star could collapse infinitely to a hole in space and that the only thing preventing that was the strange behavior of electrons. He speculated that "various accidents may intervene to save the star, but I want more protection than that. I think there should be a law of Nature to prevent a star from behaving in this absurd way!"[2]

Eddington's refusal to believe Chandra's theory is a bit of a mystery. It was not for lack of skill in physics or insight. Eddington had earned his reputation as the foremost astrophysicist of his time through many accomplishments, including his resolution to the mystery of what powers the Sun. This mystery had stubbornly resisted all attempts to solve it until Einstein published his special theory of relativity in 1905 with its most famous equation, $E=mc^2$. Einstein's equation elegantly describes the almost miraculous transformation of matter into energy and energy into matter. Eddington realized this was the answer—every second of its life the Sun was transforming a small fraction of its mass into energy through fusion reactions. It was a remarkable intuitive leap and a masterful application of a new idea in physics to an old problem. So why did Eddington resist using the new physics to solve the old problem of white dwarfs?

The answer is that Eddington fell victim to some combination of the four primordial barriers to understanding that are constantly at work in the hearts and minds of every person: limited perspective, misleading emotions, intellectual inertia, and excessive pride. Humans try to observe the vast universe from the confines of the surface of Earth, which I can tell you from firsthand experience is always difficult. People find some ideas comforting and others disturbing, and these emotions often get in the way of the search for truth. Longstanding and popular ideas are often difficult to overcome even when compelling evidence like Chandra's is presented. And, sometimes people like Eddington experience a lapse in humility that causes them to use their authority to oppose an idea they just don't like.

Fortunately, despite Eddington's eminent status, many astronomers and physicists were on Chandra's side in the controversy, including great pioneers of quantum physics like Niels Bohr and Wolfgang Pauli. Even that was not enough to convince Eddington, who steadfastly resisted the new physics and was left behind.

Part 2: More Bodies in the Stellar Graveyard

Chandra's calculations solved one problem in astrophysics while creating another. If a dying star had less than 1.4 times the mass of the Sun, it was safe from becoming a hole in the universe. In the unscientific words of Eddington, it would "find peace" as a white dwarf. However, astronomers had observed many stars far more massive. For example, Betelgeuse, the red giant star gracing the shoulder of Orion, is almost 12 times more massive than the Sun. Astronomers realized that unless Betelgeuse were to shed nearly all of this mass in its final phase of life, it appeared to be doomed. Was there anything to prevent a more massive star from collapsing infinitely into oblivion?

Chandra had been so discouraged by Eddington's resistance to his white dwarf work that he had moved on to solving other problems in physics. It would be the father of the atomic bomb, J. Robert Oppenheimer, who would discover the next body in the cosmic graveyard of stars. Oppenheimer intuitively guessed that what astrophysicists now call neutron stars[3] might be the ultimate fate of dying stars above the white dwarf threshold.

Neutron stars were theoretically possible. Neutrons, just like electrons, resist the immense squeeze of gravity by speeding up as they're compressed. Oppenheimer wondered if, like Chandra's white dwarfs, there was a limit to how massive a neutron star could be before it was crushed by its own gravity into something else. He recruited one of his students, George Volkoff, to labor through the details of the calculation, much as Chandra had done earlier with his solution to the white dwarf problem. In the days before superfast computers, this involved tedious and exhausting mathematical work that was even more difficult than the white dwarf problem.

Oppenheimer and Volkoff had to combine quantum mechanics, Einstein's general theory of relativity, and what at the time was the poorly understood nuclear force. Oppenheimer's brilliant ability to simplify problems and push aside details he thought were unnecessary led to an important discovery. He and Volkoff showed that there was indeed a limit to how much mass neutrons stars could have.[4] The most recent calculations show that limit to be 1.5 to 3 times the mass of the Sun.

However, once again, answering one question raised another. What happens to stars more massive than the neutron star limit? Oppenheimer and another student, Hartland Snyder, worked out the details of an imploding massive star, employing the same ingenious method of simplification. What they discovered was so strange, it would prevent most physicists from accepting the existence of black holes for decades.

The equations worked out by Oppenheimer and Snyder showed that light from the surface of an imploding star would become so stretched out by gravity that, to a distant observer, the star would become invisible. The flow of time would also be stretched by gravity so that this same faraway observer would eventually see the star's collapse in slow motion until it appeared to be frozen in time at some critical size.[5] Far stranger, the equations showed the opposite from the perspective of a hypothetical observer on the surface of the imploding star: It would remain visible as it imploded faster and faster. Physicists in the Soviet Union readily accepted the existence of black holes; but physicists in the West had great difficulty accepting that different observers would have entirely different experiences of the same event, even though this was what the equations said.

All of this was so mind-boggling it temporarily broke the faith Western physicists had in the methods of theoretical science—they simply couldn't accept that such a strange scenario was possible. Following this implosion scenario to the very end led to the final insult to common sense: The imploding star would shrink until it became an infinitely small and dense singularity, a literal hole in the fabric of space and time where a star once existed. Though Oppenheimer's results pointed definitively in this direction, he couldn't accept it.

Nobel laureate physicist Kip Thorne, who chronicled the history of black hole physics in his popular book *Black Holes and Time Warps: Einstein's Outrageous Legacy*, speculates that it was Oppenheimer's scientific conservatism that prevented him from following the logic of his equations to their inevitable conclusion. But there is evidence that Oppenheimer had simply lost his faith in the laws of physics, and that made it difficult, if not impossible, for him to go further in theoretical physics.

A close friend of Oppenheimer's, the Nobel laureate physicist Isidor Isaac Rabi, believed that Oppenheimer's abilities as a physicist suffered as a result of his turning away from the beliefs of the Old Testament in favor of the literature of Hindu mysticism. According to Rabi, Oppenheimer was scientifically blinded by an exaggerated sense of mystery at the boundary between the known and the unknown, and became incapable of following the laws of physics "to the very end."

"Some may call it a lack of faith," said Rabi, "but in my opinion it was more a turning away from the hard, crude methods of theoretical physics into a mystical realm of broad intuition."[6] Rabi made a distinction without a difference because faith in the laws of physics *is* the hard, crude methods of theoretical physics. The laws of physics were developed by the great pioneers of science, from Nicolaus Copernicus and Johannes Kepler to Isaac Newton and James Clerk Maxwell, whose Christian faith in a rational Creator caused them to have faith that the universe operated according to uniform, universal, and knowable laws. Oppenheimer had turned his back on that faith, and instead embraced Eastern philosophical and religious authorities who promoted mysticism instead of rationalism. This, in turn, limited his ability to contribute further to theoretical science.

Part 3: The Triumph of Optimism

After World War II, physicists turned their attention away from weapons development back to more abstract problems like imploding stars. Physicist John Wheeler used new methods developed during the war to give a final answer to what happened to imploding stars. Together with Niels Bohr, he had developed the theory of nuclear fission, and, like Oppenheimer, he had worked on atomic and hydrogen bombs. Wheeler showed that the only objects that could theoretically exist in the stellar graveyard were white dwarfs, neutron stars, and black holes. If a star is more massive than about three times the mass of the Sun when it dies, it must implode to the point of becoming a black hole.

Wheeler, like Eddington decades earlier, couldn't accept the idea that stars could collapse infinitely and become cut off from the rest of the universe. His emotional reaction was an example of the second barrier to understanding that plagues mankind. He also distrusted Oppenheimer's trademark simplifications and believed Oppenheimer and Snyder had overlooked important physics that might save stars from this absurd fate. It looked to be the Chandra-Eddington controversy all over again, except that Wheeler was fundamentally a different person than either Eddington or Oppenheimer.

What saved Wheeler was the same thing that motivated science from the time of Copernicus—an adventurous zeal for the truth no matter how strange that truth might turn out to be. In contrast to Oppenheimer's Eastern sense of mysticism, Wheeler possessed a distinctly Western attitude toward frontiers in physics: "I confess to being an optimist about things, especially about someday being able to understand how things are put together."[7] Though Wheeler was not conventionally Christian—he was raised in the Unitarian church—this adventurous optimism has its roots in the Christian faith, and it had driven the great pioneers of science to push the boundaries of knowledge for the previous four centuries. Wheeler's words are a modern-day echo of Kepler's belief that the material laws of nature "are within the grasp of the human mind" and that "God wanted us to recognize them by creating us after his own image so that we could share in his own thoughts."[8]

In spite of his initial skepticism of black holes, Wheeler became convinced of their existence by two postwar advances in the science of collapsing stars. The first was the new ability to use sophisticated computer simulations that showed Oppenheimer and Snyder had been correct in their calculations 20 years before in spite of the details they had ignored. There was now no doubt that stars exceeding the neutron star limit must implode to black holes.

The second advance was a new way of looking at the absurdities of imploding stars.

Most physicists were hesitant to accept the existence of black holes because of the paradox implied by the equations done by Oppenheimer and Snyder. This was an example of the first barrier to understanding—the problem of limited perspective. How, they wondered, was it possible for an observer far from the action to witness an imploding star become frozen in time and eventually vanish while another observer, riding on the surface of the star, watched as the star rapidly imploded all the way to its final end? This seeming paradox was resolved by physicist David Finkelstein, who realized that there was a unified way of looking at a star's implosion that reconciled what was happening both near the imploding star and far away.[9]

With the problem of differing perspectives solved, Wheeler, who had initially rejected the idea of black holes, became an ardent proponent. In fact, it was Wheeler, in his newfound enthusiasm, who popularized the term *black hole* to refer to an imploded star. The scientific community was now a little less skeptical of the existence of black holes. However, few scientists would truly believe these strange objects existed until they were presented with physical evidence.

Every person, even the greatest of scientists, is susceptible to the four human failings that act as the great barriers to the pursuit of knowledge. Eddington and Oppenheimer could only go so far in the quest to understand collapsing stars because they had reached conceptual and emotional barriers they couldn't overcome. Though he faltered at times, Wheeler succeeded where others failed by overcoming the four failings. He embodied the rational scientific spirit with his willingness to follow the physics to the very end and his ability to overcome an emotional aversion to black holes when the mathematical evidence demanded it.

The limitations of Eddington and Oppenheimer reveal the dangers posed by a combination of intellectual, emotional, and philosophical factors that act as an ever-present intellectual gravity that threatens to pull science down from its lofty pursuit of knowledge. The only force that can overcome this intellectual gravity and sustain scientific progress is faith in the Bible's promise that the universe is rational and knowable. A scientist doesn't necessarily have to be Christian to embrace this philosophy about science, but the ultimate source of that faith in science is undeniably biblical.

Einstein once said, "The eternal mystery of the world is its comprehensibility...The fact that it is comprehensible is a miracle."[10] It is a miracle indeed; but a universe that will reveal its secrets to inquisitive humans is exactly what is promised in Psalm 19:

> The heavens declare the glory of God; the skies proclaim the work of his hands. Day after day they pour forth speech; night after night they reveal knowledge. They have no speech, they use no words; no sound is heard from them. Yet their voice goes out into all the earth, their words to the ends of the world (verses 1-4).

Black Holes Revealed

"Without proper experiments, I conclude nothing."[11] These words spoken by Kepler epitomize the modern scientist. Kepler and other scientists of his time were believers, but they did not work by blind faith. These pioneers of science required physical evidence to believe something, and this basic tenet of science comes straight from the Bible with the apostle Paul's admonition to test all things and to hold onto what is true (1 Thessalonians 5:21).

Deriving equations is crucial in physical science, but without experiments and observation, you don't have true science—at best, you have philosophy. It was one thing to show that black holes were mathematically possible; but if physicists failed to find physical evidence of their existence, black holes would remain nothing more than mathematical curiosities, and it seemed in the 1960s that black holes were doomed to this status.

Even after Wheeler's definitive calculations, Western astronomers had no interest in searching the universe for black holes. They wondered about different ways they might find black holes, but all of them had insurmountable problems. Even neutron stars were thought to be too small to be detectable.

But, as often happens in science, astronomers eventually discovered evidence for neutron stars by accident. They observed objects emitting rapid and highly precise pulsations in the radio part of the electromagnetic spectrum. The pulsations were so precise that astronomers considered, for a fleeting moment, whether they could be signals from an extraterrestrial intelligence. They soon realized that such a signal could only come from a tiny yet massive object exactly like a neutron star. This led to the discovery of pulsars—rapidly rotating neutron stars with bright magnetic poles that sweep around like light from a lighthouse at a rate of up to hundreds of times per second. With this conclusive evidence for neutron stars, the possibility that black holes existed became more credible.

In the early 1970s, with a dedicated X-ray telescope in space, astronomers detected an X-ray signal from the most credible star-massed black hole candidate to date, an object in the constellation Cygnus called Cygnus X-1. It appeared to be a binary system consisting of a visually bright star and another object that was emitting X-rays. A massive decades-long effort produced evidence that the X-ray-emitting object is a black hole that is pulling material off of the surface of its stellar companion, superheating the black hole to the point that it emits X-rays. However, astrophysicists are not certain that Cygnus X-1 is a black hole because, unlike the evidence for neutron stars, the evidence for Cygnus X-1 is not conclusive. Nevertheless, the scientific community has largely accepted that this is a black hole, and that probably as many as a million such entities reside in the Milky Way.

The most compelling evidence for black holes would come in an unexpected way. Since the formation of the Milky Way, the edge of the universe has lurked in the heart of the galaxy. It is invisible, but it hasn't been silent. Whispers are emitted to us every time the constellation Sagittarius rises in the sky. Physicist Karl Jansky was the first to detect these utterances in the early 1930s, with a radio antenna he had built for Bell Laboratories in New Jersey,[12] though he had no idea of the origin of the signal.

Radio waves are part of the electromagnetic spectrum, along with visible light, X-rays, and other types of electromagnetic radiation. People encode information on radio waves and use them for communication, and natural sources of radio emission can interfere with those transmissions. Jansky was cataloging sources of natural interference with his antenna, and determined that most were due to thunderstorms. However, he noticed a periodic radio "hiss" coming from the constellation Sagittarius, where the center of the Milky Way Galaxy resides. Astronomers knew of no way for a galaxy to produce that much radio emission, so the significance of Jansky's remarkable discovery was missed by scientists.

While astronomers in the 1930s ignored the Sagittarius radio source, a radio engineer named Grote Reber was so fascinated by what was happening that he built his own antenna in his mother's back yard in Illinois to map out radio sources in the sky. After the war and the invention of radar gave birth to high-precision radio astronomy in the 1950s, astronomers raised the possibility that Reber's radio sources were distant galaxies. They were once again faced with an absurdity. Given how far away these galaxies are—millions of light-years—they must be producing enormous amounts of radio emission to be detectable, but astronomers still had no idea how galaxies could do that.

By the 1950s, the tension between the evidence and intellectual gravity grew even worse as astronomers discovered something stranger than galactic radio sources. Radio astronomers mapping out the sky found several visible points of light that also produced radio emission. They appeared to be stars rather than galaxies; but when optical astronomers studied the spectra of these quasi-stellar radio sources—or *quasars*, as these objects would eventually be called—they were shocked to discover that not only did their spectra look nothing like the normal spectra from stars, they looked like nothing they had ever seen in the universe. Quasars produced a series of emission lines corresponding to mysterious elements never before seen. At that point, astronomers desperately needed a paradigm shift because they were stuck in old ways of thinking.

In the 1960s, astronomer Maarten Schmidt made the necessary mental leap over the barriers to knowledge when he took a fresh look at the spectrum for a quasar called 3C 273.[13] In a flash of brilliance, he realized that the mysterious emission lines in its spectrum were in fact a well-known series of hydrogen emission lines that had been shifted to the red part of the spectrum by 16%. In retrospect, it was obvious, but as Thorne observed, a "mental block held sway" that for decades prevented astronomers from seeing the truth.[14]

The red-shifting of the emission lines was due to the relative motion of quasars away from Earth and the incredible speed at which they were moving. Astronomers determined that quasars were billions of light-years from our galaxy, which meant their intrinsic brightness was an incredible thousand times brighter than the entire Milky Way Galaxy. Even stranger, the rapid rate at which quasars were observed to fluctuate in brightness meant that all of this energy was coming from a region of space not much larger than our own solar system.

Additional evidence showed that something very small was producing vast amounts of energy across the electromagnetic spectrum. After ruling out chemical and nuclear power, as well as matter-antimatter interactions, astrophysicists realized that the only force capable of generating that much energy in such a small object was extreme gravity—specifically the gravity of an absurdly massive black hole on the order of millions of times the mass of our Sun.

Scientists theorized that the energy came from a disk of gaseous matter that was falling into the supermassive black hole. This gaseous matter became superheated as it swirled down into the black hole at speeds close to the speed of light, which caused the gas to shine so brightly it could be seen by astronomers on Earth billions of light-years away. Eventually astronomers discovered evidence of faint wisps around quasars that turned out to be entire galaxies. Each quasar is at the center of its own galaxy, with the brightness of the quasar all but drowning out the light from its galactic host in astronomers' telescopes. The idea of a supermassive black hole engaged in a feeding frenzy as it sits in the heart of a galaxy was astonishing by itself, but astronomers discovered something far more surprising—nearly every galaxy in the observable universe hosts one of these monsters, or at least did at one time.

By the 1970s, astrophysicists made the connection between radio emissions in distant galaxies and quasars. They then realized that the Milky Way radio emissions discovered by Jansky decades before could be emanating from a colossal black hole in our own galactic backyard. To test this hypothesis, astronomers began collecting more detailed observations from the central region of the Milky Way, located in the Sagittarius constellation.

Using radio and infrared telescopes to penetrate the obscuring dust in our galaxy's disk, they observed swirls of gas that changed color as they rapidly streamed past a particular point in space. In 1995, astronomers obtained highly detailed observations of several individual stars orbiting this same point in space located in the very center of our galaxy. Over the span of decades, the collected data on these stars showed them tearing around an invisible racetrack at speeds of up to 3.1 million miles per hour. Given the tiny volume of space to which this stellar racetrack is confined, astronomers knew, even from the rudimentary physics of Newton, that whatever it was they were orbiting must be exceedingly massive—about four million times the mass of our Sun. Astronomers are now nearly certain that this invisible mass is a supermassive black hole.

It wasn't until the end of the twentieth century, around the time I began my career as a graduate student at the University of Texas, that astronomers uncovered evidence that black holes—whether actively feeding on gaseous material or lying dormant—inhabit the centers of almost all galaxies that have been observed. Astronomers have now collected data for hundreds of thousands of these supermassive black holes. If nearly every one of the hundreds of billions of galaxies in the observable universe contains one supermassive black hole, that's hundreds of billions of holes in the space-time fabric of the universe. And if each of those galaxies also contains millions of star-massed black holes like Cygnus X-1, as astronomers believe they do, then there isn't just one or a million ends to the observable universe, there are *quintillions*.

Black holes have gained a bad reputation over the decades. They are not voracious cosmic vacuum cleaners sucking up and destroying everything around them. You would have to come very close to a black hole before you would risk falling in. But if you were so foolish as to wander too close to a star-massed black hole, the tidal forces near the event horizon would pull so hard on you that you would be "spaghettified" and torn apart before you even passed the horizon. Somewhat paradoxically, you could in theory survive a trip across the event horizon of a supermassive black hole—its event horizon is far enough away from its singularity that the tidal forces are relatively gentle there—but you would eventually be shredded after a few hours of falling toward the singularity.

Despite these frightening scenarios, scientists now know that black holes play a crucial role in the development of the universe. As an astrophysicist who studies black holes, I've come to think of them in the way C.S. Lewis described Aslan the lion in his Chronicles of Narnia series: Black holes good, but not safe. As extraordinary as it sounds, black holes have indirectly made at least one place in the universe fit for life. When a massive star collapses during a supernova, it releases the heavy elements necessary for life in the universe to be gathered up in the formation of another star system. The collapse of the star's core to a black hole prevents destructive amounts of energy from being released to its surroundings. In fact, most of the entropy (physical chaos) in the universe is safely locked up in black holes. Supercomputer simulations show that supermassive black holes probably regulate how galaxies grow, ensuring that star formation shuts off at some critical point. This is important because galaxies are the basic building blocks of the overall structure of the universe.

A black hole. (Courtesy of NASA)

God Revealed

The story of the discovery and grudging acceptance of black holes reveals a lot about the strengths and weaknesses of human beings. The scientific revolution has proven that we have the ability to unlock the secrets of the universe and use the knowledge gained to advance our well-being. But the struggle to accept and understand black holes also shows there are powerful forces at work in the human heart and mind that always threaten to hold science back or even reverse the progress mankind has made. Even the most intelligent and dedicated people are susceptible to the four ancient barriers to understanding, and great scientists struggle like everyone else with limited perspective, misleading emotions, intellectual inertia, and a lack of humility.

The black hole epic shows that people have an especially difficult time with anything that is vast, strange, and invisible. It's normal to want the emotional comfort of dealing with what is touchable, visible, familiar, and safe. But this need leads to an attitude that is a significant part of atheistic thinking and has caused science a lot of trouble: "If I can't see it or touch it, it doesn't exist, and I don't have to think about it."

Black holes explode that attitude by demonstrating in the most dramatic way possible that the universe cannot be understood on those limited terms. Black holes are too big and important to ignore; they force people to struggle with something that stretches their understanding and imagination to the breaking point. Black holes take our thinking right to the edge of the universe, where everything we know ends and the something—or nothing—on the other side is unfathomable. Black holes are frightening to the point of being unthinkable because they represent the end of everything that is familiar and reassuring.

> We can't see or touch God, but as with black holes, we have reason to believe something or someone immensely powerful is there.

I've talked to hundreds of people about religion, and have come to realize that many of them have the same reaction to God that Eddington and Oppenheimer had about black holes. God is a far greater, far more mysterious and uncomfortable concept than even black holes. We can't see or touch God, but as with black holes, we have reason to believe something or someone immensely powerful is there. But for many people the notion of God is even more unsettling than black holes because anything with the power to create this universe has to be vast and powerful beyond our ability to imagine.

We can't rationally ignore the scientific evidence for God any more than we can ignore the evidence for black holes. Those who don't want to believe in God are skeptical for many of the same reasons scientists didn't want to believe in black holes—the idea is just too big and unnerving to deal with. Eddington and

Oppenheimer dismissed black holes as improbable, unprovable, and absurd, the same way many prominent atheists dismiss the idea of God.

A natural phenomenon like black holes differs significantly from a supernatural entity like God in that black holes can't intend anything or make the choice to hide themselves from us. As an astrophysicist, I have to live with the frustration that I'll never know *for sure* that black holes exist. God, however, has the ability to reveal his full glory to us. As I've been asked countless times by atheists, "If God wants me to believe in him, why doesn't he make it easier?" It's not an unreasonable question.

Why would God choose to conceal himself from us and make faith so difficult? Some people think God is capricious and mischievous, like the willful and unpredictable pagan gods of the ancient Greeks. Albert Einstein, the scientist ultimately responsible for discovering the physics of black holes, rejected this belief when he stated his view of the invisible and mysterious force behind the universe: "God is subtle. But he's not malicious."[15] Though Einstein believed in a pantheistic God, he inadvertently described the biblical Creator very well: While God conceals himself and reveals clues about his existence in subtle ways, he is not trying to deceive or trick us. There are far different and necessary reasons for God's subtlety.

First, it would be too dangerous for us to be exposed full-force to God, just as it would be destructive to get too close to the power of a black hole. When Moses asked God to show him his glory on Mount Sinai, God replied that no one can see his face and live (Exodus 33:18-20). Our physical and spiritual fragility could no more endure being exposed to God in all his glory than our physical fragility could withstand the devastating effects of venturing too close to a black hole. We have to gain an understanding of God and black holes from a safe distance. This need for physical detachment means we will always have doubts about their existence. But most scientists now choose to believe black holes exist because the theoretical arguments are compelling and there's enough indirect evidence to support belief. The same is true of a belief in God.

The other reason God does not reveal himself to us directly is demonstrated by biblical examples of people who had a close encounter with God and were completely transformed by it—Jacob, Moses, Samson, Job, and Isaiah, for example. Part of God's expression of love for us is that he respects the free will he gave us. If God showed himself to us, we would be so overpowered by the experience that we would have no choice but to believe. It would negate our free will because the direct experience of God would make disbelief impossible.

Far from removing all doubt, God revealing himself fully would introduce a different and more serious kind of doubt than lack of belief. If we had perfect knowledge that God exists, how would we know why we chose him? Would our choice be made because God and all that he promises is what we really want? Would our decision be based on genuine love for God and a willingness to accept his terms for reconciliation? Or would we choose God because we're compelled by awe of his power and end up clinging to him like members of an entourage to a famous and powerful celebrity? The uncertainty about the hidden and untouchable God allows us to know whether we genuinely love him or not. Christians choose God because they *want* him and all that goes with having faith in him: purpose, meaning, and the hope that the underlying principle of existence is a perfect goodness. God shows enough of himself in his creation that we are justified in the kind of belief declared in Psalm 19 and Romans 1:20.

Christians must be aware of and constantly on guard against the four barriers to understanding that made the effort to understand black holes so difficult because they are also barriers to faith. Limited perspective makes it difficult for people to believe in anything they can't touch or see, so we are all doubting Thomases to some degree. God and black holes have a frightening aspect because both are powerful beyond all understanding, and the mind naturally reels at anything so threatening. The same kind of intellectual inertia that got in the way of understanding black holes prevents many from embracing the scientific evidence for God. God and black holes are so incredible, radical, and far-removed from everyday experience it is hard for some to accept that both reason and evidence strongly point to their existence.

The worst of the primordial barriers to understanding, a lack of humility, requires special attention. It is said that Satan's great sin was pride caused by his refusal to accept God's authority over him. When I listen to professional atheists who profess to be scientists, I sense a false pride amounting to a scientifically fatal arrogance behind their efforts. The most famous and influential atheist of our time is former biologist Richard Dawkins. He accepts that science can't prove that God doesn't exist, so he pronounces God "improbable." This makes Dawkins an agnostic who doesn't want God to exist. Most self-professed atheists are actually *antitheists* who don't want any deity setting limits or telling them what to do.

These antitheists demonstrate a lack of humility through their conviction that the material is all that exists, so no intellectual effort to explore beyond the material world is necessary. Because they feel no need to look beyond science for explanations, they corrupt it into a means to find evidence for what they already believe.

The search for and acceptance of the existence of black holes shows that true science succeeds only when people shed their biases and follow the evidence wherever it takes them. Even though individual scientists faltered because of their prejudices and emotions, as a group, scientists have overcome the four barriers to truth by accepting the evidence in favor of the existence of black holes. They know they can never have perfect knowledge of these remote and mysterious objects, but most scientists have taken the scientific leap of faith and accept black holes as real. It helps that the evidence is now sufficient so the leap is like that over a small stream rather than a canyon.

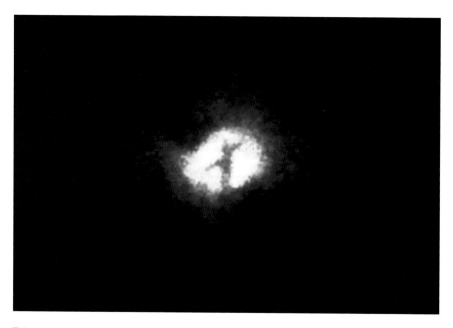

This stunning image taken by the Hubble Space Telescope in 1992[16] shows the mysterious inner workings of a massive black hole at the center of the Whirlpool Galaxy, M51. The dark X is believed to be the result of intersecting dust lanes surrounding the black hole. (Courtesy of NASA)

I entered my university education as a confirmed atheist. I didn't see any need to study religion because I felt I already knew everything anyone needed to know about it. I was especially certain that Christianity had nothing to offer a person who aspired to be a professional scientist. Then I began to learn about the incredible mysteries of black holes as I started my career researching quasars.

One beautiful summer day as I was walking across campus, I suddenly realized there was no way the universe could have "just happened" without a conscious cause. I had the sense that some Great Intellect had created a universe, complete with black holes, and left its fingerprints everywhere. Without warning, the scientific evidence had turned me into a theist.

The science of black holes is what delivered me from atheism, convinced me that God exists, and set me on a path that ultimately led to Jesus Christ. The need to understand the magnificent, mysterious, and invisible forces at play in the universe revealed the ultimate truth to me just as the Bible promised.

CHAPTER 7

TYCHO BRAHE AND JOHANNES KEPLER: THE GLORIOUSLY ODD COUPLE OF ASTRONOMY

WAYNE R. SPENCER

Tycho Brahe and Johannes Kepler lived in a tumultuous time in history. As both Christians and astronomers, their lives can teach us a lot about endurance through trials and the often-misunderstood relationship between faith and reason. Brahe and Kepler made significant contributions to the field of astronomy that would have been otherwise impossible for either of them to make on their own. As Kepler once said of his relationship with Brahe, "If God is concerned with astronomy, which piety desires to believe, then I hope that I shall achieve something in this domain, for I see how God let me be bound with Tycho through an unalterable fate and did not let me be separated from him by the most oppressive hardships."[1] Their lives provide us with a glimpse of the premodern scientific era long before any supposed conflict between science and religion existed, and even before Protestantism had fully clarified its doctrinal distinctives. From their stories, we too can learn valuable lessons about our own stories in the cosmos.

Tycho Brahe was born into Danish nobility in 1546,[2] just three years after the death of the Polish astronomer Nicolaus Copernicus and ten months following the death of the German Protestant reformer Martin Luther. Johannes Kepler, born in 1571 into humble German peasantry, barely survived his childhood,

and for much of his adult life was often on the go due to the political and eccle-
siastical conflicts of the Counter-Reformation. Brahe and Kepler came from
families who considered themselves to be Lutheran, and they both lived in the
region known at the time as the Holy Roman Empire (later called Germany).[3]

After Copernicus's death in 1543, controversy slowly began to grow in the
academic world over his suggestion that Earth revolved around the Sun, an idea
known as heliocentrism. Copernicus, interestingly enough, did not even own
a telescope (as they did not exist until the turn of the seventeenth century). His
observations and calculations relied heavily on the work of the ancient Alexandrian astronomer Ptolemy. The famed Italian astronomer Galileo Galilei, a contemporary of Kepler and Brahe, would not introduce the first telescope to the
world until the winter of 1609, stirring the wonder of Europe with his stunning
discovery of four of Jupiter's brightest Moons, an encounter that forever
changed the course of our view of the heavens.

Statue of Tycho Brahe and Johannes Kepler in Prague, Czechia. Brahe is on the left,
Kepler is on the right. Prague is where Brahe and Kepler met and worked together.
(WikiCommons)

Common people of the sixteenth and seventeenth centuries in Europe had limited education and lived with many fears and difficulties. Most people may have said they believed the Bible, but real understanding of it was severely lacking. Illiteracy prevented many from reading Scripture for themselves and usually only the priests read Scripture aloud, often in Latin. Few could read or understand Latin and virtually no one had access to a Bible in their own native tongue. Luther thus labored to translate the Bible into the common German vernacular. By 1522 he had completed the New Testament, and by 1534 he had translated the entire Bible into his native language.

There existed a great deal of cultural tension between Catholics and those who followed the teachings of Luther. Local authorities often decided whether each city would be Catholic or Lutheran. If the city was Catholic, this usually meant Protestants had to pay heavy fines or relocate. This arrangement came about because of a treaty known as the Peace of Augsburg, signed in 1555. This treaty became the law, often expressed in English by the phrase "to whom the land, to him the religion."

Amidst this chaotic world of spells, enchantments, fears, and religious strife, Tycho Brahe and Johannes Kepler kept their focus on the Creator of the heavens, navigating their way—by both their faith in Christ and the stars themselves— through the tumult in a manner much like finding one's way through a mine field.

> God seemed to be shaking up the entirety of the heavens and Earth with Luther, Kepler, and Brahe as his theological and astronomical prophets.

Astronomers of this era who were known more as mathematicians, such as Kepler, took their employment as either professors in schools and universities or were hired by kings to create calendars. These calendar books, similar to a modern-day farmer's almanac, were always expected to include advice for the coming year and prognostications regarding coming events, a guide people could use as they made their way through the seasons. The times literally were changing during the 1500s, as astronomers would soon distance themselves from astrology and the Julian calendar system. The Gregorian calendar, which we still use today, would be adopted in 1582 at the time of Pope Gregory the VIII.[4]

While Copernicus's heliocentrism slowly began to spread across Europe, Kepler and Brahe helped to further it even more.

These men lived between two worlds. They lived under the canopy of the Ptolemaic model of the universe, with Earth at its center and each planet orbiting Earth in a perfect circle within their own crystalline sphere, but they were also among the first to observe the mathematical problems this model created. Because Aristotle and Plato were considered authoritative in the academic world, many scholars initially resisted the Copernican concept. The beliefs of people very much depended on what authorities said, and in religious matters, the Catholic Church had long been considered the only authority, though Luther and Calvin and a few others had challenged that authority with great effect among the common people. God seemed to be shaking up the entirety of the heavens and Earth with Luther, Kepler, and Brahe as his theological and astronomical prophets.

Astronomers needed new mental tools, and society needed to escape the fog of astrological and theological ignorance. People's understanding of both the heavens and Earth were slowly undergoing a radical revision. Astronomical tables used for the purpose of observing the planets were inaccurate, and calendars (prior to the Gregorian calendar) also had problems that periodically required major corrections and were quite confusing and disruptive to people's daily lives. The Julian calendar year, for example, was too short. This put events out of sync with the seasons. Kepler lost ten days when he moved from Tubingen, which used the Julian calendar, to Graz, which used the Gregorian calendar. Kepler and Brahe were among some of the first astronomers who tried to comprehend the order of the Earth, Sun, and planets in geometric terms: Brahe's detailed observations and Kepler's wrestling with the implications of Brahe's data, though at first a tad obscure and difficult to understand, nevertheless began reforming the course of our understanding of the universe.

Some people today question the idea of a belief in God as being compatible with science. But Kepler and Brahe's lives demonstrate that being a faithful believer is not at odds with scientific inquiry. Knowledge of God from the Bible is essential for our understanding of ourselves and the cosmos; it is not the source of the problems having to do with science and faith. Belief in the Bible is not superstitious. *Misconceptions* about the Bible, on the other hand, are often the cause of much trouble, confusion, and superstition. Kepler and Brahe together paved a path through the astronomical and theological storms toward faith with reason. Their examples are not perfect, but they show how God had a good purpose that was bigger than either of them. Brahe's observations, combined with Kepler's laws of orbits, made it possible to predict much more accurately where and when to look in the sky to see the planets. Their work helped lead people away from superstition and toward the truth. For Kepler and Brahe, science was a tool for better understanding creation—a compliment to the faith, not a conflict.

Tycho Brahe

Unlike other men in his noble family lineage, Tycho Brahe took a somewhat unorthodox path through life. The men in the Brahe family normally became knights and often became rulers of fiefs that were given to them by Danish royalty. Tycho, however, was raised by an uncle and aunt rather than his parents. He studied at the University of Copenhagen and was heavily influenced by Martin Luther and his colleague Philipp Melanchthon. Melanchthon promoted the principle that the church could succeed in its mission to the world only if it made a broad-based education a priority—an education that included some knowledge of astronomy.

Even before the age of twenty, Brahe developed a keen interest in making careful astronomical observations. He wanted to discover and measure for himself what could be learned from a careful study of the stars and planets. During Tycho's college years, two published tables of planet positions existed for use in astronomical observations. The Alfonsine Tables of the planet positions, based on Ptolemy's Earth-centered model of the heavens, were centuries old. By contrast, the Prutenic Tables based on the Copernican Sun-centered model, were a more recent resource. Brahe found that neither set of tables were very reliable, but the Prutenic Tables were less in error.[5] Thus, as a young man he desired to make his own observational tables and this became the primary emphasis of the remainder of his life. He gave more attention to making accurate measurements of the positions of the planets and other objects than anyone before him. This was a significant challenge considering that all observations were done by the naked eye. Telescopes, as noted earlier, were not yet available. In his quest to make more accurate observations, Brahe ended up creating several ingenious mechanical instruments that proved helpful for measuring angles.

Brahe's lifelong pursuit of making careful astronomical observations is often overshadowed by his fabricated prosthetic noses. In 1566, as a young man and student at the University of Rostock, Brahe found himself in an argument with a man named Manderup Parsberg. The argument escalated into a sword fight, and Parsberg swiftly cut off the end of Tycho's nose. At that time, doctors could not do much about it, so Tycho fashioned a few metals into some simple artificial noses, none of which ever stayed attached very well. Painted portraits of Tycho, however, made his nose appear normal.

Brahe seemed to have his nose out of joint with the rest of his contemporaries too. He was willing to question commonly accepted ideas regarding astronomical objects and use his observations to test them. But his willingness to observe for himself paid off—spectacularly so. On November 11, 1572, he looked overhead toward the circumpolar W-shaped constellation Cassiopeia and noticed a new star, a very bright star that had not appeared in that area of the sky before, shining more brilliantly than early-morning Venus. His detailed knowledge of the stars helped him to be the first to record this object.

But this new star did not fit the common understanding of the universe at the time. The old Aristotelean-Ptolemaic system held that nothing in the heavens above the Moon's orbit ever underwent change of any kind. The heavens above the Moon were perfect, immutable, and without blemish. But Brahe made ongoing observations of this new star, which he called a *nova*. He found that it kept its position in the sky relative to the other stars, and eventually it dimmed. Using the shift of a star's position, what astronomers call *stellar parallax*, Brahe attempted to calculate the distance to the new star. A parallax applies the mathematics of trigonometry to measure the distance to a remote object. It requires using a known distance, called the baseline, and measuring the two angles looking at the remote object from either end of the baseline. Tycho had done this to measure the distance to the Moon. But for the new star, the angle difference was too small to measure. Thus he reasoned that the object must be farther away than the Moon; a conclusion that flatly contradicted Aristotle.

Brahe's new star is what astronomers today refer to as a supernova, a star that explodes. The death of this specific sun (now called SN 1572), and Tycho's eyewitness testimony of its radiant blast, forever changed the story of the cosmos. Convinced of his observations regarding the new star, Brahe wrote, "I doubted no longer...In truth, it was the greatest wonder that has ever shown itself in the whole of nature since the beginning of the world, or in any case as great as [when the] Sun was stopped by Joshua's prayers."[6]

Brahe also discovered a new comet. Between November 13, 1577 and January 26, 1578, he did regular observations of the object. It was believed at the time that comets were traveling within Earth's atmosphere. Tycho attempted to measure the parallax but found it was too small, thus indicating the object was not inside Earth's atmosphere after all. In fact, the comet had to be farther away than the Moon. Other observations showed that the comet's brightness and its tail varied over time. He noted that the comet moved at varying speeds in the same direction as the planets. Thus, he rightly concluded the comet was orbiting the Sun and its tail was always pointing away from the Sun. Comets were generally feared at the time, believed to be portents of future disasters. Brahe, however, was much more concerned about making good observations and learning about the comet rather than making any astrological prognostications about its appearance.

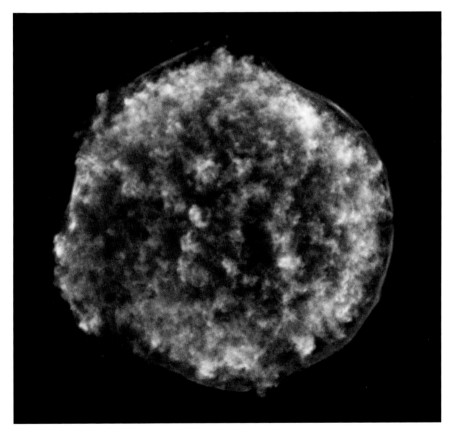

Taken by the Chandra X-ray Observatory, this is a false-color image[7] of what is left of the exploded star that Tycho Brahe observed in 1572. This supernova, SN 1572, "exploded" the medieval belief in the immutability of the heavens, forever changing our perception of the heavens. (WikiCommons)

Brahe was a colorful character, as bombastic as a supernova and as enigmatic as a comet, a star in his own right. Though a nobleman himself with connections to other noblemen, he married a commoner daughter of a Lutheran minister. Sadly, his wife, Kirsten, and her family never mingled with Brahe's noble-born family. Together, Tycho and Kirsten had eight children, two of whom died very young.

Brahe devoted much of his life to his astronomical observations. The island of Hven, given to him by King Frederick II in 1576—shortly after Brahe had discovered the supernova—was not only his home but the location of observatories, workshops, and specially constructed instruments to aid his observations.

On the island, Brahe built Stjerneborg, an underground observatory designed "to protect the instruments from vibration and wind, only the dome-shaped roofs rising above ground level; so that 'even from the bowels of the earth he could show the way to the stars and the glory of God.'"[8] Both Stjerneborg and Tycho's original and rather massive Disneyland-like island observatory Uraniborg "were full of gadgets and automata, including statues turning on hidden mechanisms, and a communication system that enabled him to ring a bell in the room of any of his assistants—which made his guests believe that he was convoking them by magic. The guests came in an unceasing procession, savants, courtiers, princes, and royalty, including King James VI of Scotland."[9]

Peasants lived on and near the island of Hven and were enlisted to help build and maintain the structures and lands there. Brahe had a somewhat exaggerated view of his own importance as a nobleman, and the peasants eventually came to hate him for his harsh treatment of them and for putting them through economic hardships. Due largely to his unpopularity with the locals, Brahe eventually moved away from Hven to the city of Prague, where he took up the position of imperial astronomer for King Rudolf II, Holy Roman Emperor. Johannes Kepler came to Prague to work with Brahe.

Brahe later put forward his own model of the solar system, which was a kind of compromise between what Ptolemy and Copernicus had proposed. In Brahe's model, Earth was at the center of the solar system. Brahe's Earth did not move in an orbit and did not rotate. Instead, the Sun orbited Earth, and the other planets orbited the Sun. The Tychonian model, as it has come to be known, was similar to the Copernican model in how it explained the planets. It is important to note, however, that Brahe had no conceptual understanding of gravity. Scholars of the time believed gravity did not operate in outer space. The understanding of gravity would not be available for several more decades,

Tycho Brahe's mural quadrant as it was in his Uraniborg mansion on the island of Hven. Approximately six feet and four inches in radius, it was an arc making a quarter of a circle. The quadrant was used to measure the angle to observe an object viewed toward the upper left. Tycho sat pointing to objects in the sky, such as the Moon. Three assistants helped with the observation. One at point F, on the right, looked at the object in the sky and observed the angle. The second, below at point H, observed two accurate clocks to note the time. The third, at the lower left point N, wrote down the observation at the time it is made. (WikiCommons)

through the work of the polymath Isaac Newton. Though Brahe's system was not entirely correct, his innovative approach toward making careful astronomical observations and measurements not only challenged the accepted cosmological models, but also laid the groundwork for Kepler's revolutionary discoveries about planetary motion. Brahe died in 1601 at the age of 54, and Johannes Kepler became his successor.

Johannes Kepler

Unlike Brahe, Kepler was born into a common family without much to recommend his future astronomical successes. He grew up in a small city called Weil der Stadt. The Kepler family was Lutheran. His father, Heinrich, often away from home, worked as a mercenary soldier. Thus, Johannes's grandfather, Sebald, was the primary father figure in Johannes's life.

Johannes was born premature, and as a boy and young man he was considered slight in build. He became ill with smallpox when he was four and managed to survive, although this viral disease did some damage to his fingers and sometimes his left eye was afflicted by double vision. In 1577, when Johannes was six, his mother took him outside to see the same comet that Tycho Brahe wrote about.

In his college years, Kepler became known for holding controversial points of view. He spoke in defense of Copernican cosmology, a significant concern to the university faculty. Johannes was appalled at the tension and sometimes outright hatred that existed between differing theological camps. The doctrinal issues he had with Lutheran communion, for example, made his superiors believe he should not be allowed to go into ministry in the Lutheran church. Though Kepler desired to enter the ministry, events seemed to conspire against this.

Kepler's coursework prepared him well for his future planetary endeavors. With an emphasis on Greek philosophy, Latin, Greek, Hebrew, and theology, as well as some mathematics and astronomy, Kepler's meticulous attention to detail had been honed through his studies, preparing him to sift through the volumes of Tycho's celestial data. In 1591 he finished his master's degree at the University of Tubingen.[10] The university had arranged for him to continue another four years for advanced study, but this was cut short largely due to the death of a mathematics teacher in Graz, Austria. Lutheran church leaders seized this as an opportunity to keep Kepler out of the ministry—they arranged for him to be offered the position of teaching mathematics rather than continuing his theological studies. This turned out to be a pivotal moment in Kepler's life, moving him toward a career in mathematics and astronomy.

In Graz, Kepler was both a teacher and a district mathematician, which involved preparing calendar books containing astrological predictions about the coming year. Kepler came to have a good reputation for the prognostications that he published. Yet he admittedly disliked writing these books because it was "nourishing the superstition of fatheads."[11] In various letters to acquaintances he often commented that he took no pride in those writings himself. In one document he sent to a physician he stated that astrology was the "foolish little daughter of the respectable, reasonable mother astronomy."[12] Kepler considered astrological predictions questionable at best, but royalty and political leaders of the day considered this the "practical" aspect of an astronomer's work.

While in Graz, Kepler encountered an uneasy tolerance between Catholics and Protestants. This remained tenuous until 1598, when Archduke Ferdinand II came to power over inner Austria. Ferdinand determined to undo any Protestant influence from his land and restore Catholic rule. This meant that Protestant schools and colleges were shut down and many Protestants were fined and forced to leave. Protestants were sometimes refused care at hospitals and were required to have their children married in a Catholic ceremony. When Kepler and his wife lost a baby daughter and refused to have a Catholic burial ceremony, they were subsequently fined. Sometime after the loss of his daughter, Kepler suffered the indignity of being forced to leave Graz along with other teachers. Officials later permitted him to return because of his position as the district mathematician. Yet Kepler began looking for another means of employment so he could move out of Graz permanently.

The year 1600 was eventful for both Brahe and Kepler as a turn of events soon brought them face to face. Brahe and Kepler knew of one another and had sent each other letters, but up until 1600, had never met in person, nor did their letters always reach each other. Brahe moved to Prague and had managed to come under the support of Emperor Rudolph II. In the move, Brahe lost some of the assistants he had at Hven. His massive amount of data needed sorting and analyzing, but he needed help from someone with mathematical acuity far beyond his own. Brahe, however, was unwilling to entrust his research to Kepler because of a misunderstanding.

The source of the misunderstanding involved their mutual acquaintance with a young astronomer by the name of Ursus, as well as their differing views on Copernicus. As one of Brahe's young protégés, Ursus plagiarized Tycho's model, publishing it in a book as his own work. In the same publication, Ursus also printed a personal letter from Kepler, but without Kepler's knowledge or consent. The letter obviously made Brahe somewhat suspicious of Kepler's allegiance—he suspected Kepler might have been spying for Ursus. But Kepler had also written a book of his own, the title of which could be loosely translated *The Cosmic Mystery*, which he had sent to Brahe. Impressed, Brahe decided to take a chance on Kepler and invited him to visit Prague.

Despite their differences, Brahe the careful observer-experimentalist and Kepler the adroit mathematician-theoretician needed each other's abilities to make sense of the heavens. Even to the present day, in the fields of physics and astronomy, some scientists are known as experimentalists because of their emphasis on observational techniques, and others are known as theoreticians because they emphasize the mathematical and conceptual side of research.

The unlikely duo had a tense working relationship, but one that eventually led to a complete restructuring of our concept of the universe. By himself, Kepler would have had difficulty with the observations due to his eye problems, while Brahe had a keen eye for observation but did not have Kepler's mathematical prowess. Kepler eagerly desired to get access to Brahe's observational data on the planets and also needed Brahe's assistance to intercede on his behalf with Emperor Rudolph II and obtain for him a paid position. Both men thus earnestly desired to test their own models of the heavens against good observational measurements of the planets. Kepler orbited Brahe as the Moon orbits Earth, an odd couple of orbs tidal-locked in a cosmic struggle that would eventually yield one of the greatest chapters in the story of the cosmos. As James R. Voelkel aptly says,

> The two men could not have been more different. Tycho was a nobleman, self-assured, domineering, and combative. Kepler was a commoner, sincere, reflective, peace-loving, and unassuming. Yet they fit together like a lock and key…Both brilliant, and each one's skills complemented the other's. But neither was there by choice.[13]

Brahe eventually requested that Emperor Rudolph make it possible for Kepler to obtain a paid position. But circumstances prevented that arrangement from working out. At one point Kepler became quite angry with Brahe about the terms of Kepler's employment by the emperor. As a result, Brahe almost parted ways with Kepler, but the latter quickly realized he had caused offense and apologized. Brahe quickly forgave him and they resumed working together.

Eventually Kepler obtained access to some of Brahe's observations of Mars. Though Brahe stubbornly refused to give Kepler the data for all the planets, he did make a proposal to the emperor to prepare a new astronomical tables book from the observations of the planets. Such a publication would be the culmination of Brahe's dream as a young man of creating an accurate star and planet catalogue. He proposed to the emperor that it should be called the Rudolphine Tables and that Kepler would work with him on the project. Emperor Rudolph very much liked the idea. Sadly, Brahe would not live long enough to see the tables completed. He died in October of 1601, approximately one year and eight months after he and Kepler met. Kepler continued his work on the tables and eventually had them published in 1627, some years after Emperor Rudolph had died.

After Brahe's death, Kepler was quickly appointed as Brahe's successor, but became embroiled in difficult conflicts with the Brahe family. Despite this, Kepler persevered and published his important works that would eventually revolutionize all of astronomy. While Kepler continued his work on the Rudolphine Tables, he published a series of important works on the science of optics in 1604 and 1611. Kepler was apparently the first to write about the basic principles of ray optics—principles that explain how the eye works, with images being inverted as they are captured upon the back of the eye (the same way a pinhole camera works).

In 1609, the same year Galileo made his first telescope, Kepler published a book called *Astronomia Nova*. This book went into great detail about how Kepler arrived at his discoveries regarding the orbit of Mars. It mentioned the first two of his laws of planetary motion but applied them solely to Mars. This landmark book made a persuasive case that the planets did not move in perfect circles as Aristotle imagined, but rather, had elliptical orbits. He also stated that the Sun was at the center of the planets and somehow influenced their motions. *Astronomia Nova* was a supernova in its own right, stirring not a little controversy upon its publication, and forever changing the way we understand the heavens.

After *Astronomia Nova*, Kepler published some lesser-known works: in 1610 a book in German about his views on astrology, and in 1614 a book known as *De Vero Anno*. This book dated the birth of Jesus Christ and related the magi mentioned in the New Testament to planetary conjunctions. Kepler's date is consistent with modern scholarship, placing Jesus's birth at around 4 or 5 BC.

DE MOTIB. STELLÆ MARTIS

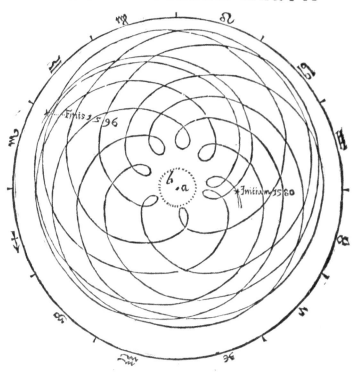

Depiction of the motion of Mars, originally from Johannes Kepler's book *Astronomia Nova*. The diagram graphs what would be the actual motion of Mars if Earth were stationary in space. Around the outside of the circular diagram are symbols of the zodiac, marking out the constellation positions. Virgo and Leo are at the top and Aquarius and Pisces are at the bottom. The point in the center marked *a* is Earth. To the right of point *a* is marked the starting position of the observation of Mars in the year 1580. To the upper left of point *a* is marked the ending position in 1596. Kepler used this diagram to argue against both the Ptolemaic and Tychonian models for the motion of the planets. He argued that these models were contrary to observations because in this motion Mars would never come back to the same position in the sky, as observed from Earth. (WikiCommons)

The period from 1611 to 1619 was full of political turmoil and painful loss for Kepler. His first wife, Barbara, died in 1611, and the conflict between the Catholics in power and resident Protestants intensified. In 1612 Emperor Rudolph II died, which brought changes in the political situation for Protestants. Kepler remarried in 1613 and moved his family to the city of Linz to escape trouble in Prague. He also had to find new employment. From sometime in late 1617 into

1618, two of Kepler's children died within a six-month period. In 1618 came the beginning of the terrible Thirty Years' War between Protestants and Catholics. This war caused the deaths of many either directly from the fighting or indirectly from various diseases. And if all of that was not trouble enough, in 1619 Kepler was excommunicated by the Lutheran church. Yet in spite of his personal Job-like calamities, he managed to publish a book that same year titled *The Harmony of the World*. By God's grace, Kepler managed to move his family away from the wars and conflicts and provide for them, mainly from his writings.

From 1617 to 1621, Kepler published a set of books known in English as *The Epitome of Copernican Astronomy*. Intended as a complete course on astronomy, these volumes explained all three of his laws of planetary motion. These laws were applied not only to Mars, but all the planets, the Moon, and to certain Moons of Jupiter, which at the time had recently been discovered by Galileo. Kepler had a general idea for what we now call gravity, but many other scholars of Kepler's day resisted the concept.

It is nothing short of remarkable that Kepler not only endured so many personal difficulties, but that he also pioneered one of the foundational tenets of modern astronomy. His three laws of planetary motion described three important properties of planetary orbits. The first is that the orbit of a planet is the shape of an ellipse, with the Sun at one of the two focal points of the ellipse. Second, a straight line drawn from the Sun to a planet will sweep out equal areas in equal amounts of time as a planet moves along its orbit. And third, there is a mathematical relationship between the time it takes for a planet to make one orbit and the distance to that planet. Kepler used his laws of motion to predict how astronomers could observe Mercury as it passed in front of the Sun in 1631.

Kepler, unfortunately, did not live to see his prediction confirmed. He laid his earthly troubles aside for the final time in November of 1630. His prediction turned out to be within about five hours of the correct time for viewing Mercury, a great accomplishment for that era. Unlike subjective astrological prognostications, this was a mathematical prediction based on what Kepler had learned about the orbit of Mercury.

Kepler demonstrated exceptional character and resilience in his personal life. He lived in difficult times and faced personal loss, occasional mistreatment for his Protestant faith, financial trouble, political upheavals, church conflicts, and other challenges. He had children from both of his marriages—five from the first, of which three died, two in infancy. He had seven children from his second marriage, but only one or two of them lived to adulthood. His life stands as a testimony and encouragement to us that despite the challenges and difficulties we face, through faith in Christ, we, too, can overcome and persevere for his glory.

Kepler's faith in Christ was central to his life and work. It gave him a strong sense of meaning in his scientific endeavors and the strength to persevere through personal trials. Influenced by the times in which he lived, he partially accepted astrology and had some mystical leanings. Yet he set an excellent example in not blindly accepting prevailing ideas. In both theological matters and in astronomy, he tested ideas against reason and evidence.

On biblical issues, Kepler had the ability to examine Scripture in Greek and Hebrew for himself. He also steadfastly resisted capitulating to Catholicism even though it could have benefitted him and spared his family hardship. He also tried to persuade Protestants to accept the Gregorian calendar on its own merits and look past the fact that it came from the Pope. The sometimes-petty disagreements between people of faith appalled Kepler, even though he was quite firm on essential issues. Lutherans too often misunderstood Kepler. He once said, "It makes me heartsick that the three big factions have so miserably torn up the truth among themselves that I have to gather the little scraps together wherever I find them."[14]

Kepler often wrote about how he related his faith to life and his astronomical work. He wrote about loving his philosophical speculations more than the hours of long calculations. In *The Harmony of the World*, for example, Kepler wrote about similarities between the planet orbits (or orbital periods) and musical notes and chords. On the surface, this seems like an odd connection to make. But both sound and planet orbits are periodic phenomena, and Kepler noticed similarities expressible in mathematical ratios. He wrote, "I am writing the book—whether to be read by my contemporaries or by posterity matters not. Let it await its reader for a hundred years, if God Himself has been ready for His contemplator for six thousand years."[15] Kepler believed God had a purpose for his book *The Harmony of the World*, though some astronomers who knew Kepler would have considered it a waste of time. Kepler believed God had waited for him to write this book since the creation of the world. He also believed God created the universe with the deliberate intent that human beings would search it out and discover its mysteries. In one of his letters, he addressed the matter of what good astronomy was to people. He wrote,

> Should…the kind creator who brought forth nature out of nothing…deprive the spirit of man, the master of creation and the Lord's

own image, of every heavenly delight? Do we ask what profit the little bird hopes for in singing? We know that singing in itself is a joy to him because he was created for singing. We must not ask therefore why the human spirit takes such trouble to find out the secrets of the skies.[16]

Kepler believed that God had created the universe with order and harmony. But to Kepler it wasn't enough to merely acknowledge this. He wanted to understand the order God created and know the reasons behind how the heavens appeared as they do. His task was made more difficult by the fact that we, as human beings, tend to build on the assumptions made by our predecessors to the point that we no longer know another way to view the world around us. Kepler had to work through a long process to arrive at real answers. He spent many hours comparing Ptolemy, Copernicus, and Brahe's ideas, holding them up to good observations, and working out the numbers through longhand calculations. The harmony God had created turned out to be an order of a kind that Kepler, and even the whole scholarly world, had never expected. One of the surprises Kepler discovered was that the planets, including Earth, follow elliptical orbits. Somehow God did not seem to have the same concept of perfection as human scholars! The planets did not orbit in perfect circles after all.

The Meaning of Exploration

When Tycho Brahe lay dying, he repeatedly said something to the effect of "let me not seem to have lived in vain." Brahe wanted Kepler to show that the Tychonian model could explain the motion of the planets. But Kepler went where the evidence led him, and this brought him to the Copernican model but with the modification of replacing circular orbits with elliptical ones. Yet to arrive at this conclusion, Kepler had depended on the careful observations Brahe had made over the course of many years. Tycho Brahe's observations could have ended up being ignored or forgotten if it were not for Kepler and his mathematical skills. In this sense, one could say that Brahe and Kepler were like two binary stars that shone brighter together than either of them could do alone.

Brahe and Kepler also set an example in how they exercised faith with reason, even though their assumptions about the universe were not always correct. They both believed there was a divine purpose behind their efforts to understand the order God created. Even their mistakes contributed to the process of them coming to answers. Both Brahe and Kepler helped lead people away from superstition and ignorance, and Kepler's writings show how faith gave meaning and purpose to his scientific and mathematical discoveries.

In Kepler's *The Epitome of Copernican Astronomy* there is a section where Kepler pauses to explain what astronomy meant to him. It expresses beautifully the meaning of the human exploration of space and the human desire to understand the universe. The quote below comes out of Kepler's biblical mindset, which held that human beings are made in God's image. For us as human beings to possess this image means we don't merely discover facts and figures in scientific investigation, we discover something of the Creator behind them all. To Kepler, this is our place in the cosmos.

> With a pure mind I pray that we may be able to speak about the secrets of His plans according to the gracious will of the omniscient Creator, with the consent and according to the bidding of His intellect. I consider it a right, yes a duty, to search in cautious manner for the numbers, sizes and weights, the norms for everything He has created. For He Himself has let man take part in the knowledge of these things and thus not in a small measure has set up His image in man. Since He recognized as very good this image which He made, He will so much more readily recognize our efforts with the light of this image also to push into the light of knowledge the utilization of the numbers, weights and sizes which He marked out at creation. For these secrets are not of the kind whose research should be forbidden; rather they are set before our eyes like a mirror so that by examining them we observe to some extent the goodness and wisdom of the Creator.[17]

PART II:

EXPRESSIONS OF THE COSMOS IN ART AND LITERATURE

CHAPTER 8

THE COSMOS AND THE STARRY NIGHT

TERRY GLASPEY

When I stand in a field in the middle of night, far from the light pollution of the cities and civilization, I look up and am filled with breathless awe and an almost overwhelming curiosity. As I think about my own natural responses, I recognize there is little question about how the science of astronomy came to be. Surely it began when the first humans looked up into the night sky and were filled with wonder. Throughout history, people have lifted their eyes toward the dark vastness of space and all its shimmering stars and contemplated the mysteries they saw there. They have asked questions about where all this majestic beauty came from and tried to make sense of its expanse. Those with a scientific bent naturally gave themselves to investigating the secrets of the universe and exploring and mapping its immensity.

But scientists are not the only ones who have been fascinated by the stars twinkling so brightly in the night skies. Those with a poetic and artistic bent have also meditated on what they have seen there and what it might mean. They have gazed upward to learn what such beauty might have to say to us. One such poet authored many of the psalms. The psalmist suggests that the heavens above are a revelation of the glory of the one who created them. So clear is the message from the stars that he uses the metaphor of speech as he contemplates their communicative powers:

> The heavens declare the glory of God; the skies proclaim the work
> of his hands.

Day after day they pour forth speech; night after night they reveal knowledge.

They have no speech, they use no words; no sound is heard from them.

Yet their voice goes out into all the earth, their words to the end of the world (Psalm 19:1-4).

The heavens speak with a "voice that goes out into all the earth" and proclaim God's glory, majesty, and power. Looking into the sky, whether by day or by night, the psalmist suggests, we can better understand the nature of the Creator by contemplating the creation. Psalm 29 parallels this same metaphorical understanding of God being heard in his creation—in the thunder of the mighty waters, the towering cedars and oaks, the flashes of lightning racing across the skies, and the stillness of the barren deserts. The psalmist pictures God enthroned on the praises of his created world, which is why Psalm 148 calls upon the Sun and Moon, the shining stars, and all the inhabitants of Earth—both human and animal—to offer up praise to the one who made them.

That the created order could offer such praise not only tells us something about its nature, but also about the nature of the one who fashioned it. A Person and a Personality stand behind all that has been made. The universe itself, the Psalms would have us understand, is a wondrous living creation—not, as some materialistic scientists suggest, a machine slowly winding down. The whole order of living things is a witness to meanings and purposes almost beyond imagining.

> If the out-of-doors is a grand natural cathedral,
> then the artist can invite people who stand
> before their work to enter that cathedral,
> their brushstrokes pointing like fingers
> toward the glory of God to be found there.

The poets who penned these psalms understood the natural world to be a revelation of the God who had created it. Artists have found the same to be true as they record the grandeur of the creation with their paints and brushes. If nature is speaking, then perhaps we can think of the work of the artists who paint these glories as *transcribers* of that divine message, helping us to see and appreciate it in new ways. If nature is a source of revelation, illumination, consolation, and wisdom, then artists can offer such experiences through their transcriptions of that beauty. If the out-of-doors is a grand natural cathedral, then the artist can invite people who stand before their work to enter that cathedral, their brushstrokes pointing like fingers toward the glory of God to be found there.

Hugo of St. Victor, a medieval theologian, wrote that "the whole world, perceivable through the senses, is, after all, like a book written by the finger of God."[1] And Thomas Aquinas wrote of the natural world being one of God's "two books" that offer revelatory insights into his nature and character. There is the book of Scripture and the book of nature, both of which are vehicles through which God makes himself known. In other words, nature can be "read," and the attentive reader will gain a deeper understanding of God and his ways. All things, both great and small, are the individual letters of a mysterious and beautiful book that provide us with glimpses of the power and majesty of what lies beyond them. Which is why John Calvin saw this world as a "theater of God's glory" and "a living painting of God's majesty."[2]

The Scientist and the Artist

Of course, some have looked up into a night sky and seen nothing but the outworking of a random cosmic event somewhere in the imperceivably distant past. Similarly, some can stand at the precipice of the Grand Canyon and feel no sense of awe or wonder, remaining content to explain it by way of geological convulsions and describe it merely through taking measurements and commenting upon the coloration of its variegated strata. They see nothing more than what their eyes can behold and find there no meaning or purpose or evidence of something more. Could it be that the power of materialistic naturalism blinds them from seeing anything beyond what imprints itself upon their retina? As children of the Enlightenment, they have settled for a world that asks no questions and offers no answers. They have become dulled to the wonders in the heavens above and Earth below and failed to comprehend the messages that are written across the expanse of the universe. But artists can challenge them, and us, to take a second look, to see once again the beauty and majesty and mystery that stretches out before us, to be reenchanted by the magic of the heavens.

The artist reminds us that the proper human responses to the things we behold in nature are to sigh and wonder and puzzle over our place in the family of things. For the artist is one whose purpose is always to help us see, to draw out specific things from all the phenomena that surrounds us and help us really look at them, as though seeing them for the first time—whether it be the vastness of a landscape, the fragile beauty of a single leaf, a bunch of oranges clustered together on a table, or the mysterious terrain of a human face. The artist foregrounds what he or she wants us to see. And in doing so, raises questions about the things we are looking at.

Just as the scientist focuses upon individual realities to help us understand how they work and function, so the artist focuses upon asking questions about what they *mean*. And while science is focused upon finding answers, sometimes art is satisfied with simply evoking the right kinds of questions.

As we think about the cosmos and about the environs of our planetary home, the artists provide us with kinds of data that mere scientific experimentation will never be able to explain. For artists not only reproduce the phenomena of nature, but through their artistry evoke emotional responses, such as awe, wonder, and the sense that this planet upon which we dwell is our home, a gift offered by the one who created it—and who created us. They give us a glimpse of the order, the symmetry, the perfections to be found even in the imperfect. They offer us wordless "words" that can lead us to expressions of praise and gratitude. They may even stir up a feeling of ecstasy, the feeling that we are standing outside ourselves and participating in something truly remarkable. They are not offering an argument in the usual sense of the word. Instead, they are offering an invitation for us to see what they see.

And what many artists have seen in nature, and shared with us through their creations, is a manifestation of a divine presence that haunts every inch of the cosmos. The transcendent God who is beyond everything he has made is immanent in every star and constellation, every mountain peak and lush valley, every barren desert and singing stream, the vast expanse of the sky and the depth of the ocean, every single crack and crevice and microbe and atom. It all sings a visual hymn to its creator and invites us to join the chorus.

A Brush with Glory

For many centuries, religious expression in art was focused almost exclusively on retelling the sacred stories of Scripture and of the saints. In these paintings, the landscape was mostly just an artistic backdrop—if it even appeared at all. Such paintings often told a story that existed in a timeless realm beyond our earthly one, and if there were elements to ground the narrative on earthly soil, they were limited—such as a couple of trees against a simple landscape. It wasn't until after the Reformation that artists began to consider nature on its own to be a worthy subject and to rediscover the truths of which the psalmist sang regarding how it could communicate spiritual realities by representing physical ones. Landscape painting began to emerge as a serious genre of visual art, though it failed to be highly esteemed as a genre until the middle of the nineteenth century.[3]

It was at the hands of Dutch artists like Jacob van Ruisdael (c. 1628–1682) that the landscape itself became a primary subject for an artist's work and landscape painting as a genre was born. As a member of the Reformed Church in Amsterdam, van Ruisdael trained as both a surgeon and a painter—a man whose steady hands could capture even the smallest details of nature with the same precision that is required to perform an operation. He recognized the spiritual significance of the visible world and what it pointed toward. In his art, we see mystery and majesty in stately weathered trees, the play of light on the rolling countryside and in the movement of clouds. He painted a transient and ever-changing world, but it is one in which humans can live in harmony. And his work arouses an attitude of contemplation, where nature becomes a ladder on which our thoughts may climb toward God.

In van Ruisdael's painting *Landscape with a View of Haarlem* (c. 1665),[4] we see the human world dwarfed by the immensity of the nature in which it exists. The sky is immense, taking up nearly two-thirds of the painting, which is a signature motif for Van Ruisdael's work. The clouds are in movement, creating alternating bands of shadow and sunlight that fall in succession across the expansive view. The painting suggests a providential sense of well-being and peace, and a distant church steeple might be seen as a finger pointing upward, out beyond this world. Van Ruisdael blazed a path for landscape painting that many artists would eventually follow.

During the Romantic period, nature was widely embraced as the language of God. For the Romantics, the visual arts and poetry could be used as windows into the natural world, making connections between our human emotions and the beauties of nature which provoked them. As William Wordsworth wrote, "To me the meanest flower that blows can give / Thoughts that do often lie too deep for tears."[5] For many artists, the thoughts that "lie too deep for tears" were meditations about the divine order of things and our place within it.

Jacob van Ruisdael, *Landscape with a View of Haarlem* (c. 1665), Kunsthaus Zurich (WikiCommons)

The German artist Caspar David Friedrich (1774–1840) was raised in a devout Lutheran home and deeply influenced by the theologian Ludwig Gotthard Kosegarten, whose notions of nature as a revelation of God were important to Friedrich's development as an artist. Friedrich often sought to portray supernatural realities through natural ones. Hence, his paintings frequently portray a solitary individual surveying an awe-inspiring panorama of nature. The individuals in his paintings are generally not saints or biblical characters, but ordinary people. And usually their backs are turned, investing them with a sense of "standing in" for the viewer. A prime example is the iconic *Wanderer Before the Sea of Fog* (1818).[6] In it, we stand alongside the lone gentleman who has clambered up to the top of a mountain peak and stands gazing over the fog-shrouded world that stretches out before him. He is an adventurer whose own path has taken him as far as it can go, and now he stands alone before God. He is prepared to receive whatever nature will reveal to him about the one who created it—the presence of God which is palpable in the natural world.

Caspar David Friedrich, *Wanderer Above the Sea of Fog* (1818), Kusthalle Hamburg (WikiCommons)

In the mid-nineteenth century, a group of American painters who came to be known as the Hudson River School (as its founders lived and painted in the Hudson River Valley in the northern part of New York state) painted grand scenic vistas that called attention to the unspoiled wilderness of the youthful nation and celebrated the beauties of the natural world. All the most important members of this artistic circle were Christians who saw God's handiwork in the grandeur of the landscape. Humans are largely absent from their paintings, and any signs of human existence were usually dwarfed by the natural surroundings.

The first of the Hudson River painters was Thomas Cole (1808–1848), whose paintings of the American landscape celebrated the wild and sublime beauty of the natural world. At a time when forests were beginning to be destroyed to make way for railways, Cole was concerned that the progress of civilization would damage the pristine beauty he found all around him, and he sought to hold this beauty up for inspection through his art. He was convinced that God was the ultimate artist and that nature was his canvas, writing, "There are spots on this earth, where the sublime and beautiful are united—where the heart of man feels its own nothingness or rises with the most ecstatic emotions—when the lips are sealed in reverence, but the soul feels unutterably."[7] He and the other Hudson River painters sought out such spots to paint. They believed that nature could be a spiritual refuge from an increasingly materialistic culture and that it should be celebrated and protected.

One of Cole's most famous works is *View from Mount Holyoke: The Oxbow*, painted in 1836.[8] In it he included a tiny self-portrait of himself working away in the lower right portion of the painting, illustrating a scene of the wilderness giving way to cultivation, which was not an entirely welcome phenomenon. A storm is passing through, and sunlight spotlights the view in the valley below. On the side of the mountain in the distance he has given us a subtle hint of his intentions. The Hebrew letters for the word *Shaddai* ("the Almighty") can be made out, painted upside-down in the spots of clearing on the mountain. Perhaps this is Cole's reminder that God leaves his mark even when humans tamper with their natural surroundings.

Thomas Cole, *View from Mount Holyoke: The Oxbow* (1836), Metropolitan Museum of Art (WikiCommons)

Cole's most famous protégé was Frederic Edwin Church (1826–1900), his only full-time student, and one whose work many thought surpassed his teacher. Like Cole, Church was fascinated by the effects of light. He saw it as a symbol for spiritual realities breaking into the natural order. His paintings, many of them quite large, display the drama and the majesty of the physical world. Church, himself an amateur scientist, read widely in the scientific literature of his day, especially geology and botany. He belonged to the American Geological and Statistical Society, an organization comprised of scientists, artists, and literary men who were "united in their fascination with the natural world."[9] The accuracy and power that Church evoked in his landscapes has caused some to refer to him as "the painter of scientific eloquence."[10]

Not content to work from secondhand descriptions or photos of faraway places, Church traveled to South America, the tropics, the Arctic circle, the Alps, and the Middle East to experience these places for himself and to sketch what he saw in preparation for the paintings he would later create in his studio. He once traveled five days on a donkey to get a glimpse of a South American mountain peak he desired to see and paint. The resulting works are filled with intricate details and emphasize the effects of light as it plays over the landscape. He put that knowledge to use in making his paintings both precise and alive, bringing a sense of poetry to his accurate representations of the landscape.

Frederic Church, *The Heart of the Andes* (1859), Metropolitan Museum of Art (WikiCommons)

One of Church's most popular paintings, *The Heart of the Andes* (1859),[11] was composed after a harrowing journey into the jungles of South America to study the flora and fauna and make extensive sketches of them. From these he fashioned a canvas that is over five feet high and almost ten feet wide. He wanted the painting to be an immersive experience for those who viewed it, and he rented space in New York City just to exhibit this single masterpiece. Church set up palms around the perimeter and bordered the painting with curtains to suggest the effect of gazing out a window. The room was darkened, and the painting lit by spotlight. More than 12,000 people paid an admission fee to see this single work, and opera glasses were provided so that they viewers could search out the smallest details of this immense masterpiece. What they saw was a reminder of how God's glory is displayed through his work. As Church's friend and biographer the Reverend Louis Noble explained, this painting leads the mind "into the presence of the Maker."[12] As one takes the time to let the painting fully reveal itself, it produces a stillness that can usher the viewer into a state akin to contemplation. A reviewer for the *New York Daily Tribune* summarized one of Church's paintings in this way: Here is "art, science, and holiest sentiment."[13]

Other important members of the Hudson River school included Asher Durand (who once expressed the belief that "the true province of art is the representation of the work of God in the visible creation"[14]), Thomas Moran, Jasper Cropsey, and Albert Bierstadt. Cropsey believed that landscape painting would "be great in proportion as it declares the glory of God."[15] The Hudson River artists rarely introduced religious symbols or direct references to Christianity into their work. They believed that nature itself could tell the story and that it was up to the artist to display God's majesty through an accurate depiction of what he had created. As Cropsey wrote, "The voice of God came to me through every motionless leaf…on every blade of grass…in every breath of air…in all these things I could see the beauties of holiness and the greatness of the Lord."[16]

Through their work, these artists showed God as both transcendent and immanent in his creation. In viewing their paintings, one didn't need to travel to the wilds, hike up a jagged mountain peak, or delve into the dark forests to witness what nature had to say. Nature is a book of revelations, and it was giving voice to the book's message. As Thomas Cole wrote, "…in gazing on the pure creations of the Almighty, he [the viewer] feels a calm religious tone steal through his mind, and when he has turned to mingle with his fellow men, the chords which have been struck in that sweet communion cease not to vibrate."[17] His paintings sought to do just that, which is why, when William Cullen Bryant spoke at the funeral of Thomas Cole, he could say, "The paintings of Cole are of that nature that it hardly transcends the proper use of language to call them acts of religion."[18]

Looking Up

These landscape painters saw their canvases as sacred works that testified to the glory of God every bit as much as a painting of a biblical scene or an episode from the lives of the saints. They saw the very fingerprints of God in his creation.

When we circle back to where we started, we look again to the night sky and observe the wonders that great artists have seen when they gazed up into its illuminated darkness.

Giotto, vault of the Scrovegni Chapel (c. 1305), Padua, Italy (WikiCommons)

The first great painter of the Western tradition was Giotto di Bondone (c. 1267–1337), an Italian painter and architect whose frescoes were the first to express the deeply human emotions that lay beneath the stories of the Bible and the saints. He made these characters come alive through his depiction of these emotions, whether joy or grief or confusion. Giotto's masterpiece was the series of frescoes he created for the Scrovegni Chapel in Padua, Italy (completed about 1305).[19] These frescoes portrayed key scenes from the life of Jesus, as well as the life of his mother, Mary. But for our purposes, we should look up. Towering high above these biblical scenes and painted upon the ceiling of the small chapel is a sky full of stars. A rich deep blue pigment called *lapis lazuli* was used for the sky itself. It was a color associated with the divine, a pigment costlier than gold. It provided the frame for the bright stars. By painting the night sky in all its glory, Giotto gave us a vision of the very vault of heaven itself.

Unknown, *Studying Astronomy and Geometry* (early fifteenth century), The British Library (WikiCommons)

Some years later, an unknown artist of the early Renaissance illustrated the growing interest in the sky as more than just a beautiful backdrop.[20] This painter portrayed it as a phenomenon worthy of investigation. Against a setting of trees and rolling hills, a group of men are seen examining the night sky. While one of them offers a blessing, the others set their gaze above with intensity, or consult their various early astronomical instruments. One of them reads aloud from a book, which is probably meant to represent the Bible. In this painting, then, we see science and faith working hand in hand, using both the Scriptures and scientific inquiry to gain a deeper understand of the star-strewn heavens. There is no war between faith and science in evidence here; just the use of differing— and complementary—tools. It illustrates the way that faith, art, and science can work together to tell the fullest story about the cosmos.

Un missionnaire du moyen âge raconte qu'il avait trouvé le point
où le ciel et la Terre se touchent...

Unknown, Flammarion woodcut (sixteenth century?) (WikiCommons)

Another early work by an unknown artist, *Beyond Earth Unknown*,[21] pro- vides a powerful illustration of the idea that there is more to the created order than the unaided human eye can see. This woodcut, which first appeared in a French book on meteorology, proposes that it takes a *spiritual* vision to penetrate beyond what appears before our eyes. There is a divine order that ungirds phys- ical reality, but we must have eyes to see it. This woodcut suggests that spiritual sight can help us pierce through to a deeper level of comprehension. A pilgrim, staff in hand and crawling along the ground, has pushed through the veil of the physical world so that he is receiving a vision of what lies beyond. He catches a glimpse of an invisible divine order that upholds and sustains the visible realities. There are beauties beyond what our eyes can behold, this unknown artist seems to be saying, and it takes a spiritual vision to glimpse behind the curtain.

Frederic Church, *Meteor of 1860* (1860), private collection (WikiCommons)

Earlier we referred to the work of the great American landscape painter Frederic Edwin Church. Perhaps the clearest illustration of how his interest in science informed his work as an artist is a lesser-known painting entitled *The Meteor of 1860*,[22] which was inspired by a meterological event that he witnessed. Church assigned the title of his painting to a particular event at a specific time. But the painting is more than just a piece of scientific reportage, for he draws our attention to a rare and mysterious occurence in the night sky—an incandescent bit of matter entering Earth's atmosphere, streaking across the darkness, and lighting up the cobalt heavens. Church was evoking something bigger than mere science; he was evoking mystery.

With *The Sower of Systems* (1902),[23] English painter George Watts offered one of the most fascinating interpretations of the relationship between God and the world he has made. The title clearly references the biblical parable of the sower, which had also been the theme of famous paintings by Millet and van Gogh. Watts was an amateur stargazer with an admiration for the work of scientists, and he once wrote that scientists were "dwelling...in a kingdom of infinite wonder."[24]

He was fascinated by early long-distance photographs of the solar system, which inspired this dynamic image of the cosmos. In the painting we see a blue-robed divine presence sweeping through the heavens, radiating swirling golden arcs that form galaxies and scattering stars and constellations as though they were seeds. Sparks of light shoot forth from divine hands. Watts combines a theological and a scientific understanding of the universe, an expanse that has a purpose behind it. God is the Creator and Sustainer, ever at work in his own cosmos.

G.F. Watts, *The Sower of the Systems* (1902), Watts Gallery (WikiCommons)

Vincent van Gogh, *The Starry Night* (1889), The Museum of Modern Art (WikiCommons)

Then there is the most popular modern painting of the night sky, Vincent van Gogh's iconic *The Starry Night*, painted in 1889. It was likely inspired by one of Vincent's favorite poems, "Under the Stars," composed by the Victorian novelist and poet Diana Maria Craik. In letters to his brother, Theo, Vincent quoted this poem no fewer than three times, and the line that seemed to move him most was this: "When earth sounds cease, God's voice is heard." Perhaps that was one of the things that stimulated him to paint what he saw in this way. We can certainly "hear" God make himself known in this vibrant painting. The voice of God is the music of the swirling, pulsing, undulating night skies punctuated with vivid stars and alive with an energy that is palpable in the animated brushwork. There is a pyrotechnic display in the heavens that hovers above the stillness of the sleepy town below. Here is a world alive with God's presence, and the cosmos that van Gogh evokes is not a machine grinding away above us, but a fiery dance. The night sky does not whisper the reality of God's glory, but positively shouts it aloud.

Ultimately, science and art are telling the same story about the mysterious glory of the cosmos. When Jupiter's swirling clouds were photographed by NASA's Juno probe, the resulting images surprised some researchers in that they looked so much like works of abstract art. When Amelia Carolina Sparavigna, an amateur astronomer, saw these photos, they reminded her of the famous *Starry Night* painting by van Gogh, so she used computer technology to replace the sky of his painting with the photograph that Juno had captured.[25] The resulting juxtaposition is a prescient reminder that perhaps art and science are not really so far apart—just two different ways of seeing the same wondrous things.

(Wikimedia Commons)

The Heavens Are Telling

There is, the artists are telling us, an evidentiary power to the beauty of the cosmos and the created world. It is a different kind of evidence than that offered by science or philosophy, an evidence based more on intuition than on proofs.

But that beauty can tell us something important about who made this world and about our place in it. The artists call us to pay attention, to see more clearly and fully, to quiet our hearts and minds before the great artistic creation of the Great Creator.

When I look up into the night skies on a clear night, I experience several different responses. I consider my own smallness in the vast scheme of things, as if I were the tiniest dab of paint on a huge canvas. At the same time, I experience a sense of connection with the very glories I am perceiving, as though I were being lifted up and embraced by the bigness of it all. I feel a deep sense of belonging—that the universe is my home, made for me to live in, to enjoy, to investigate and try to understand, to appreciate, to be grateful for. And it arouses a longing for something more.

What we see above us is wondrous, yet it points to so much more. Surely one of the purposes of nature is to remind us of paradise. The dense leafy forests, the fields of jocund wildflowers, the singing and surging rivers, the pounding surf, the clouds scudding across the blue expanse of sky, the Sun, the planets, the stars, and the constellations whirling above—they all remind us that the world was once an unspoiled paradise and that even the most irresponsible environmental actions of humankind cannot quiet its voice. And that someday all of it will be restored to its full perfection. Like humanity, the groaning creation will be redeemed.

In the interim, both science and art encourage me to look up, examine more closely, and seek to understand. Both the questions of *how* and *why* come into focus as I explore the heavens and earth and celebrate what they have to say about the one who created them and how I fit into the unfolding story of the cosmos. At its heart, it is not only a story of power and glory; it is a story, in Dante's words, "of a love that moves the sun and other stars."[26]

CHAPTER 9

Imagine There's No Heaven?: C.S. Lewis on Making Space for Faith

Michael Ward

In 1961, the Russian cosmonaut Yuri Gagarin became the first man to travel in space as well as the first man to orbit Earth. His Vostok 1 spacecraft was launched on April 12 of that year, and the entire flight took less than two hours. In recognition of his achievement, Gagarin was awarded the title Hero of the Soviet Union, the nation's highest honor. Fifty years later, in 2011, the United Nations marked the event by declaring April 12 to be the International Day of Human Space Flight. As Humpty Dumpty would have said, "There's glory for you!"

One interested observer of Gagarin's pioneering adventure was a certain professor of medieval and Renaissance English at the University of Cambridge, C.S. Lewis. In a letter he wrote shortly after Gagarin's flight, Lewis described this first journey into space as "exciting,"[1] a reaction he might have been expected to have given his longstanding interest in interplanetary travel. But his more substantial response to Gagarin's historic voyage came two years later when he published in an American periodical an article entitled "Onward, Christian Spacemen."[2] Lewis opened the piece by writing, "The Russians, I am told, report that they have not found God in outer space." It was a report that left him unperturbed because finding God "by astronautics" was, in his

view, impossible: "the methods of science do not discover facts of that order…
What is required is a certain faculty of recognition…Much depends on the
seeing eye."[3]

The report by the Russians that they had not found God in outer space
originated, so I understand, with remarks made not by Yuri Gagarin, but by
the Soviet leader Nikita Khrushchev, who told a meeting of the Central Committee of the Communist Party that "Gagarin flew into space, but didn't see
any god there." But it wasn't long before Khrushchev's words *about* Gagarin were attributed *to* Gagarin, thus misrepresenting Gagarin's own Christian belief.[4]

But why would the Russians think God *might* have been found in outer
space? I suppose it must be because of the opening line of the prayer that Jesus
taught his disciples, which, as we know, runs as follows: "Our Father, who art
in space, hallowed be Thy name." Or perhaps the Russians were thinking of the
first verse of the Bible: "In the beginning God created space and the earth." Having created space first, God presumably chose to live there, having previously
had nowhere to rest his head. Or maybe the Russians had in mind that crucial
article of the Creed: "On the third day he rose again; he ascended into space."

Whether it be in the Lord's Prayer or the book of Genesis or the Apostles'
Creed, *heaven* is a key term in Christian belief. Heaven, however, is not space;
the two terms are not synonymous and interchangeable. But Khrushchev and
the atheist propagandists whom he oversaw deliberately elided the two terms for
their own purposes. If God is supposed to reside in heaven and heaven equals
space yet God can't be seen in space, then God evidently isn't in heaven. Therefore, God doesn't exist. QED.

Khrushchev's linguistic sleight of hand does, however, raise a legitimate
question: Why should we not say *space* instead of *heaven*? What truly distin-
guishes these words from each other? That was a question that greatly exercised
C.S. Lewis, and in this essay, I will examine three aspects of his involvement
with this issue: first, what he had to say about the history of the term *space*; second, how he viewed the implications of this term as being almost entirely negative; and third, his response to those negative implications.

The History of Space

C.S. Lewis is best known for his Chronicles of Narnia and his Christian
apologetics, but these parts of his output were sidelines to his professional work

as an academic. Lewis's scholarly career was that of a literary historian and critic. In those expert capacities he taught as a fellow and tutor in English at Oxford for nearly thirty years before being appointed the first Professor of Medieval and Renaissance English at Cambridge. The biggest book Lewis wrote was a 700-page tome entitled *English Literature in the Sixteenth Century Excluding Drama* (1954). It was his contribution to a multivolume series called The Oxford History of English Literature—or, as he nicknamed it, "O Hell!"

Lewis's "O Hell!" volume begins not with hell but heaven. More precisely, it begins with the heavens and how they were understood during the period under discussion, for the sixteenth century saw perhaps the greatest change there has ever been in man's understanding of the heavens, as the old geocentric system gave way to the modern heliocentric model, the "new astronomy" as Lewis calls it. The volume opens with a 14-page treatment of this astronomical revolution that Nicolaus Copernicus ushered in with his epoch-making work *De Revolutionibus Orbium Coelestium* ("On the Revolutions of the Heavenly Spheres"), published in 1543. At first this revolution was purely theoretical in nature.[5] It was not verified until after the telescope had been invented in the early seventeenth century and observations had been made by Kepler and Galileo.

Lewis was interested in the imaginative effects of the Copernican Revolution. As a literary historian and critic, he wanted to see how the new heliocentric cosmos affected the course of English literature. The cosmology that a given generation accepts has immense consequences for its thoughts and emotions, and in every age, there is a "mythology which follows in the wake of science" (an important phrase, to which we will return),[6] a mythology that feeds into our understanding of ourselves and the way we imaginatively interpret the world and our place in it. Garrett Green makes the point well:

> From Galileo and Newton to Einstein and Stephen Hawking, the reigning scientific models of the cosmos have provided the larger culture with powerful analogies and metaphors that shape its epistemology, its poetry, its politics, and its religion…many of the leading postmodernist ideas borrow much of their imagery and not a little of their social prestige from scientific notions of relativity, uncertainty, and incommensurability.[7]

In his "O Hell!" volume, Lewis concludes that what proved important about the newly developing astronomy of the sixteenth century was not the mere alteration in our map of the cosmos but the methodological revolution that verified it:

> By reducing Nature to her mathematical elements [the new astronomy] substituted a mechanical for a genial or animistic conception of the universe. The world was emptied, first of her indwelling spirits, then of her occult sympathies and antipathies, finally of her colours, smells, and tastes. (Kepler at the beginning of his career explained the motion of the planets by their *animae motrices* [motive spirits]; before he died, he explained it mechanically.)[8]

A mathematically expressed and mechanically understood paradigm became operative and dominant. The older view of nature as a veritable organism teeming with humors, planetary influences, and the four elements disposed in particular realms or homes—that older view was overthrown: we have abandoned that world picture. Hence the title of Lewis's final book, *The Discarded Image* (1964).

The new model of the cosmos did not, as it turned out, immediately enter the public consciousness during the sixteenth century, let alone affect the literature that was produced at that time. Shakespeare, who died in the second decade of the seventeenth century, wrote all his plays almost exclusively from the presupposition of pre-Copernican or Ptolemaic or Aristotelian cosmology.

However, in due course, the Copernican Revolution did trickle down to affect writers and, through them, the general populace. Indeed, Copernicus would eventually become a kind of totemic figure, a champion borne aloft by Whig historians who wished to caricature the Middle Ages as an intellectually primitive period from which humanity did well to escape. Lewis humorously satirized the simplistic thinking that lay behind this caricature in the inaugural lecture he delivered upon assuming his professorial chair at Cambridge, when he invited his audience to reread the first chapter of J.M. Berdan's *Early Tudor Poetry*:

> It is still in many ways a useful book; but it is now difficult to read that [opening] chapter without a smile. We begin with twenty-nine pages…of unrelieved gloom about grossness, superstition, and cruelty to children, and on the twenty-ninth comes the sentence, "The first rift in this darkness is the Copernican doctrine"; as if a new hypothesis in astronomy would naturally make a man stop hitting his daughter about the head.[9]

That was one effect that the Copernican Revolution had: it allowed lazy writers to start hitting the Middle Ages about the head! But obviously it was not an important effect, and Lewis mentions it principally to amuse his audience at the start of his lecture.

The more serious effects of the Copernican Revolution had to do with the way the cosmos was progressively evacuated of its hidden qualities, inner meanings, and spiritual factors. The seven planets influencing the four elements (earth, air, fire, water) and the four humors (black bile, yellow bile, phlegm, blood) and their bearing on the four temperaments (melancholic, choleric, phlegmatic, sanguine). These intricate, interdependent relationships—along with various other features of the medieval model—were all gradually discarded. The theory of ether lingered longest and was not finally disproven until the Michelson-Morley experiments of 1887.

For the inhabitants of Earth—*planet* Earth as it was now known—home had been relocated. It had not just been removed from the central place it had hitherto enjoyed, it was now situated in "space," a neologism with all sorts of unpredictable imaginative trajectories. The heavens that had previously surrounded mankind's home were dismantled and the universe progressively "disenchanted," to use the term deployed to such influential effect by the German sociologist Max Weber. Eventually this new cosmology, or at least a dream version thereof, would be celebrated as a liberation from religious constraint: John Lennon, in his signature solo album, "Imagine," invited us to dream of a cosmos without either a heaven above us or a hell beneath us. Above us there would be only sky. And above the sky, what? To the modern imagination, space. And space is a vacuum. And in a vacuum no one can hear you scream![10]

Lewis traces the process whereby we have "come to know the universe" as a single one-way progression:

> At the outset the universe appears packed with will, intelligence, life and positive qualities; every tree is a nymph and every planet a god. Man himself is akin to the gods. The advance of knowledge gradually empties this rich and genial universe…But the matter does not rest there. The same method which has emptied the world now proceeds to empty ourselves…[W]e were just as mistaken…when we attributed "souls," or "selves" or "minds" to human organisms as when we attributed Dryads to the trees…Man is indeed akin to the gods: that is, he is no less phantasmal than they…

> And thus we arrive at a result uncommonly like zero…The Subject is as empty as the Object. Almost nobody has been making linguistic mistakes about almost nothing. By and large, this is the only thing that has ever happened.[11]

It was this "empty universe" that constituted the "mythology which follows in the wake of science." Lewis often uses the word *mythology* in a positive sense, but in this case he is using it much more ambiguously. The mechanical, mathematical, materialist mythology (that is to say, value-laden explanatory narrative) that followed in the wake of Copernicus was not a necessary or even a logical consequence of the scientific progress in question. "It is the glory of science to progress,"[12] and the advance represented by the Copernican Revolution was not one that Lewis wished to undo: "I hope no one will think I am recommending a return to the Medieval Model."[13]

However, Lewis did wish to enter some serious reservations about the imaginative effects of the vocabulary that accompanied the new astronomy. By all means, let us believe that the cosmos is heliocentric and admit that the old scheme of the seven "heavens" revolving around a static Earth "was not true."[14] But must we therefore of necessity abandon *heaven* and henceforth use only the word *space*? That terminological change carries with it all sorts of connotations and implications that may not be warranted. Lewis was sensitive to the semantic shift that *space* underwent in the post-Copernican period because, as a literary historian, he knew something about the history of the word.

Medieval writers, such as the author of the fourteenth-century poem "Pearl," had used the phrase *in space* to mean "in a space of time" or "presently."[15] For these authors, "*space* usually meant a temporal rather than a local extension." (Lewis, incidentally, being such a medievally minded author himself, adopts that usage himself in at least one place—his poem "Old Poets Remembered."[16]) As for the modern meaning of "local extension," Lewis writes that "*space* as… the abyss, the vacuity in which all material objects exist" cannot be found recorded earlier than the seventeenth century. He continues:

> [T]his modern meaning of space could not have existed in the fourteenth century because the thing meant did not exist for the human mind. The drama of existence was not performed against any such forbidding backcloth. There was no abyss. Man looked up at a patterned, populous intricate finite cosmos; a builded thing, not a wilderness; "heaven" or "spheres" not "space."[17]

One of the great strengths of Lewis as a literary historian is that he reminds us that human sensibility has differed hugely over time according to linguistic usage. Our forebears referred to those in the governing class as their *rulers*, whereas we tend to refer to our *leaders*, a change with "subtle and far-reaching effects."[18] Once upon a time, *gentleman* denoted a man with a coat of arms; it has now become a general term of approbation for a male of the human species.[19] *Love* was the term used in olden times for the greatest virtue; now, Lewis claims, *unselfishness* takes that top spot—a negative term has been substituted for a positive one.[20] We look out on *space*; our ancestors did not do so and could not have done so. There was no such category in their cosmos.

The word *cosmos*, incidentally, comes from the Greek verb *kosmein*, meaning "to arrange" or "to organise or embellish," whence "cosmetics."[21] One applies cosmetics to one's face in order to bring out its structure in a way considered attractive—to highlight certain features while masking or downplaying others. Cosmologists likewise bring out certain features in the physical world according to the criteria that they have determined to be most useful for expressing the model being developed. The patterned and finite cosmos depicted by medieval sculptors, painters, and writers in the centuries before Copernicus was classical in sensibility—ordered, balanced, hierarchical. The modern cosmos, by contrast, is romantic—that is to say, free-roaming, unstructured, unbounded.

As a literary historian, Lewis does not concern himself with the scientific basis of the modern model; he is interested only with the terminology used to convey it and with the imaginative and emotional effects thereof:

> [T]o look out on the night sky with modern eyes is like looking out over a sea that fades away into mist, or looking about one in a trackless forest—trees forever and no horizon. To look up at the towering medieval universe is much more like looking at a great building. The "space" of modern astronomy may arouse terror, or bewilderment or vague reverie; the spheres of the old present us with an object in which the mind can rest, overwhelming in its greatness but satisfying in its harmony.[22]

This explains why there is no agoraphobia, no sense of pathlessness or bafflement when medieval poets lead us into the sky. Dante, in *Paradiso*, was more like a guide to an immense cathedral than a landsman gesturing over a shoreless sea. The sense of the sky as something alien and disorientating enters English poetry only with John Milton when, in "Il Penseroso," he sees the wandering Moon "riding near her highest noon":

> Like one that has been led astray
> Through the heav'ns wide pathless way.

Interestingly, Milton has this pathless way wind through "the heav'ns"—the new adjective is still attached to the old noun. Soon, however, *the heavens* would be discarded and it would be the noun *space* that would become the substantive term; *heaven* or *the heavens* would be reserved more and more consistently for the pre-Copernican cosmos in which tracklessness did *not* feature.

The first writer on record as using *space* in the modern sense is again, interestingly, John Milton. (Lewis, of course, knew Milton's poetry intimately; one of his most important academic works was *A Preface to Paradise Lost*.) Milton "is perhaps the first writer to use the noun *space* in its fully modern sense," Lewis says,[23] quoting as his source Book 1 of *Paradise Lost*, published in 1667:

> Space may produce new worlds…
> Thither, if but to pry, shall be perhaps
> Our first eruption, thither or elsewhere:
> For this Infernal Pit shall never hold
> Celestial Spirits in Bondage…

The speaker of these lines in the poem is Satan—a rather inauspicious originator of *space* in its modern meaning. Lewis evidently paid close attention to this passage, for it supplied him with the title of his first published work, *Spirits in Bondage, a Cycle of Lyrics* (1919). But although he studied these lines closely, he is cautious regarding what they demonstrated about semantic change: They contain what is "perhaps" the first appearance of *space* in its fully modern sense. Lewis covers his back by inserting "perhaps" as a qualifier here, but his prudence appears to have been unnecessary. At any rate, the Oxford English Dictionary gives no earlier citation than this 1667 usage for *space* in the sense of "the immeasurable expanse in which the solar and stellar systems, nebulae, etc., are situated." Before the second half of the seventeenth century there is no documentary evidence to show that *space*, in that sense, existed for the human mind.

Milton lived in the period when the two cosmoses were jostling alongside one another in the popular consciousness. The pre-Copernican heavens still held some sway over the public imagination; the new heliocentric space had not yet been fully embraced. Wanting to combine the two models in *Paradise Lost*, Milton came up with a clever device for retaining the former scheme while simultaneously expressing the new one. He put his cosmos "in a spherical envelope within which all could be light and order, and hung it from the floor of Heaven. Outside that he had Chaos, the 'infinite Abyss'…where 'length, breadth and highth / And time and place are lost.'"[24] And thus he got to enjoy, almost literally, the best of both worlds.

When Milton wrote *Paradise Lost*, more than 100 years had elapsed since Copernicus published *On the Revolutions of the Heavenly Spheres*. The astronomical paradigm shift was clearly not instantaneous. Eventually, however, the divide between the two cosmological models would no longer be thought worth bridging and the triumph of the heliocentric system would be complete. And so we arrive at the modern position. The cosmic imaginings of a modern person, who conceives of Earth as adrift in a void, are quite different from those of people who lived in Tudor times, whose universe was "tingling with anthropomorphic life, dancing, ceremonial, a festival not a machine… a vast, lighted concavity, filled with music."[25] No one nowadays holds Earth to be the center of a network of celestial influences and significant interplanetary relationships. The music of the spheres is now considered illusory and *astrology* has become a dirty word. The new sense of *space* carries with it, Lewis claims, "the idea that the heavenly bodies move in a pitch-black and dead-cold vacuity."[26]

Let us now turn to examine further the implications—the almost exclusively negative implications—of this newly dominant cosmological conception.

Space: Negative Implications

In his earliest work of nonfiction apologetics, *The Problem of Pain* (1940), Lewis opened his argument with the following confession:

> Not many years ago when I was an atheist, if anyone had asked me, "Why do you not believe in God?" my reply would have run something like this: "Look at the universe we live in. By far the greatest part of it consists of empty space, completely dark and unimaginably

cold. The bodies which move in this space are so few and so small in comparison with the space itself that even if every one of them were known to be crowded as full as it could hold with perfectly happy creatures, it would still be difficult to believe that life and happiness were more than a by-product to the power that made the universe."[27]

This cosmological argument for atheism was one that Lewis eventually abandoned as he moved first to theism and then to Christianity, but it is clear how strongly he once believed it, or perhaps we should say felt it. For, as he would later point out in "Dogma and the Universe" and *Miracles*, the argument from size proves nothing, not if we are thinking entirely rationally. But, of course, human beings are more than mere reasoners: our imaginations, our nerves, our emotions, and indeed our wills are also important factors in the way we conceive of the universe. For all that Lewis came to distrust about "the argument from size," at one time he accepted it and was much affected by it. This may explain why he spilled so much ink on the imaginative impact of the word *space*. It had exerted a powerful spell over him personally, existentially. The term for him connoted not just emptiness, darkness, coldness, but also meaninglessness. In his poem "The Salamander," he captured the bleakness (and also, by the way, the hidden flaw) of the cosmological view that had once enthralled him with its talk of "the vertigo of space," "the fear / Of nothingness," "negation's final sovereignty."[28]

The contrast between *heaven* and *space* is a topic Lewis returns to in his address "Imagination and Thought in the Middle Ages" (1956), where he goes so far as to describe the modern cosmological model as not just a shoreless sea or a pathless forest, but "a great jungle." He writes:

> You can lose yourself in infinity; there is indeed nothing much else you can do with it. It arouses questions, it prompts to a certain kind of wonder and reverie, usually a sombre kind, so that Wordsworth can speak of "melancholy space and doleful time"…But it answers no questions; necessarily shapeless and trackless, patient of no absolute order or direction, it leads, after a little, to boredom or despair or (often) to the haunting conviction that it must be an illusion.[29]

Lewis gives voice to this sense of boredom, despair, and illusion in a powerful scene in his novel *Perelandra*, where the protagonist, Elwin Ransom, becomes overwhelmed by the vastness of the ocean on the planet Venus. For if this ocean was too big for him, well…

> Beyond this ocean was space itself. In vain did Ransom try to remember that he had been in "space" and found it Heaven, tingling with a fulness of life for which infinity itself was not one cubic inch too large. All that seemed like a dream. That opposite mode of thought which he had often mocked and called in mockery The Empirical Bogey, came surging into his mind—the great myth of our century with…its nightmare perspectives of simple arithmetic in which everything that can possibly hold significance for the mind becomes the mere by-product of essential disorder. Always till now he had belittled it, had treated with a certain disdain…its glib munificence of ciphers…Part of him still knew that the size of a thing is the least important characteristic…But this knowledge remained an abstraction. Mere bigness and loneliness overbore him.[30]

In this passage Lewis is trying to give expression to what he regards as a modern imaginative tendency—to think too exclusively in terms of arithmetic, of measurable quantities, to be "more sensitive to bigness"[31] than our ancestors were.

Our contemporary valorization of numerical ciphers is a subject Lewis addresses at some length in his essay "The Language of Religion," where he lists three different sentences, as follows:

(1) It was very cold

(2) There were 13 degrees of frost

(3) Ah, bitter chill it was!
   The owl, for all his feathers was a-cold;
   The hare limped trembling through the frozen grass,
   And silent was the flock in woolly fold:
   Numb were the Beadsman's fingers.[32]

These three sentences reflect three different linguistic paradigms. The first Lewis calls "Ordinary language," the second, "Scientific language," and the third, "Poetic language" (it's a quotation from John Keats's "The Eve of St Agnes"). Each linguistic paradigm has its particular strength. The strength of Scientific language is that it gives a precise quantitative description of the cold that can be tested by a thermometer. If the thermometer confirms that there are indeed 13 degrees of frost, various inferences can be drawn: we can confidently predict certain effects on vegetable and animal life. The Scientific language description "is therefore of use in what Francis Bacon called 'operation.' We can take action on it. On the other hand it does not, of itself, give us any information about the quality of a cold night."[33]

Ordinary language would convey the quality of a cold night better than Scientific language, and Poetic language would do it better still. Lewis says that Keats gave us "all that concrete, qualitative information which the Scientific statement leaves out. But then, of course, he is not verifiable, nor precise, nor of much use for operation."[34]

While poetry conveys qualitative information, science conveys quantitative information. Science finds meaningful those things that are enumerable, measurable, and instrumentalisable—that is, useful in "operation": they can be put to work; they have a utilitarian value. It's for this reason that scientific statements are so verifiable or falsifiable—they are, as Lewis put it, more easily "cashed" than statements made either in Ordinary language or Poetic language: "But the poet might of course reply that it always will be easier to cash a cheque for 30 shillings than one for 1,000 pounds, that the scientific statements are cheques, in one sense, for very small amounts, giving us, out of the teeming complexity of every concrete reality only 'the common measurable features.'"[35] Poetic language, on the other hand, usually tries to get beyond the common measurable features and convey the uniqueness, the never-to-be-repeated peculiar tone or flavor of a certain human experience or sensation.

Without a doubt, quantities are useful, but the universe we live in is one of liberality and peculiarity, not mere functionality and uniformity. Numbers, though extremely handy when we are treating the cosmos as a machine to be measured, weighed, manipulated, and so on, cannot take us into the realm of the human spirit, let alone the Holy Spirit. We lose not only the divine but also ourselves if we take that track: both subject and object become vacuous. Numbers count for a lot, but they are too univocal to capture the fullness of life: reality is richer than even the most complicated equation. Which is why we tend to tuck our children in at night with a chapter from a fairy tale, rather than reciting the wonders of the telephone directory or the thrills and spills of the railway timetable.

Treating the cosmos scientifically—that is to say, mathematically—is a proper undertaking for the human mind. We can say that the planets are so far away, that they move at such and such a speed, that they are comprised of materials with the following chemical numbers. Lewis fully respected this scientific enterprise: the asking of *how* questions, *what* questions, *where* questions. *How* does light penetrate Earth's atmosphere? *What* makes it appear as if there are canals on Mars? *Where* is that as-yet-unidentified planet beyond Uranus whose existence was deduced before it was even observed? These are all good questions, and successfully answering them and their like has done much to improve the average human life so that it is less solitary, poor, nasty, brutish, and short than it once was. But in addition to the *how*, *what*, and *where* questions, there are the *why* and *who* questions. Questions of purpose, not function. Questions of personality, not regularity. Questions of quality, not quantity.

Lewis was sometimes concerned that people would think he was attacking science,[36] but the fact that it was a poet (John Milton), and not a scientist, who was the first to introduce the element of agoraphobia into the universe should help exculpate him on that score. If Lewis was attacking anything, it was not science but poetry—that is to say, misconceived or misused language, for, as Percy Bysshe Shelley said, it is the poets who "are the unacknowledged legislators of the world."[37] This emphasizes the point that Lewis made in *The Abolition of Man*: it is not the great scientists but "little scientists, and little unscientific followers of science"[38] who muddy the waters for the rest of us, linguistically speaking. It is they who devise and perpetuate "the mythology that follows in the wake of science."[39] New scientific terminology feeds out into the wider culture and is taken up and put to all sorts of uses with all sorts of implications that have nothing to do with whether Earth goes around the Sun or not. Astronomers cannot be held responsible for every use and misuse made of the language they employ to describe a scientific advance.

If the poet Milton had unwisely extrapolated from Copernicus, Lewis became determined to do what he could as a poet himself to undo Milton's error. (By *poet* I mean a creative writer in prose as well as verse.) Lewis set himself to counteract that disenchanting mythology, to show that "Blind Nature" wasn't a necessary concomitant of belief in the heliocentric cosmos. It was still possible to conceive of our home as more than just "a fading spark / Enisled amid the boundless dark."[40]

One of only a few deep-sky objects visible to the unaided eye, the Orion Nebula (M42) is one of the most stunning clouds (nebulae) ever imaged by a telescope. Look to the constellation Orion and find his "sword" hanging from his belt. This nebula is the third "star" in the lower portion of the sword. "Astronomers used 520 Hubble images, taken in five colors with Hubble's Advanced Camera for Surveys, to make this picture."[41] (Courtesy of NASA)

Counteracting the Negative Implications

Between 1938 and 1945, Lewis published three novels about interplanetary adventures. In the first book, *Out of the Silent Planet*, the hero, Ransom, travels to Mars. He looks out of the window of his "spaceship" (there is, unfortunately, no other word for it!) and marvels at what he sees: "[T]he stars, thick as daisies on an uncut lawn, reigned perpetually with no cloud, no Moon, no sunrise, to dispute their sway. There were planets of unbelievable majesty, and constellations undreamed of: there were celestial sapphires, rubies, emeralds and pinpricks of burning gold."[42] As Ransom boggles at the awesome sight, he becomes aware that

> [a] nightmare, long engendered in the modern mind by the mythology that follows in the wake of science, was falling off him. He had read of "Space": at the back of his thinking for years had lurked the dismal fancy of the black, cold vacuity, the utter deadness, which was supposed to separate the worlds. He had not known how much it affected him till now—now that the very name "Space" seemed a blasphemous libel for this empyrean ocean of radiance in which they swam…He had thought it barren; he saw now that it was the womb[43] of worlds, whose blazing and innumerable offspring looked down nightly even upon the Earth with so many eyes—and here, with how many more! No: Space was the wrong name. Older thinkers had been wiser when they named it simply the heavens—the heavens which declared the glory—the
>
> > "happy climes that ly
> > Where day never shuts his eye
> > Up in the broad fields of the sky."
>
> He quoted Milton's words to himself lovingly, at this time and often.[44]

It is worth repeating two phrases from this memorable passage: "The very name 'Space' seemed a blasphemous libel…Space was the wrong name." How ironic, then, that publishers now issue these three books as The Space Trilogy! As far as I know, Lewis himself never called the series The Space Trilogy. It is much better to call it The Ransom Trilogy or The Cosmic Trilogy. At the end of *Out of the Silent Planet*, Ransom says, "If we could even effect in one per cent of our readers a changeover from the conception of Space to the conception of Heaven, we should have made a beginning."[45] To call it The Space Trilogy runs completely counter to Lewis's entire project.

It is significant that Ransom should quote from Milton yet again. The passage he cites on this occasion is from the masque *Comus* (1634). Yet Milton, though he retained a pre-Copernican awareness of the heavens, was, as we have seen, the first writer to use the word *space* in its modern sense. In a very gentlemanly way, Lewis here uses what we might call "traditional Milton" to offset "modernist Milton" as he attempts to depict a universe that was not empty but packed with life. Lewis's use of Psalm 19 is worth noting too: the heavens are telling the glory of God. "*There's* glory for you!" as Humpty Dumpty would do well to say. Lewis described the nineteenth psalm as "the greatest poem in the Psalter and one of the greatest lyrics in the world."[46]

It is not just in The Ransom Trilogy but throughout his work that Lewis celebrates "quality" and "quiddity," the peculiar flavors of particular things and particular places: "the Londonness of London or the Donegality of Donegal."[47] He is hostile toward that calculating, Gradgrindian tendency of mind that would neutralize, depersonalize, or homogenize. The modern habit of treating individual men and women as "counters or identical machines," mere "hands" or "voters," like ants in an anthill or bees in a hive, is a mistake: we should rather consider them in their fullest contexts and respect each as a "concrete entirety."[48] In a similar vein, Lewis objects to the equalizing, regularizing mentality of those "to whom pebbles laid in a row are more beautiful than an arch."[49] Nature "stripped of its qualitative properties and reduced to mere quantity" is not wholly real, so he argues in *The Abolition of Man*.[50]

"Reducing Nature to her mathematical elements"[51] is in one sense understandable, for pure mathematics is "the type of successful thought."[52] But its success in unlocking the mysteries of physics has led some of its practitioners, and not a few of those practitioners' followers, to suppose that it has also unlocked the mysteries of metaphysics. As Lewis remarks in the epilogue to *The Discarded Image* while discussing the twentieth century's increasing reliance upon arithmetical interpretations of the cosmos:

> The mathematics are now the nearest to the reality we can get. Anything imaginable, even anything that can be manipulated by ordinary (that is, non-mathematical) conceptions, far from being a further truth to which mathematics were the avenue, is a mere analogy, a concession to our weakness. Without a parable modern physics speaks not to the multitudes.[53]

Alluding here to St. Matthew's description of Christ's teaching method,[54] Lewis implies his own view of the present situation: Modern science—or rather, "scientism"—has arrogated to itself a pseudo-dominical authority. It has attempted to reduce all knowledge to the scientific form of knowledge, supplanting ordinary and poetic language with impersonal numeric terminology.

Everywhere one looks in Lewis's works, one sees this recurrent aim: to reenchant the universe, to reignite a sacramental view of nature and of man, and to question the conceptual paradigm that would "ignore [Nature's] final cause (if any) and treat it in terms of quantity."[55]

We quite rightly draw up our charts and our tables. We quite rightly conduct and repeat our tests and establish our findings, our highly prized "scientific facts." But as the philosopher Alasdair MacIntyre once quipped, "facts, like telescopes and wigs for gentlemen, were a seventeenth-century invention."[56] If we are not careful about the reductive implications of the methodology that led to the scientific revolution, we will end up knowing more and more about less and less. ("Almost nobody has been making linguistic mistakes about almost nothing."[57]) If we trust overmuch to one particular form of knowledge, one particular kind of language, we will find, as Lewis puts it in a poem, that "heaven has given us the slip."[58] The "Empirical Bogey," like the attitude of the cynic, will keep us in the world of price, not value. What we need, rather, is a *gestalt* embrace of the data, a truly holistic approach in which the knowing subject, the known object, and the language used to describe the knowledge in question are all properly weighed and balanced factors.

A star is telling the glory of God, if we have ears to hear. A star is a messenger, if we have eyes to see. Things are more than the sum of their parts.

In Lewis's third book in The Chronicles of Narnia series, *The Voyage of the Dawn Treader*, Eustace, a boy from England, meets a character named Ramandu, who in that world is a star and has trodden the great dance in the sky, looking down on everything from above. Eustace says to Ramandu, "In our world, a star is a huge ball of flaming gas." Ramandu replies, "Even in your world, my son, that is not what a star is but only what it is made of."[59] This is a pithy encapsulation of Lewis's whole case against materialistic reductionism. Eustace is an unwitting exponent of the mythology that follows in the wake of science. He thinks of a star in purely quantitative, nonqualitative terms. He's interested in size, shape, constituent materials, and their measurable activity. But that is not what a star *is*. A star is telling the glory of God, if we have ears to hear. A star is a messenger, if we have eyes to see. Things are more than the sum of their parts.

Thinking Clearly and Speaking Wisely

What I think Lewis is suggesting in his dissection of the difference between *heaven* and *space* is that we need to be careful about the collateral effects of linguistic change and to ask whether all the apparent implications of a new term need be embraced. As a literary historian and critic, Lewis had a great concern to "purify the dialect of the tribe," in T.S. Eliot's phrase. One only needs to read Lewis's fascinating book *Studies in Words* to see how minutely he inspected the subtle shades, the tiny ramifications discoverable in certain semantic shifts. (Many contributors to religion-versus-science debates would benefit from reading his chapters titled "Nature," "World," and "Life.") Human language, like every other human undertaking, is susceptible to corruption. There are diseases, abuses, hidden traps, and fashions in language: we need to be on our watch against these if we are to think clearly and speak wisely.

As Lewis's friend Owen Barfield once wrote, "Of all devices for dragooning the human spirit, the least clumsy is to procure its abortion in the womb of language."[60] Kill off a way of speaking and, in due course, you will kill off a way of thinking and feeling and knowing and believing. Eradicate the term *heaven* from your cosmological vocabulary and you will find that sooner or later, whether you intended it or not, you have less space for faith.

CHAPTER 10

RECOVERING A VISION OF THE COSMOS: TOLKIEN'S CREATION NARRATIVE IN *THE SILMARILLION*

HOLLY ORDWAY

We look up at the starry expanse of the night sky, or at the lavish colors of a sunset, or we gaze at the ceaseless movement of the ocean, or the wind blowing through a field of wildflowers, or a sudden frost that has coated everyday objects with a glittering coat of ice. What do we see? First we recognize beauty. Next, if we see rightly, we recognize that this beauty is patterned and orderly at some level even in seeming chaos, and that it is meaningful in some way. These intuitions of meaning are age-old; even a passing familiarity with art and literature reveals that the natural world and the cycle of the seasons—ever repeated and ever new—are productive of countless associations with our own lives.

One does not have to believe in God to recognize that the created world we live in is marvelous: complex, mysterious, and somehow deeply meaningful and compelling. It is possible to admire the beauty of nature and hold to an agnostic or atheistic view of reality, but the very act of finding meaning in nature and of responding to beauty is itself a challenge to the materialistic, naturalistic paradigm. Why should we find anything beautiful at all, much less something as "useless" as a colorful sunset? Is the incredible complexity and organization of the material world, from the movements of the planets in their orbits down to the microscopic structures of a cell, really the result of nothing more than blind chance operating over time? The beauty and order of the cosmos are divine irritants, unsettling the viewer and providing a call to look deeper and to discover that, in the words of the psalmist, "The heavens are telling the glory of God; and the firmament proclaims his handiwork" (Psalm 19:1 RSV).

> The beauty and order of the cosmos are divine irritants, unsettling the viewer and providing a call to look deeper.

That is, if one looks at nature—really looks at it and sees it. However, our modern consumer culture increasingly pushes against such seeing or fully engaging with the outside world at all. We need to recover a right vision of the world, to see the cosmos in such a way as to appreciate its meaning. Such a recovery is neither easy nor quick to effect, but it is possible. J.R.R. Tolkien provides us with both a theory of recovery and an example of its application in *The Silmarillion*, his collection of tales from the history of Middle-earth before *The Hobbit* and *The Lord of the Rings*.[1] Yet before we consider any possible remedy for our cultural problem, we should take a few moments to reflect on the factors that make it difficult for us to see properly.

A Disconnected Culture

The apostle Paul tells us that "ever since the creation of the world his invisible nature, namely, his eternal power and deity, has been clearly perceived in the things that have been made" (Romans 1:20 RSV). Yet the rise in Western culture of both professed atheists and "nones"—people who claim no religion at all—suggests that God's handiwork in creation is no longer "clearly perceived." Certainly, some atheists and agnostics may deny the hand of the Creator out of rebellion or resentment, but many people who lack faith simply have been left adrift by a secular culture. Their nonbelief is passive, and they seek to fill the God-shaped hole in their hearts with a substitute of some kind: sex, an obsession with health, physical appearance, consumerism, drugs, money, or power. They long for meaning but fail to see any hint of it in the natural world around them.

What has led to this disconnect?

First, we are physically removed from the natural world and its cycles. Often we live, work, and shop in fully climate-controlled spaces, driving from one place to another in our climate-controlled cars, literally insulating ourselves against experiencing the seasons. At the supermarket we buy produce shipped from around the world so that our consumption makes no concession to the natural rhythms of fruitfulness and fallowness. We no longer recognize the spring-ness of asparagus, the summer-ness of strawberries, the autumnal quality of apples.

Second, we increasingly choose to mediate our experiences of the natural world. Faced with a beautiful sunset, our first response is often to take a picture and post it on social media—and having done that, to move on. The photograph then becomes an object of interest not for what it displays, but for how many "likes" or "shares" or comments it generates. It is not wrong to take pictures or share them; the problem is that the *secondary* aspect of the experience (capturing and sharing it) now usually precedes and often excludes the *primary* experience—that is, our own immediate engagement with it. Such mediation can be observed in the widespread popularity of television programs such as *Cosmos* and *Planet Earth*. People are drawn to the extraordinary wonders of the natural world but are conditioned to accept the media representation of it as sufficient. The images become substitutes for encounters with the ordinary world right at hand. Like carved idols, we have "eyes, but do not see...ears, but do not hear; noses, but do not smell" (Psalm 115:5-6 RSV).

Third, the media and technology element of our cultural environment creates a state of continuous distraction. Messages and notifications of all sorts buzz, beep, and flash on our smartphones and computers, fragmenting our attention with out-of-context information. Our entertainment is interrupted by advertisements—something that has become so normal for us that we no longer recognize just how strange and intrusive it is. News is broken into bite-sized pieces, presented largely without context, and with no logical transitions between one news article or soundbite and the next. Cell phones and work email blur or erase the boundary between work and home with the result that uninterrupted time is an ever-scarcer commodity.

All of these things, perhaps small in themselves, produce in us a far deeper state of constant disquiet and distraction than we often recognize. In one of my classes, I require my graduate students to set aside three 20-minute blocks of time for silent reflection, with nothing to read, listen to, watch, or do. The results are fascinating: Some of them find the experience distressing or anxiety-producing; many are shocked to realize the extent of their own impatience and distracted habits.

This constant disruption of attention is far from inconsequential. If we are distracted about the small things, we will be distracted about the greater things. The natural law is available for all to grasp—both inwardly in one's conscience and outwardly in the intelligible, ordered cosmos—but this natural law does not force itself upon the individual. It is possible (and all too easy in our present culture) to be so distracted as never to ponder the significance of what we see.

Nor is this merely an intellectual problem. Failing to see the order in the cosmos, we often fail to see that we are made by God in his image, that there is a moral order that comes from God, and that our actions have consequences which resound into infinity. We become vulnerable to relativism and the abuse of power. C.S. Lewis, in *The Abolition of Man*, notes the modern naturalistic worldview has lost "the doctrine of objective value, the belief that certain attitudes are really true, and others really false, to the kind of thing the universe is and the kind of things we are,"[2] as well as the related idea that "emotional states can be in harmony with reason (when we feel liking for what ought to be approved) or out of harmony with reason (when we perceive that liking is due but cannot feel it)."[3] Lacking this grounding of value in something objectively real, the naturalist or materialist is reduced to treating "good" and "bad" as mere statements of personal preference. Among other problems, this leaves our culture utterly vulnerable to the abuse of power, for as Lewis notes, "When all that says 'it is good' has been debunked, what says 'I want' remains."[4]

One of the most fundamental ways of addressing this loss of moral vision is to address the problem of *meaning*. As I have written at length elsewhere,[5] before we care whether something is true or false, we must find the idea meaningful. Arguments for the existence of God can be based on natural law or on the design that we observe in the created order, but as Michael Ward has pointed out, unless those arguments are "imaginatively realized," the words—and indeed, the ideas themselves—will be nothing more than "counters in an intellectual game."[6] Only if people have a view of the cosmos as meaningful will they be genuinely open to the idea of a Creator who not only made all that is, but who sent his Son to become incarnate, entering into creation in order to rescue and restore us in our fallen and alienated state.

This beauteous celestial ornamentation is the Pleiades star cluster (not a constellation but an asterism, a group of stars within a constellation). Taken by the Hubble Space Telescope,[7] these luminous diadems have inspired and guided mankind for eons. They are also one of the few star patterns specifically named in the pages of Scripture (see Job 38:31). (Courtesy of NASA)

J.R.R. Tolkien

The author of *The Hobbit* and *The Lord of the Rings* might seem at first an unlikely figure to guide us in a cosmic renewal of vision, but Tolkien's stories of Middle-earth are compelling in no small part because they were *not* the result of a purely inward-looking imaginative process. Rather, Tolkien's imaginative vision reached both inward and outward, and his interests extended beyond literary and linguistic matters. It is worth noting some of the evidence for Tolkien's attention to science and natural history, as it helps us understand how he was able, in his fiction, to portray the cosmos as richly meaningful.

When asked to recall a book that was especially important to him as a teenager, Tolkien wrote that "botany and astronomy" were his favorite subjects at the time, and that his "most treasured volume" was a botanical work, C.A. Johns' *Flowers of the Field*.[8] His interest in natural history extended throughout his life; Clyde Kilby recalled that Tolkien once gave him a tour of his garden "and described every tree, every shrub, every flower, and even the grass and had some scientific knowledge of all of it."[9] Tolkien's granddaughter Joanna recalled that he "encouraged" her "interest of different species of plants, trees, birds and animals, particularly horses," and gave her "two pocket-books of British Birds, and an Encyclopaedia of horses, so that [she] could study them further."[10] Tolkien's visual art contains many depictions of landscapes, flowers, and plants. In his 1938 "Dragons" lecture at the Ashmolean Museum, he spoke knowledgeably about specific types of dinosaurs that had once lived in Oxfordshire. Tolkien's interest in astronomy is evident in his careful attention to calculating the phases of the Moon for the various stages of the journey of the Fellowship in *The Lord of the Rings*, and in the special significance of Durin's Day in *The Hobbit*.

Tolkien could recognize the hand of his Creator in the cosmos because he was interested in the world around him: he looked and paid attention to what he saw. And having seen, he could use his immense creative talents to produce imaginative literature that helps us see too.

The Need for Recovery

In his great essay "On Fairy-stories," Tolkien notes that the things and people we see every day can become affected by the "drab blur of triteness or familiarity."[11] In particular, he argues that this familiarity can become a kind of possessiveness: "They have become like the things which once attracted us by their glitter, or their colour, or their shape, and we laid hands on them, and then locked them in our hoard, acquired them, and acquiring ceased to look at them."[12] The everyday, familiar things around us are the things most likely to be affected by our distraction and self-absorption; ordinary life feels dull and boring, and we require greater and greater shocks even to get our attention.

One example of this can be observed in Hollywood action movies, whether they are set in the "real" world or are superhero or fantasy films. It is no longer enough for the protagonist's family or friends to be in danger: the entire city, or world, or even universe must now be put in danger to raise the stakes high enough for moviegoers to care. It is not enough to have one exciting car chase or shootout at a film's climax: we must have nonstop action, noise, and explosions. More action yields diminishing returns, as it becomes more and more difficult to produce an adrenaline rush in jaded viewers. Tolkien would not have been surprised by this state of affairs. Speaking of art in terms that can readily be applied to other media, he suggests that

> the true road of escape from such weariness is not to be found in the wilfully awkward, clumsy, or misshapen, not in making all things dark or unremittingly violent; nor in the mixing of colours on through subtlety to drabness, and the fantastical complication of shapes to the point of silliness and on towards delirium.[13]

One of the functions of fantasy, according to Tolkien, is to promote *recovery* from such a state. He says,

> Recovery (which includes return and renewal of health) is a regaining—regaining of a clear view. I do not say "seeing things as they are" and involve myself with the philosophers, though I might venture to say "seeing things as we are (or were) meant to see them"—as things apart from ourselves.[14]

We need to see the world around us afresh: to really see it, not merely to glance at it and look away. As Tolkien puts it, "We should look at green again, and be startled anew (but not blinded) by blue and yellow and red. We should meet the centaur and the dragon, and then perhaps suddenly behold, like the ancient shepherds, sheep, and dogs, and horses—and wolves."[15]

The "clear view" that Tolkien describes involves seeing things as separate from ourselves, thus breaking us free from the constraints of possessiveness and overfamiliarity. At the most basic level, a story can provide a helpful shock of unfamiliarity: Tolkien points out that "things that have become trite" can become fresh and new for us "when they are seen suddenly from a new angle."[16]

G.K. Chesterton was a master at this sort of defamiliarization. But Tolkien holds out fantasy stories as especially powerful, in being able not just to startle us into seeing things from a new perspective, but also to make our experience of ordinary things more meaningful.

> By the forging of Gram cold iron was revealed; by the making of Pegasus horses were ennobled; in the Trees of the Sun and Moon root and stock, flower and fruit are manifested in glory…It was in

fairy-stories that I first divined the potency of the words, and the wonder of the things, such as stone, and wood, and iron; tree and grass; house and fire; bread and wine.[17]

Trees, stone, bread, wine—these are things we can see, touch, and taste. The cosmos, however, can seem too big to see, or at least to take in. Can Tolkien's idea of recovery extend to the heavens? Indeed it can. Tolkien shows us in *The Silmarillion* that fantasy literature can help us to recover our right vision at the cosmic as well as the local level.

The Silmarillion

The Silmarillion is strikingly different from *The Lord of the Rings* or *The Hobbit*. It is written throughout in a stately and formal style, with a rhythm and sonority that often evokes the Bible, and—like the Bible—is not a single narrative, but rather is comprised of different tales recounting various stories from Middle-earth's history. The first part of *The Silmarillion* is its Genesis-story: the tale called the *Ainulindalë*, or "The Music of the Ainur."

The *Ainulindalë* tells how God created the world. In its opening sentences, Tolkien boldly sets out the origins of Middle-earth in a way that is entirely consistent with Christian theology, yet presented with a degree of strangeness that distances it for us:

> There was Eru, the One, who in Arda is called Ilúvatar; and he made first the Ainur, the Holy Ones, that were the offspring of his thought, and they were with him before aught else was made. And he spoke to them, propounding to them themes of music; and they sang before him, and he was glad.[18]

Ilúvatar calls the Ainur to "make in harmony together a Great Music." This they do, but one of them, Melkor, who has been given "the greatest gifts of power and of knowledge,"[19] becomes impatient and introduces discord into the music of the Ainur. Ilúvatar intervenes and introduces a new theme that incorporates these disruptions into a new harmony. Melkor persists in asserting his own way so that an opposing music is created: "it was loud, and vain, and endlessly repeated; and it had little harmony…And it essayed to drown the other music by the violence of its voice, but it seemed that its most triumphant notes were taken by the other and woven into its most solemn pattern."[20] Then Ilúvatar decisively intervenes: "in one chord, deeper than the Abyss, higher than the Firmament, piercing as the light of the eye of Ilúvatar, the Music ceased."[21]

Ilúvatar then shows the Ainur a vision of the world (Arda) and its future that, unbeknownst to them, he has woven from their music. Declaring *"Ea! Let these things Be!"*[22] he brings it to being and allows the Ainur to enter into the created order if they wish; those who do are called Valar, "the Powers of the World."[23] Melkor still tries to dominate Arda, but he is opposed by another of the Valar, Manwë. Thus "there was strife between Melkor and the other Valar; and for that time Melkor withdrew and departed to other regions, and did there what he would."[24] The loyal Valar continue to labor to prepare the world for the new races, Elves and humans, who are to come, but always with opposition by Melkor: "for as surely as the Valar began a labour so would Melkor undo or corrupt it."[25]

The Silmarillion continues with the doings of the Valar, Elves, and men, but our focus in this essay is on the *Ainulindalë*. Here we can see that Tolkien is providing the material for the experience of "recovery" for his readers on several levels.

Order in Creation

The opening of the *Ainulindalë* emphasizes that all that comes to be in Middle-earth comes from the mind of its eternally existent Maker: "There was Eru, the One…and he made first the Ainur…and they were with him before aught else was made."[26] The role of the Ainur in the musical themes with which Ilúvatar weaves the created world is also significant: Tolkien would have been well aware of the passage in Job in which God responds to Job's questioning by asking him, "Where were you when I laid the foundation of the earth?…when the morning stars sang together, and all the sons of God shouted for joy?" (Job 38:4, 7 RSV). Creation is not random or chaotic, but structured and intentional. Tolkien here is reminding us, in and through his literary creation, of the inherent order, beauty, and meaning of the cosmos.

Interestingly, here we can also get a glimpse of how Tolkien handles the Christian revelation. Middle-earth takes place in a pre-Christian context; elsewhere in his legendarium, Tolkien has the Elves allude to a tragic event which befell humans before they came into the Elves' ken: this is clearly an allusion to the fall of man, and indeed human sin is very much in evidence throughout the tales. But Tolkien discreetly keeps it off-stage, developing his stories with

called Morgoth) is the original "fallen angel," and that Sauron, the Dark Lord of *The Lord of the Rings*, is merely his lieutenant, one of the lesser spiritual beings who has been corrupted by Melkor. Which one is the Satan figure—Melkor or Sauron? The answer is both and neither. Tolkien is not writing an allegory in *The Silmarillion* any more than he is in *The Lord of the Rings*. Rather, what he is doing is creatively expressing, in this secondary world of Middle-earth, certain things that are true of primary reality: that there is evil in the world; that it is present not because God (Ilúvatar) created it but because some of his creatures freely chose to reject him; that there are spiritual beings of great power who have rebelled against God, just as there are others who serve and obey him; and that evil is a corrupting force. Given the existence of Melkor, we should not be surprised by the existence of Sauron—and vice versa.

Tolkien is not naive about the reality or destructive power of evil, not least because of his own experiences in war. As a young man, he fought in the trenches of World War I, where most of his close friends were killed;[27] as an older man, he lived through World War II, with one of his sons, Christopher, serving as an RAF pilot, one of the most dangerous roles in the war. Most of the tales of *The Silmarillion* are deeply tragic, and we see the harm wrought by Melkor and by those who believe his lies. Tolkien shows how devastating sin is, and how pervasive, but his vision, set forth in that first tale and consistently upheld, is that God is working through and in it all, and will redeem all the suffering that we experience.

Looking at the most deep-rooted corruption, exploitation, and cruelty in our own world, we should recognize both that the immediate cause of this evil can be found in human choices to do evil, and also that diabolic activity has a role as well. In the tragic events of *The Silmarillion*, Fëanor, one of the Elves and the creator of the precious Silmarils, is caught up in possessiveness; he and his people succumb to the "lies and evil whisperings and false counsel"[28] of Melkor to the point of rebelling against the Valar, a rebellion that leads to the first slaying of elf by elf, and to lasting division and tragedy among the peoples of Middle-earth. Tolkien invites us to "recover" a more richly complex view of the cosmos, which recognizes the reality and insidiously corrupting nature of evil while refusing the oversimplification of a dualist perspective.

Scripture

Thus far, we have been attending to specific aspects of the cosmos that

Tolkien's *Ainulindalë* helps us to see more clearly. But our reading of *The Silmarillion* also helps in recovering a sense of wonder at, and interest in, the Bible itself.

Lifelong Christians may not always realize how easy it is to be put off or even jaded by reading the Bible. It can seem alien, distant, obscure: From talking snakes to extended genealogies, the Old Testament in particular is difficult for anyone to engage with if they are not previously convinced of its merits.

The Silmarillion is in many ways very much like the Old Testament. It is written in a formal, "high" register that evokes the language of the Bible (if we exclude paraphrase translations that aim for a distinctly modern tone). Unlike many, or perhaps most, fantasy authors who try this, Tolkien succeeds at writing in this style, with variations on it (some tales are more terse and formal, others more detailed and narrative) naturally occurring throughout *The Silmarillion*. It feels natural because for Tolkien it is natural; his lifelong immersion in sagas and myth, as well as his lifelong immersion in Scripture—as a Catholic, heard as well as read, and in Latin as well as in English—allowed him naturally to compose in a style that drew on epics both pagan and biblical. Linguistically, then, he provides us with the familiar made strange so that the strange has the potential to become familiar.

If we get into the rhythm of *The Silmarillion* and become interested in the fates of the different families of the Elves, perhaps consulting the glossary or the genealogical trees at the back of the book, then the narratives of the Bible may well begin to seem both less and more strange. Less strange, because we will have learned from Tolkien how to follow multigenerational stories that are sometimes told in the starkest manner (like Cain and Abel) and sometimes in an almost novelistic way (like Joseph and his brothers). More strange, because reading the Bible after *The Silmarillion* suggests that we are, in a sense, reading a fantasy story: entering into a secondary world.

Here the Christian may well balk. Is it not counterproductive to encourage someone to read the Bible as if it were a fantasy story? There are two points to be made in response to this. The first is that the Bible has *no* chance of resonating with a person who never bothers to read it. The experience of reading it purely as a story—because it really does contain excellent stories—means that the reader is at a bare minimum given the opportunity to recognize it as more than a story. We can't be moved by Scripture if we never bother to read it.

The second, and more significant, point has to do with what Tolkien believed about revelation. As he helped C.S. Lewis to see, the Gospels are, in a sense, a myth, but (in Lewis's words), "a true myth."[29] As Tolkien later put it:

> The Gospels contain a fairy-story, or a story of a larger kind which embraces all the essence of fairy-stories…But this story has entered History and the primary world; the desire and aspiration of sub-creation has been raised to the fulfillment of Creation…this story is supreme; and it is true. Art has been verified. God is the Lord, of angels, and of men—and of Elves. Legend and History have met and fused.[30]

The Christian story is both historical fact and the greatest tale ever told. To reduce the Gospels to bare facts about the historical events recounted there, or to a set of propositions to be asserted, is to make them less meaningful. But if we can encounter as a myth (in the positive sense) a fairy tale, a fantasy story, we open ourselves up to encounter it as profoundly meaning-full, as both fact *and* fantasy. In our meaning-starved culture, this is precisely what we need. We do not lack for opportunities to read Scripture. In fact, never before has the text of the Bible been more readily available to anyone who wants to read it. What we lack is a meaningful engagement with it, and this—via the "recovery" of fantasy—Tolkien helps us to have.

And so we can see that fantasy stories can do a great deal to alleviate a problem that might at first seem to be only a problem of reason. If science and faith are thought to be incompatible, scientific apologetics such as the argument from design may not help very much by themselves. The evidence of a Creator is stamped in the creation itself, if we have but eyes to see it—but the problem of our modern culture is that we so often do not have eyes to see it.

Tolkien was a tremendously effective *indirect* apologist; his writings, above all his stories set in Middle-earth, are powerful works of pre-evangelism. They present the truth about our meaning-rich cosmos and its Creator in ways that subtly challenge skepticism and apathy about religious issues. A tale such as *The Silmarillion* addresses the issue from a different angle: helping us to clean our windows, to see clearly what is before us. We may still reject the truth that we see, but we now have the possibility of seeing it, and perhaps even, if recovery has done its work thoroughly, of finding the truth meaningful and worth investigating.

PART III:

EVIDENCES POINTING TO THE CREATION OF THE COSMOS

CHAPTER 11

CREATION *EX NIHILO*: THEOLOGY AND SCIENCE

WILLIAM LANE CRAIG

I n the beginning God created the heavens and the earth" (Genesis 1:1). With majestic simplicity the author of the opening chapter of Genesis thus differentiated his viewpoint not only from the ancient creation myths of Israel's neighbors, but also effectively from pantheism, such as is found in religions like Vedanta Hinduism and Taoism, from panentheism, whether of classical neo-Platonist vintage or twentieth-century process theology, and from polytheism, ranging from ancient paganism to contemporary Mormonism. The biblical writers give us to understand that the universe had a temporal origin and thus imply *creatio ex nihilo* in the temporal sense that God brought the universe into being without a material cause at some point in the finite past.[1]

Moreover, the church fathers, though heavily influenced by Greek thought, dug in their heels concerning the doctrine of creation, staunchly insisting on the temporal creation of the universe *ex nihilo* in opposition to the prevailing Hellenistic doctrine of the eternity of matter.[2] A tradition of robust argumentation against the past eternity of the world and in favor of *creatio ex nihilo*, issuing from the Alexandrian Christian theologian John Philoponus (d. 580?), continued for centuries in Islamic, Jewish, and Christian thought.[3] In 1215, the Catholic Church promulgated temporal *creatio ex nihilo* as official church doctrine at the Fourth Lateran Council, declaring God to be "Creator of all things, visible and invisible...who, by His almighty power, from the beginning of time has created both orders in the same way out of nothing."[4] This remarkable declaration not only affirms that God created everything apart from himself without recourse to any material cause, but even that time itself had a beginning. The doctrine of creation is thus inherently bound up with temporal considerations and entails that God brought the universe into being at some point in the past without any antecedent or contemporaneous material cause.

Contemporary Cosmology and Creation *Ex Nihilo*

In this chapter we leave aside the fascinating philosophical questions raised by the doctrine of creation *ex nihilo*, which I have sought to address elsewhere[5] in order to focus upon the relevance of contemporary science—in particular, astrophysics and, still more specifically, physical cosmogony—to creation *ex nihilo*. Two independent but closely interrelated lines of physical evidence are relevant to the doctrine of creation *ex nihilo*: *evidence from the expansion of the universe*, and *evidence from the thermodynamics of the universe*.

The Expansion of the Universe

Pre-Relativistic Physics

In Aristotelian physics, prime matter, of which all physical substances are composed, is, like God himself, eternal and uncreated. It underlies the eternal process of generation and corruption undergone by things in the sublunary realm. In its large-scale structure, the universe has remained unchanged from all eternity.

Even with the demise of Aristotelian physics in the scientific revolution completed by Isaac Newton, the assumption of a static universe remained unchallenged. Although Newton himself believed that God had created the world, the universe described by his physics was to all appearances eternal. The assumption that the universe was never created was only further reinforced by Hermann Helmholtz's statement in the nineteenth century of the laws of the conservation of matter and energy. Since matter and energy can be neither created nor destroyed, there must have always been and will always be a universe—that is to say, the universe is temporally infinite in the past and the future.

To be sure, there were already clues in pre-relativistic physics—like Olbers' paradox of why the night sky is dark rather than aflame with light if an infinity of stars has existed from eternity past, or like the second law of thermodynamics, which seems to imply that the universe, if it has existed from eternity, ought to lie moribund in a state of equilibrium—that there is something wrong with the prevailing assumption of an eternal, static cosmos. But these niggling worries could not overturn what was everywhere taken for granted: that the universe as a whole has existed and will exist unchanged forever.

The Revolution Wrought by General Relativity

Tremors of the impending earthquake that would demolish the old cosmology were first felt in 1917, when Albert Einstein made a cosmological application of his newly discovered gravitational theory, the general theory of relativity (hereafter, GR).[6] Einstein assumed that the universe is homogeneous and isotropic and that it exists in a steady state, with a constant mean mass density and a constant curvature of space. To his chagrin, however, he found that GR would not permit such a model of the universe unless he introduced into his gravitational field equations a certain "fudge factor" Λ in order to counterbalance the gravitational effect of matter and so ensure a static universe. Einstein's static universe was balanced on a razor's edge, however, and the least perturbation—even the transport of matter from one part of the universe to another—would cause the universe either to implode or expand. By taking this feature of Einstein's model seriously, the Russian mathematician Alexander Friedman and the Belgian astronomer Georges Lemaître were able to formulate independently, during the 1920s, solutions to the field equations that predicted an expanding universe.[7]

The monumental significance of the Friedman-Lemaître model lay in its historization of the universe. As one commentator remarked, up to this time the idea of the expansion of the universe "was absolutely beyond comprehension. Throughout all of human history the universe was regarded as fixed and immutable and the idea that it might actually be changing was inconceivable."[8] But if the Friedman-Lemaître model were correct, the universe could no longer be adequately treated as a static entity existing, in effect, timelessly. Rather the universe has a history, and time will not be matter of indifference for our investigation of the cosmos.

In 1929 measurements by the American astronomer Edwin Hubble of the red-shift in the optical spectra of light from distant galaxies,[9] which was taken to indicate a universal recessional motion of the light sources in the line of sight, provided a dramatic verification of the Friedman-Lemaître model. Incredibly, what Hubble had discovered was the isotropic expansion of the universe predicted by Friedman and Lemaître on the basis of Einstein's GR. It was a veritable turning point in the history of science. "Of all the great predictions that science has ever made over the centuries," exclaims John Wheeler, "was there ever one greater than this, to predict, and predict correctly, and predict against all expectation a phenomenon so fantastic as the expansion of the universe?"[10]

The Standard Big Bang Model

According to the Friedman-Lemaître model, as time proceeds, the distances separating galactic masses become greater. It is important to understand that as a GR-based theory, the model does not describe the expansion of the material content of the universe into a pre-existing, empty, Newtonian space, but rather the expansion of space itself. The ideal particles of the cosmological fluid constituted by the matter and energy of the universe are conceived to be at rest with respect to space but to recede progressively from one another as space itself expands or stretches, just as buttons glued to the surface of a balloon would recede from one another as the balloon inflates. As the universe expands, it becomes less and less dense. This has the astonishing implication that as one reverses the expansion and extrapolates back in time, the universe becomes progressively denser until one arrives at a state of infinite density at some point in the finite past. This state represents a singularity at which space-time curvature, along with temperature, pressure, and density, becomes infinite. It therefore constitutes an edge or boundary to space-time itself. P.C.W. Davies comments,

> If we extrapolate this prediction to its extreme, we reach a point when all distances in the universe have shrunk to zero. An initial cosmological singularity therefore forms a past temporal extremity to the universe. We cannot continue physical reasoning, or even the concept of spacetime, through such an extremity. For this reason most cosmologists think of the initial singularity as the beginning of the universe. On this view the big bang represents the creation event; the creation not only of all the matter and energy in the universe, but also of spacetime itself.[11]

The term *big bang*, originally a derisive expression coined by Fred Hoyle to characterize the beginning of the universe predicted by the Friedman-Lemaître model, is thus potentially misleading, because the expansion cannot be visualized from the outside (there being no "outside," just as there is no "before" with respect to the big bang).

The standard big bang model, as the Friedman-Lemaître model came to be called, thus describes a universe that is not eternal in the past, but that came into being a finite time ago. Moreover—and this deserves underscoring—the origin it posits is an absolute origin *ex nihilo*. For not only all matter and energy, but space and time themselves come into being at the initial cosmological singularity. As John Barrow and Frank Tipler emphasize, "At this singularity, space and time came into existence; literally nothing existed before the singularity, so, if the Universe originated at such a singularity, we would truly have a creation *ex nihilo*."[12] On the standard model the universe originates *ex nihilo* in the sense that at the initial singularity it is true that *there is no earlier space-time point* or it is false that *something existed prior to the singularity.*

Beginningless Models

Although advances in astrophysical cosmology have forced various revisions in the standard model,[13] nothing has called into question its fundamental prediction of the finitude of the past and the beginning of the universe. Indeed, as James Sinclair has shown, the history of twentieth-century cosmogony has seen a parade of failed theories trying to avert the absolute beginning predicted by the standard model.[14] These beginningless models have been repeatedly shown either to be physically untenable or to imply the very beginning of the universe which they sought to avoid. Meanwhile, a series of remarkable singularity theorems has increasingly tightened the loop around empirically tenable cosmogonic models by showing that under more and more generalized conditions, a beginning is inevitable. In 2003 Arvind Borde, Alan Guth, and Alexander Vilenkin were able to show that any universe that is, on average, in a state of cosmic expansion throughout its history cannot be infinite in the past but must have a beginning.[15] In 2012 Vilenkin showed that cosmogonic models that do not fall under this single condition fail on other grounds to avert the beginning of the universe. Vilenkin concluded, "There are no models at this time that provide a satisfactory model for a universe without a beginning."[16] In an article in the online journal *Inference* published in the fall of 2015, Vilenkin strengthened that conclusion: "We have no viable models of an eternal universe. The BGV theorem gives reason to believe that such models simply cannot be constructed."[17]

Cosmologist Sean Carroll, in an effort to subvert the implications of the Borde-Guth-Vilenkin theorem, has recently cited privately communicated remarks from Alan Guth to the effect that "I don't know whether the universe had a beginning. I suspect that the universe *didn't* have a beginning. It's very likely eternal—but nobody knows."[18] Carroll rightly asks, "Now, how in the world can the author of the Borde-Guth-Vilenkin theorem say the universe is probably eternal?"[19] More aptly, how can one of its authors say that it is probably eternal and the other that it is probably not? Carroll assured his audience that the reason is that "the theorem is only about classical descriptions of the universe, not about the universe itself."[20] That would not, however, explain how Vilenkin could be so desperately mistaken about the theorem's implications.

But now new light has been shed on Guth's enigmatic remarks through correspondence with the philosopher Daniel Came.[21] There, Guth reveals that he favors models of the universe featuring a reversal of time's arrow at some point in the past and that his remarks to Carroll had reference to such models. Such models do not fall under the BGV theorem because they do not satisfy the single condition of that theorem that the universe is, on average, in a state of cosmic expansion throughout its history. Thus, neither Guth nor Vilenkin are mistaken about the theorem's implications; rather, Guth just advocates a model to which the theorem does not apply. Unfortunately for hopefuls of a past-eternal universe like Guth and Carroll, such time-reversal models are highly unphysical and, even if successful, do not in fact avert the beginning of the universe but rather imply it.[22] For that time-reversed expansion is in no sense in our past but represents a universe sharing the same beginning point yet expanding in another direction. Vilenkin had already considered such models in his previous discussions and rejected them. That is why he said, "All the evidence we have says that the universe had a beginning."[23]

The BGV theorem proves that classical spacetime, under a single, very general condition, cannot be extended to past infinity but must reach a boundary at some time in the finite past. Either there was something on the other side of that boundary or not. If not, then that boundary is the beginning of the universe. If there was something on the other side, then it will be a nonclassical region described by the yet-to-be discovered theory of quantum gravity. In that case, Vilenkin says, *it* will be the beginning of the universe.[24]

For consider: If there is such a nonclassical region, then it is not past eternal in the classical sense. But neither does it seem to exist literally timelessly, akin to the way in which philosophers consider abstract objects to be timeless or theologians take God to be timeless. For it is supposed to have existed *before* the classical era, and the classical era is supposed to have *emerged* from it, which seems to posit a temporal relation between the quantum gravity era and the classical era.[25] In any case, such a quantum state is not stable and so would either produce the universe from eternity past or not at all. As Anthony Aguirre and John Kehayias argue,

> it is very difficult to devise a system—especially a quantum one—that does nothing "forever," then evolves. A truly stationary or periodic quantum state, which would last forever, would never evolve, whereas one with any instability will not endure for an indefinite time.[26]

Hence, the quantum gravity era would itself have to have had a beginning in order to explain why it transitioned some 14 billion years ago into classical time and space. Hence, whether at the boundary or at the quantum gravity regime, the universe began to exist.

The Thermodynamics of the Universe

If this were not enough, there is a second line of scientific evidence for the beginning of the universe based on the laws of thermodynamics. According to the second law of thermodynamics, processes taking place in a closed system always tend toward a state of equilibrium. Our interest in the law has to do with what happens when it is applied to the universe as a whole. The universe is, on a naturalistic view, a gigantic closed system, because it is everything there is and there is nothing outside it. What this seems to imply, then, is that given enough time, the universe and all its processes will run down, and the entire universe will come to equilibrium. This is known as the heat death of the universe. Once the universe reaches this state, no further change is possible. The universe is dead.

The question this implication of the Second Law inevitably forces upon us is this: *If, given enough time, the universe will reach heat death, then why is it not in a state of heat death now, if it has existed forever, from eternity?* If the universe did not begin to exist, then it should now be in a state of equilibrium. Like a ticking clock, it should have run down by now. Because it has not yet run down, this implies, in the words of one baffled scientist, "In some way the universe must have been *wound up*."[27]

Pre-Relativistic Physics

As alluded to earlier, nineteenth-century physicists were already aware of this conundrum. The German scientist Ludwig Boltzmann offered a daring proposal in order to explain why we do not find the universe in a state of heat death or thermodynamic equilibrium.[28] Boltzmann hypothesized that the universe as a whole *does*, in fact, exist in an equilibrium state, but that over time fluctuations in the energy level occur here and there throughout the universe so that by chance alone there will be isolated regions where disequilibrium exists. Boltzmann referred to these isolated regions as "worlds." We should not be surprised to see our world in a highly improbable disequilibrium state, he maintained, because in the ensemble of all worlds there must exist by chance alone certain worlds in disequilibrium, and ours just happens to be one of these.

The problem with Boltzmann's daring Many Worlds Hypothesis is that if our world were merely a fluctuation in a sea of diffuse energy, then it is overwhelmingly more probable that we should be observing a much tinier region of disequilibrium than we do. In order for us to exist, a smaller fluctuation, even one that produced our world instantaneously by an enormous accident, is inestimably more probable than a progressive decline in entropy over 14 billion years to fashion the world we currently see. In fact, Boltzmann's hypothesis, if adopted, would force us to regard the past as illusory, everything having the mere appearance of age, and the stars and planets as illusory, mere "pictures" as it were, because that sort of world is vastly more probable given a state of overall equilibrium than a world with genuine, temporally and spatially distant events. Therefore, Boltzmann's Many Worlds Hypothesis has been universally rejected by the scientific community, and the present disequilibrium is usually taken to be just a result of the initial low entropy condition mysteriously obtaining at the beginning of the universe.

General Relativistic Physics

Today eschatology is no longer merely a branch of theology; rather, it has become a field of cosmology. Just as cosmogony studies the origin of the universe, so physical eschatology studies its end. In contemporary cosmological eschatology there are two possible types of death for the universe. If the universe will eventually recontract, it will die a "hot" death. Beatrice Tinsley describes such a state:

> If the average density of matter in the universe is great enough, the mutual gravitational attraction between bodies will eventually slow the expansion to a halt. The universe will then contract and collapse into a hot fireball. There is no known physical mechanism that could reverse a catastrophic big crunch. Apparently, if the universe becomes dense enough, it is in for a hot death.[29]

If the universe is fated to recontraction, then as it contracts, the stars gain energy, causing them to burn more rapidly so that they finally explode or evaporate. As everything in the universe grows closer together, the black holes begin to gobble up everything around them, and eventually begin themselves to coalesce. In time, "All the black holes [will] finally coalesce into one large black hole that is coextensive with the universe,"[30] from which the universe will never re-emerge.

But suppose, as is more likely, that the universe will expand forever. Tinsley describes the fate of this universe:

> If the universe has a low density, its death will be cold. It will expand forever at a slower and slower rate. Galaxies will turn all of their gas into stars, and the stars will burn out. Our own Sun will become a cold, dead remnant, floating among the corpses of other stars in an increasingly isolated Milky Way.[31]

At 10^{30} years the universe will consist of 90 percent dead stars, 9 percent supermassive black holes formed by the collapse of galaxies, and 1 percent atomic matter, mainly hydrogen. Elementary particle physics suggests that thereafter protons will decay into electrons and positrons, so that space will be filled with a rarefied gas so thin the distance between an electron and a positron will be about the size of the present galaxy. Some scientists believe that at 10^{100} years, the black holes themselves will dissipate by a strange effect predicted by quantum mechanics. The mass and energy associated with a black hole so warp space such that they are said to create a "tunnel" or "wormhole" through which the mass and energy are ejected in another region of space. As the mass of a black hole decreases, its energy loss accelerates so that it is eventually dissipated into radiation and elementary particles. Eventually all black holes will completely evaporate, and all the matter in the ever-expanding universe will be reduced to a thin gas of elementary particles and radiation. Yet because the volume of space constantly increases, the universe will never actually arrive at equilibrium, since there is always more room for entropy production. Nonetheless, the universe will become increasingly cold, dark, dilute, and dead.

Recent discoveries provide strong evidence that there is effectively a positive cosmological constant that causes the cosmic expansion to accelerate rather than decelerate. Paradoxically, because the volume of space increases exponentially, allowing greater room for further entropy production, the universe actually grows farther and farther from an equilibrium state as time proceeds. But the acceleration only hastens the cosmos's disintegration into increasingly isolated material patches no longer causally connected with similarly marooned remnants of the expanding universe. Each of these patches faces, in turn, thermodynamic extinction. Therefore, the grim future predicted on the basis of the second law remains fundamentally unaltered.

Thus, the same pointed question raised by classical physics persists: Why, if the universe has existed forever, is it not now in a cold, dark, dilute, and lifeless state? In contrast to their nineteenth-century forbears, contemporary physicists have come to question the implicit assumption that the universe is past eternal. Davies, an expert in the physics of temporally asymmetrical processes, reports,

> Today, few cosmologists doubt that the universe, at least as we know it, did have an origin at a finite moment in the past. The alternative—that the universe has always existed in one form or another—runs into a rather basic paradox. The Sun and stars cannot keep burning forever: sooner or later they will run out of fuel and die.

> The same is true of all irreversible physical processes; the stock of energy available in the universe to drive them is finite, and cannot last for eternity. This is an example of the so-called second law of thermodynamics, which, applied to the entire cosmos, predicts that it is stuck on a one-way slide of degeneration and decay towards a final state of maximum entropy, or disorder. As this final state has not yet been reached, it follows that the universe cannot have existed for an infinite time.[32]

Davies concludes, "The universe can't have existed forever. We know there must have been an absolute beginning a finite time ago."

Multiverse Scenarios

Inflationary theory has been exploited by some theorists in an attempt to revive Boltzmann's explanation of why we find ourselves in a universe thermodynamically capable of sustaining observers. According to generic inflationary theory, our universe exists in a true vacuum state with an energy density that is nearly zero; but earlier it existed in a false vacuum state with a very high-energy density. If we hypothesize that the conditions determining the energy density and evolution of the false vacuum state were just right, then the false vacuum will expand so rapidly that, as it decays into bubbles of true vacuum, the "bubble universes" formed in this sea of false vacuum, though themselves expanding at enormous rates, will not be able to keep up with the expansion of the false vacuum and so will find themselves increasingly separated over time.

Moreover, each bubble is subdivided into domains bounded by event horizons, each domain constituting an observable universe. Those who are internal to such a universe will see it to be open and infinite, even though externally the bubble universe is finite and geometrically closed. Despite the fact that the multiverse is itself finite and geometrically closed, the false vacuum will, according to the theory, go on expanding forever. New bubbles of true vacuum will continue to form in the gaps between the bubble universes and become themselves isolated worlds. The question, then, in the words of Dyson, Kleban, and Susskind, is "whether the universe can be a naturally occurring fluctuation, or must it be due to an external agent which starts the system out in a specific low entropy state?"[33]

The proposed solution to the problem is essentially the same as Boltzmann's. Among the infinity of worlds generated by inflation there will be some worlds that are in a state of thermodynamic disequilibrium, and only these worlds can support observers. It is therefore not surprising that we find the world in a state of disequilibrium, because that is the only kind of world that we could observe.

But then the proposed solution is plagued by the same failing as Boltzmann's hypothesis. In a multiverse of eternally inflating vacua, most of the volume will be occupied by high-entropy disordered states incapable of supporting observers. There are two ways in which observable states can exist: first, by being part of a relatively young low-entropy world, or second, by being a thermal fluctuation in a high-entropy world. Even though young universes are constantly nucleating out of the false vacuum, their volumes will be small in comparison to the older bubbles. Disordered states will therefore be, on average, strongly predominant. That implies that observers are much more likely to be the result of thermal fluctuations than the result of young low-entropy conditions.

But then the objection once again arises that it is incomprehensibly more probable that a much smaller region of disequilibrium should arise via a fluctuation than a region as large as our observable universe. Roger Penrose calculates that the odds of our universe's initial low-entropy condition coming into existence is on the order of one part in $10^{10^{(123)}}$.[34] He comments, "I cannot even recall seeing anything else in physics whose accuracy is known to approach, even remotely, a figure like one part in $10^{10^{(123)}}$."[35] By contrast, the odds of our solar system's being formed instantly by random collisions of particles is about $1:10^{10^{(60)}}$, a vast number, but inconceivably smaller than $10^{10^{(123)}}$. (Penrose calls it "utter chicken feed" by comparison.[36]) Thus, in the multiverse of worlds, observable states involving such an initial low-entropy condition will be an incomprehensibly tiny fraction of all the observable states present. If we are just one random member of an ensemble of worlds, we should therefore be observing a smaller patch of order.

Adopting the multiverse hypothesis to explain our ordered observations would thus result once more in a strange sort of illusionism. It would be overwhelmingly probable that there is really not a vast, orderly universe out there, despite our observations; it is all an illusion. Indeed, the most probable state that is adequate to support our ordered observations is an even smaller "universe" consisting of a single brain that appears out of the disorder via a thermal fluctuation. In all probability, then, you alone exist, and even your physical body is illusory! Some cosmologists have, in melodramatic language reminiscent of grade-B horror movies of the 1950s, dubbed this problem "the invasion of the Boltzmann brains."[37]

Boltzmann brains are much more plenteous in the ensemble of universes than ordinary observers, and, therefore, each of us ought to think that he is himself a Boltzmann brain if he believes that the universe is but one member of an ensemble of worlds. Because that seems crazy, that fact strongly disconfirms the hypothesis that there is a multiverse old enough and big enough to have evolved sufficient volume to account for our low-entropy condition's appearing by chance. These and other problems make the multiverse solution less plausible than the standard solution that the universe began to exist with an initial low-entropy condition.

Quantum Cosmology

Those preferring a universe without a beginning might hope that quantum cosmology might serve to avert the implications of the second law of thermodynamics. But now a new singularity theorem formulated by Aron Wall seems to close the door on that possibility. Wall shows that, given the validity of the generalized second law of thermodynamics in quantum cosmology, the universe must have begun to exist, unless, with Guth, one postulates a reversal of the arrow of time at some point in the past, which, Wall rightly observes, involves a thermodynamic beginning in time that "would seem to raise the same sorts of philosophical questions that any other sort of beginning in time would."[38] Wall reports that his results require only certain basic concepts so that "it is reasonable to believe that the results will hold in a complete theory of quantum gravity."[39]

Thus, we have good evidence both from the expansion of the universe and from the second law of thermodynamics that the universe is not past eternal but had a temporal beginning.

Creation *Ex Nihilo*

Davies raises the inevitable question:

> "What caused the big bang?"…One might consider some supernatural force, some agency beyond space and time as being responsible for the big bang, or one might prefer to regard the big bang as an event without a cause. It seems to me that we don't have too much choice. Either…something outside of the physical world…or…an event without a cause.[40]

It might seem metaphysically absurd that the universe should come into being without a cause and therefore a supernatural agency is to be preferred. But some scientists have contended that quantum physics can explain the origin of the universe from nothing.

"Nothing"

Unfortunately, some of these scientists have an outrageously naïve grasp of language. The word *nothing* is a term of universal negation. It means "not anything." So, for example, if I say, "I had nothing for lunch today," I mean, "I did not have anything for lunch today." If you read an account of World War II in which it says that "nothing stopped the German advance from sweeping across Belgium," it means that the German advance was not stopped by anything. If a theologian tells you that God created the universe out of nothing, he means that God's creation of the universe was not out of anything. The word *nothing*, to repeat, is simply a term of universal negation, meaning "not anything."

There is a whole series of similar words of universal negation in English: *nobody* means "not anybody." *None* means "not one." *Nowhere* means "not anywhere." *No place* means "not in any place."

Because the word *nothing* is grammatically a pronoun, we can use it as the subject or direct object of a sentence. By taking these words not as terms of universal negation but as words referring to something, we can generate all sorts of amusing statements. If you were to say, "I saw nobody in the hall," the wiseacre might reply, "Yeah, he's been hanging around there a lot lately." If you were to say, "I had nothing for lunch today," he might say, "Really? How did it taste?"

These sorts of puns are as old as literature itself. In Homer's *Odyssey*, Odysseus introduces himself to the Cyclops as "No man" or "Nobody." One night Odysseus puts out the Cyclops' eye. His fellow Cyclopses hear him screaming and yell to him, "What's the matter with you, making so much noise that we can't sleep?" The Cyclops answers, "Nobody is killing me! Nobody is killing me!" They reply, "If nobody is attacking you, then you must be sick, and there's nothing we can do about it!" Euripides, in his version of the story, composed a sort of Abbott and Costello "Who's on first?" routine:

"Why are you crying out, Cyclops?"

"Nobody has undone me!"

"Then there is no one hurting you after all."

"Nobody is blinding me!"

"Then you're not blind."

"As blind as you!"

"How could nobody have made you blind?"

"You're mocking me! But where is this Nobody?"

"Nowhere, Cyclops!"

The use of these words of negation like *nothing*, *nobody*, and *no one* as substantive words referring to something *is a joke*.

How astonishing, then, to find that some physicists, whose mother tongue is English, have used these terms precisely as substantive terms of reference. Lawrence Krauss, for example, has made these statements with a straight face:

There are a variety of forms of nothing, [and] they all have physical definitions.

The laws of quantum mechanics tell us that nothing is unstable.

Seventy percent of the dominant stuff in the universe is nothing.

There's nothing there, but it has energy.

Nothing weighs something.

Nothing is almost everything.[41]

All of these claims take the word *nothing* to be a substantive term referring to something—for example, the quantum vacuum or quantum fields. These are physical realities and therefore clearly something. To call these realities nothing is at best misleading and guaranteed to confuse laypeople, and at worst a deliberate misrepresentation of science. Such statements do not even begin to address, much less answer, the question of why the universe exists rather than nothing.

In his review of Krauss' book *A Universe from Nothing*, David Albert, an eminent philosopher of quantum physics, explains that with respect to Krauss' first kind of nothing,

> vacuum states are particular arrangements of elementary physical stuff…the fact that some arrangements of fields happen to correspond to the existence of particles and some don't is not a whit more mysterious than the fact that some of the possible arrangements of my fingers happen to correspond to the existence of a fist and some don't. And the fact that particles can pop in and out of existence, over time, as those fields rearrange themselves, is not a whit more mysterious than the fact that fists can pop in and out of existence, over time, as my fingers rearrange themselves. And none of these poppings…amount to anything even remotely in the neighborhood of a creation from nothing…[42]

He concludes, "Krauss is dead wrong and his religious and philosophical critics are absolutely right."

Coming into Being from Nothing

Alexander Vilenkin has a different proposal as to how the universe could have come into being from literally nothing. In response to the claim of a supernatural agency, he says,

> Regarding the BGV theorem and its relation to God, I think the theorem implies the existence of a rather special state at the past boundary of classical spacetime. Some mechanism is required to impose this state. Craig wants this mechanism to be God, but I think quantum cosmology would do just as well.[43]

Just what does Vilenkin have in mind? In his *Inference* article he explains,

Modern physics can describe the emergence of the universe as a physical process that does not require a cause. Nothing can be created from nothing, says Lucretius, if only because the conservation of energy makes it impossible to create nothing [*sic*; something?] from nothing…

There is a loophole in this reasoning. The energy of the gravitational field is negative; it is conceivable that this negative energy could compensate for the positive energy of matter, making the total energy of the cosmos equal to zero. In fact, this is precisely what happens in a closed universe, in which the space closes on itself, like the surface of a sphere. It follows from the laws of general relativity that the total energy of such a universe is necessarily equal to zero…

If all the conserved numbers of a closed universe are equal to zero, then there is nothing to prevent such a universe from being spontaneously created out of nothing. And according to quantum mechanics, any process which is not strictly forbidden by the conservation laws will happen with some probability…

What causes the universe to pop out of nothing? No cause is needed.[44]

I think this is a terrible argument. Grant the supposition that the positive energy associated with matter is exactly counterbalanced by the negative energy associated with gravity so that on balance, the energy is zero. The key move comes with the claim that in such a case "there is nothing to prevent such a universe from being spontaneously created out of nothing." Now this claim is a triviality. Necessarily, if there is nothing, then there is nothing to prevent the universe from coming into being. By the same token, if there is nothing, then there is nothing to permit the universe to come into being. If there were anything to prevent or permit the universe's coming into being, then there would be something, not nothing. If there is nothing, then there is nothing, period.

The absence of anything to prevent the universe's coming into being does not imply the metaphysical possibility of the universe's coming into being from nothing. To illustrate, if there were nothing, then there would be nothing to prevent God's coming into being without a cause, but that does not entail that such a thing is metaphysically possible. It is metaphysically impossible for God to come into being without a cause, even if there were nothing to prevent it because nothing existed.

Vilenkin, however, infers that "no cause is needed" for the universe's coming into being because the conservation laws would not prevent it and "according to quantum mechanics, any process which is not strictly forbidden by the conservation laws will happen." The argument assumes that if there were nothing, then both the conservation laws and quantum physical laws would still hold. This is far from obvious, however, because in the absence of anything at all, it is not clear that the laws governing our universe would hold. In any case, why think that, given the laws of quantum mechanics, anything not strictly forbidden by the conservation laws will happen? The conservation laws do not strictly forbid God's sending everyone to heaven, but that hardly gives grounds for optimism. Neither do they strictly forbid his sending everyone to hell, in which case both outcomes will occur, which is logically impossible, as they are logically contrary universal generalizations. The point can be made nontheologically as well: The conservation laws do not strictly forbid something's coming into existence, but neither do they forbid nothing's coming into existence, but both cannot happen. It is logically absurd to think that because something is not forbidden by the conservation laws, it will therefore happen.

> Given the metaphysical impossibility of the universe's coming into being from nothing, belief in a supernatural Creator is eminently reasonable.

Finally, it is hard to take seriously Vilenkin's inference that because the positive and negative energy in the universe sum to zero, no cause of the universe's coming into being is needed. This is like saying that if your debts balance your assets then your net worth is zero, and thus there is no cause of your financial situation. Vilenkin would, I hope, not agree with Peter Atkins that because the positive and negative energy of the universe sum to zero, therefore nothing exists now, and so "nothing did indeed come from nothing."[45] For as Descartes taught us, I, at least, undeniably exist, and so something exists. Christopher Isham, Britain's premier quantum cosmologist, rightly points out that there still needs to be "ontic seeding" to create the positive and negative energy in the first place, even if on balance its sum is naught.[46] Even if one were to concede the absence of a material cause of the universe, the need of an efficient cause is patent.

In Line with the Empirical Evidence

We thus have two independent lines of scientific evidence in support of the beginning of the universe. First, the expansion of the universe implies that the universe had a beginning. Second, thermodynamics shows the universe began to exist. Because these lines of evidence are independent and mutually reinforcing, the confirmation they supply for a beginning of the universe is all the stronger. Of course, as with all scientific results, this evidence is provisional. As Sean Carroll reminds us,

> Science isn't in the business of proving things. Rather, science judges the merits of competing models in terms of their simplicity, clarity, comprehensiveness, and fit to the data. Unsuccessful theories are never disproven, as we can always concoct elaborate schemes to save the phenomena; they just fade away as better theories gain acceptance.[47]

Science cannot force us to accept the beginning of the universe; one can always concoct elaborate schemes to explain away the evidence. But those schemes have not fared well in displaying the aforementioned scientific virtues.

Given the metaphysical impossibility of the universe's coming into being from nothing, belief in a supernatural Creator is eminently reasonable. At the very least we can say confidently that the person who believes in the doctrine of *creatio ex nihilo* will not find himself contradicted by the empirical evidence of contemporary cosmology, but on the contrary, fully in line with it.

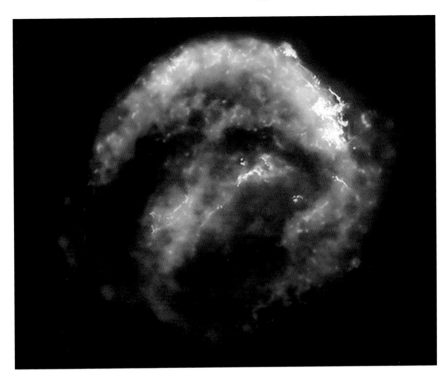

SN 1604, Kepler's Supernova,[48] is the last supernova to have been observed in the Milky Way Galaxy. When it first appeared, the brightness of this stellar cataclysm was visible throughout Europe. (Courtesy of NASA)

CHAPTER 12

THE COSMIC COINCIDENCES OF FINE TUNING

LUKE BARNES AND ALLEN HAINLINE

> The universe that we observe has precisely the properties we should expect if there is, at bottom, no design, no purpose, no evil, no good, nothing but blind, pitiless indifference. DNA neither knows nor cares. DNA just is. And we dance to its music.[1]

RICHARD DAWKINS

This famous quote shows a scientist's instinct. A crucial question to ask of any scientific theory—from atoms to zebras—is this: if it were true, what would we expect? For example, if Earth's landmass were once part of a single supercontinent, we would *expect* today's continents to fit together like a jigsaw puzzle. If the solar system formed from a swirling cloud of gas and dust, we would *expect* all the planets to orbit in the same direction. If our kids had really cleaned their room, we would expect them *not* to panic when we announce, "I'm coming in to check!"

So if the story of the cosmos had no author, what would we expect? If matter and energy in spacetime are all that exists, with no purpose or design, what kind of physical world would we expect? Any old universe seems to be Dawkins's answer, a universe *as if* chosen at random.

And yet while Dawkins wants to draw conclusions about the universe *at bottom*, he speaks of DNA, the carrier of genetic information. Well, if you're going to be a reductionist,[2] then be a reductionist. The most fundamental rules of the universe are the domain of physics and cosmology. We should be asking, What if the universe had any old set of fundamental laws and properties? Over the last 40 years, physicists and cosmologists have stumbled across a novel way of answering this question. To explain, we'll need to look more closely at how a physicist writes the story of the universe.

A Physicist's View

At bottom, science explains natural phenomena in terms of dynamical laws of nature and initial conditions. For example, given Isaac Newton's understanding of the pull of gravity (dynamical laws) and the motion of the planets around the Sun today (initial conditions, for our purposes), we can predict where they will be tomorrow, and even when the next solar eclipse will take place.

Within the laws of physics we find a set of numbers that represent foundational properties of the universe, such as the strengths of the fundamental forces and the masses of its basic particles. Furthermore, the initial conditions of the universe as a whole have been accurately measured by cosmologists over the last few decades, including the amount of ordinary and dark matter.[3]

While we have measured these numbers, we don't know why they are what they are. The equation doesn't tell us; everything is still *mathematically* fine if we consider different values for the constants. The laws of physics leave room to explore other ways that the universe could have been. We can ask what the universe *would* have been like had we chosen a different set of fundamental properties. Is this just any old universe?

In recent decades, physicists have found an unexpected pattern among many of the fundamental parameters and initial conditions of the laws of nature: they must have values in a very narrow range for life to exist. This is called the fine-tuning of the universe for life. Similarly, most initial conditions would have resulted in a lifeless universe. The simple fact is that Dawkins is wrong—the universe does *not* have precisely the properties we should expect of a world without purpose or design. Far from it. Based on what has been discovered, the universe calls out for a deeper story.

Isn't This Just a God of the Gaps Argument?

"Not so fast," you might say. "I know where this is going—you're going to try to shove God into a gap in our knowledge! All that follows from 'I don't know' is that we don't know something. Leave God out of it!"

Is God ruled out of court before we even begin? We'd better address this point before we go on. It is crucial to be clear about the kind of explanation that God is supposed to provide. Consider a simplistic analogy: books have authors.

- Why does Harry Potter go to Hogwarts? Because Hagrid, Keeper of Keys at Hogwarts, takes him there to begin his schooling as a wizard.

- Why does Harry Potter go to Hogwarts? Because the author, J.K. Rowling, wanted to write the story that way, for artistic reasons.

These explanations don't exclude each other. We do not propose an "author of the gaps" when we infer from the coherence of the plot to the ingenuity of its author. These explanations apply at different levels—the first is within the internal logic of the world of Hogwarts School of Witchcraft and Wizardry, and the second with respect to the creator of that world. Similarly, describing the natural world in greater detail does not exclude its creator. Nothing happens to God when we discover that God's world is made of atoms.

> Scientific explanations start from initial conditions and laws of nature. We can and should ask whether these are better explained by atheism or theism.

In the Christian tradition, God is more fundamental to reality than nature and thus cannot be studied by the methods of science. However, we can follow the same principles of reasoning used in evaluating scientific theories to explore the metaphysical hypothesis that God exists. We consider the implications of rival theories and ask which best explains the universe we see. This is the methodology behind Dawkins's claim—atheism makes predictions, and our universe bears them out. We accept his methodology, but we challenge his conclusion.

"But," you retort, "you're still seizing on current scientific ignorance!" On the contrary, our argument is based on the best physics that we have. In particular, we examine what these laws tell us about the fundamental properties of the universe. We do not focus on specific observations that these laws may fail to explain. Scientific explanations start from initial conditions and laws of nature. We can and should ask whether these are better explained by atheism or theism.

Now, of course, we haven't heard the last word in physics. New discoveries could reveal deeper laws. But *any* argument that relies on science could be overturned by new scientific discoveries. Far from disqualifying this hypothesis, this should be seen as a virtue. If we're trying to decide on the best ultimate explanation for the physical universe (or whether it needs one at all), the best we can do is use our best scientific understanding of how our universe works.

The Universe Is Finely Tuned for Life

We both enjoyed playing with Lego[4] as kids, and now as parents we have an excuse to play with them as adults! Suppose you were to see an advertisement for a new construction toy with the following features: it ships within a tiny volume and weight, but over time, it expands to a larger size. No assembly is required because it self-assembles into cool toys that can fly, swim, and run.[5] These building blocks can form a variety of highly sophisticated machines. They can even replicate themselves so that you can share toys with others. They require no batteries because they harness energy from the environment. They are completely recyclable—existing toys can use old toys to make new toys! Would you believe it?

This, of course, is a description of life. It's easy to take life for granted, but it is an astonishing phenomenon, from the smallest cellular machine to the largest ecosystem. Living things all depend in one way or another on the fundamental particles and the rules by which the universe operates.

The fine tuning of the universe for life, in short, is the realization that even small changes to the properties and rules of our universe often prohibit the existence of life of any conceivable kind. Making a universe that is devoid of any complex structure is rather easy. Imagine Lego pieces that don't connect to each other, or are unable to hold together for more than a few seconds. In short, life-permitting physics[6] is rare.

But how can we know this, given that biologists do not even agree on a definition of life? For our purposes, we don't need to precisely know *sufficient* conditions for life—we need only to conservatively assess what is minimally *necessary*. John von Neumann[7] demonstrated constraints on what is necessary for any self-replicating system, even one running on a computer. Storing and replicating information is crucial to building a copy of a cell. Thus, if there were no stable building blocks for life, or there was no way of harnessing the energy necessary to perform replication, then intelligent life would not be possible.

For example, astrobiologists do not believe that life could exist in the Sun because the temperature is too high for atoms to form stable, long-lived arrangements of any kind. Heat acts like an annoying younger brother who keeps breaking your Lego creations! This makes information storage practically impossible. Similarly, in the vacuum of intergalactic space, atoms interact too infrequently for much information to be stored, and too little energy is available to drive replication.

We can reasonably (if not certainly) conclude, then, that if the entire universe were like the inside of the Sun or the vacuum of space, life would be very unlikely to exist. Our universe, by contrast, permits a vast range of possible arrangements of atoms, thanks to chemical bonding.

Laws of Nature Could Have Easily Been Life-Prohibiting

What if the laws of nature had been different? What if we changed the mathematical form of the basic rules of our universe? While it is difficult to be systematic in searching through all the possibilities—the set of all mathematical laws is, to put it mildly, large—we can consider general classes of different laws.

- If gravity were a repulsive rather than attractive force, then matter would not have collected into large, complex structures. The universe would be uniform and structureless, without planets, stars, or life.

- If *opposite* electrical charges repelled and *like* charges attracted each other, then electrons would be pushed away from the positively-charged atomic nuclei, and so chemistry would not be possible. Positive charges and negative charges would form separate, featureless conglomerations.

- If the strong nuclear force—the "glue" that holds the nucleus of an atom together—were a long-range force (such as gravity or electromagnetism), then the only structures formed would be uniform, spherical, undifferentiated lumps—not suitable for information storage or replication of the type required by intelligent life.

- Without the electromagnetic force, there would be no atoms and molecules. There also wouldn't be galaxies, whose formation relies on electromagnetic cooling of gas clouds. And there wouldn't be stable stars, even if they could form at all.

Moreover, if the universe were fundamentally classical rather than quantum, matter as we know it would not be stable. Much is made of the weirdness of quantum mechanics: the rules that govern atoms and light are very different from the rules of billiard balls and waves at the beach. The theory is believed by some to show that the universe is fundamentally fuzzy and random. However, regardless of how we interpret the theory, without these fundamental quantum rules chemistry would be impossible: electrons orbiting nuclei would very quickly emit radiation and spiral inward.

What if we considered a completely different kind of mathematical structure to underlie the laws of a possible universe? Luke's book with Geraint Lewis, *A Fortunate Universe*, considered a "universe" simulated on a computer, known as John Conway's *Game of Life*.[8] Despite its simplicity, interesting and lifelike things can happen: Structures can form, grow, and interact, and information can be processed. But such interesting laws are rare within the set of possible laws. Conway and his students proposed and tested a large number of rules. Eventually, and taking some cues from biology, they found laws that could mimic aspects of life.

More could be said, but this sample provides evidence that the laws of nature look rigged for life. And there's more we can say. If we restrict our attention to the fundamental constants and initial conditions, we can systematically search a large range of possible universes. As we explore the consequences of these properties of our universe, we'll tell the story of the universe. Or rather, we'll tell the *alternative* history of the universe.

A Brief History of the Universes

In the Beginning, Order

While popular descriptions of the big bang can give the impression that the universe began in a chaotic, messy state, from its very beginning our universe was orderly. To understand this, we must remind ourselves of what a physicist means by *order*.[9]

In the days of the industrial revolution, physicists noticed that not all forms of energy were equally useful. A single match can turn a pile of timber into heat and ashes; however, it is practically impossible to turn heat and ashes back into timber. Physicists realized that for any given system, the vast majority of the ways to arrange all the constituent atoms and molecules were useless—like a pile of ashes in a warm room, nothing happens.

By contrast, systems with useful energy are very rare. There is something about the way that they are arranged, some orderliness, that means that they don't just sit there. It is precisely because these arrangements are so rare that they tend to turn into the more common, less orderly states. If we want to know what a disorderly arrangement of a particular system looks like, just wait and watch.

Let's use the law of physics, argues Oxford physicist Roger Penrose, to watch a possible future of our universe. Suppose that the universe as a whole recollapses eventually, with space contracting instead of expanding.[10] As this happens, the energy in the universe will evolve toward more useless forms. In particular, the collapse of matter under gravity will continue to lock away particles inside black holes. The universe will end in a lumpy "big crunch" full of black holes. Thus, says Penrose, a disorderly beginning of the universe looks like this ending, but played in reverse. In a disorderly big bang, the matter in the universe is born inside black holes.

Our universe is not like that. In the earliest stages of our universe, the matter is spread out, not collapsed in black holes. As the universe evolves, the attractive force of gravity harnesses this energy to make galaxies, stars, and planets.

Orderliness is rare, but how rare is it? Penrose compares our universe to one that is maximally useless, with *all* its energy locked in one black hole. The odds of getting our kind of useful beginning, given a blind choice of initial conditions, is 1 part in 10 to the power of 10 to the power of 123. Writing out all the digits for this number requires more zeros than there are subatomic particles in the known universe! Most of the alternative histories of the universe don't involve anything remotely resembling life, or even complexity. They consist of black holes: simple, useless, and dead.[11]

Inflation

Many cosmologists think that in the very early universe there was a brief period of very rapid expansion known as inflation. This would smooth out a universe that was initially somewhat lumpy in its distribution of matter. Does this negate the conclusion that the universe began in an orderly state?

Not at all. Penrose's argument does not rely on identifying *exactly* what it was about the early universe that made it orderly. While we understand why smoothness is orderly, physics and cosmology will continue to study the early universe, and if some even earlier process caused the "initial" smoothness of the universe, then Penrose's argument implies that this process must begin from an *even more orderly* useful state. Special initial conditions are required for inflation to happen at all. The problem of the orderly *smooth* beginning is simply shifted to the problem of the orderly *inflationary* beginning. In other words, as physicists pull back the layers of the cosmic onion, they will continue to discover order.

Matter and Antimatter

As the universe cooled, matter and radiation of all kinds were being produced and destroyed. However, if the particle reactions we know about were the only ones operating in the early universe, equal amounts of matter and antimatter would have been created. When a matter particle collides with its antimatter opposite, they annihilate—that is, they transform into two particles of light. So, in a universe with equal amounts of both, almost all matter would annihilate into light. Thankfully, some not-yet-fully understood physical process (called *baryogenesis*) caused a slight asymmetry, producing a tiny excess of matter over antimatter—about 1 part in a billion. This *looks* an awful lot like fine-tuning, but in the absence of a standard theory of baryogenesis we can't confirm what would happen if we altered the fundamental constants.

The Nuclear Fires

Between about 1 second and 20 minutes after the big bang, the universe had the right temperature for nuclear reactions to produce elements heavier than hydrogen. The universe's protons and neutrons bound together, producing a universe that is about 25% helium-4 and less than a percent of the other light elements (deuterium, helium-3, lithium). The big bang model predicts these abundances with remarkable accuracy.[12] The hydrogen left over from these early reactions will go on to power long-lived stars and become part of molecules, such as water and 99.97% of organic compounds.

With a few tweaks to the fundamental constants, however, we order a very different early universe from our menu of possible universes. For example, if the neutron were lighter than the proton (rather than 0.1% heavier), then there would be virtually no hydrogen in the universe. This makes for significantly shorter-lived stars and a drastically impoverished menu of available molecules. We could achieve the same outcome by changing the strengths of the fundamental forces.

Making Galaxies

A universe whose beginning is too smooth is no good for life because the useful energy of gravitational collapse is not released. Structure does not form, which leaves the universe a perpetually thin gaseous soup of hydrogen and helium. Matter is never cool enough and dense enough for solids or liquids to form, or for any chemical reactions to take place. The initial "lumpiness" of the universe (known as Q) is very small—one part in 100,000. If Q were a factor of 10 or smaller, then only very diffuse gravitationally bound structures would form, unable to collapse into stars and planets.

Perhaps the best and most famous case of fine-tuning is the cosmological constant (CC). Cosmologists have discovered that about 70% of the energy in our universe is in a form that causes its expansion to accelerate. Ordinary matter and radiation will not do this, but there is a term in the equations of gravity known as the CC, which can cause the universe to accelerate in its expansion.

What would a universe with a different CC be like? A universe with a large CC will expand extremely rapidly from very early times. Matter will be driven apart and will not collapse under its own gravity into any form of structure. With a large and negative CC, the universe will recollapse in a very short time.

What might explain the value of the CC? Our best theory of matter proposes that the universe is filled with quantum fields. Fundamental particles, such as electrons and quarks, are described as travelling waves in these fields. We can arrange the fields so that there are no particles in a given region—that is, a particle detector will not register anything. When a field is in this vacuum state, any energy that remains in the field will behave like a CC. Each field contributes to the overall CC, positive or negative, and the typical size of these contributions is enormous.

In our universe, it seems that these positive and negative contributions almost perfectly cancel out, to 120 decimal places! If only 100 decimal places cancelled out, structure in the universe would cease to form after about one year. Which is to say there would be no stars, no planets, and no chemistry—no structure at all.[13] Or, if the CC were negative, the universe would have recollapsed in about one year. Again, not very hospitable.

Stars

Stars have two essential roles to play in a life-permitting universe. First, they make useful elements. The big bang only produced hydrogen, helium and lithium, which together form fewer than 10 chemical compounds. Hydrogen and carbon, on the other hand, can form 29,019 chemical compounds.[14] Heavier elements are crucial for life based on chemistry, and these elements are made in stars. Second, stars are a stable, long-lived source of useful energy for planetary life, as well as a source of the gravity that holds planets in their orbits.

A number of finely tuned parameters are necessary to allow long-lived, stable, useful-element-producing stars to exist in the universe. In many ways, stars are remarkably robust.[15] For example, as Luke showed in a paper written in 2015,[16] changing the constants of nature so that two protons can stick to each other (the diproton) would increase the rate of nuclear reactions in stars—*at fixed temperature and density*—by 10^{18}. However, it seems that stable stars are still possible; they simply have cooler, less dense cores.

Nevertheless, there are universes that won't have useful stars. The clearest way is by increasing the strength of gravity.[17] The extra squeeze means that the star burns out faster. Gravity in our universe is extremely weak—10^{40} times weaker than electromagnetism. If it were only 10^{30} times weaker, all stars would burn out in less than one million years. This is probably too fast for the surface of a rocky planet to cool from its initial molten state, let alone for life to form and evolve.

Another interesting coincidence, and one beneficial to life, is that a typical photon from a star has the right energy to catalyze chemical reactions. For example, there is a molecule in your eyes (known as 11-cis retinal) that has a bend in the middle. The light from the Sun has the right amount of energy to make the bend straighten, which sends a signal to your brain, which is how you see. An infrared photon doesn't have enough energy to straighten the bend, and an X-ray photon would break the molecule into pieces.[18] The reason that the energy from stars and the energy in chemical bonds are roughly similar is because of a coincidence between the gravitational constant, Planck constant, speed of light, proton mass, electron mass, and the strength of electromagnetism.[19] The relationship involving these parameters hold to within 15% in our universe, meaning that stars are able to power chemical reactions and rearrange molecules, rather than merely heating them or destroying them.

The production of two of the most important elements for life, carbon and oxygen, seems to require a degree of fine-tuning, though this has been the subject of considerable recent research. Carbon's ability to form long-chain molecules like DNA is unparalleled in the periodic table, and oxygen is both a constituent of water and an important element for storing and releasing energy. On the one hand, only a small change in the masses of the light quarks would result in a change in the internal structure of carbon, resulting in significantly less carbon or oxygen (or both) in our universe. On the other hand, other changes (specifically, binding beryllium-8) seem to provide an alternative pathway to carbon. Regardless, a number of coincidences between the fundamental constants seem to be required to make a universe in which the most abundant element (after hydrogen and helium) is *also* the element most suitable for life (carbon).

Supernovae

To make life, the useful elements formed in stars need to be released into the wider universe. Without additional fine-tuning, life-friendly elements would remain sequestered inside dead stars. Thankfully, large stars explode as supernovae. While modelling supernovae explosions is difficult, UK Astronomer Royal Sir Martin Rees has estimated that a change in the strength of the weak nuclear force by about 1 part in 10,000 relative to the strength of the strong force would have prevented core-collapse supernovae from occurring.[20] This case, however, is not totally clear cut: another rarer type of supernova (known as Type 1a) would still distribute some elements, as would the ejection of the outer layers of aging stars in planetary nebulae. But these would be much less efficient, making the occurrence of planets much rarer.

Atoms and Chemistry

Some of the clearest cases of fine-tuning come from the basic structure of atoms and molecules. When we simultaneously spin the dials that control the mass of the up quark, the down quark, and the electron, we find that it takes a very rare combination of settings for the building blocks of atomic nuclei to be stable.[21] With a relatively small increase in the mass of the up quark, for example, we can arrange for all protons to decay into neutrons, even if they are locked inside nuclei. There would be no nuclei and no atoms at all in the universe; matter would only be capable of forming (at most) spherical clumps, not the intricate and useful molecules known in our universe.

Similarly, a small increase in the mass of the down quark will result in universes in which the only stable element is hydrogen, and the universe can manage a grand total of one chemical reaction ($H + H \rightarrow H_2$). When we consider all the relevant restrictions on these fundamental masses, the "living island" is extremely small—the associated probability is at most 1 chance in 10^{20}.

Further, stable nuclei and atoms require forces to hold them together. If the strength of the strong nuclear force were much smaller, the nuclei of elements required by life would not be stable. If electromagnetism were too strong, atoms would not be stable—nuclei would capture orbiting electrons.[22] Our universe has a remarkable and seemingly rare capacity for order and complexity.

Fine-Tuning as Evidence for God

Let's return to Dawkins's view of the universe as being only matter in motion, energy and spacetime, with no purpose or design. Is our universe just *any old universe,* a universe *as if* chosen at random?

We can answer this question, or at least a reasonable approximation to this question. What if the universe had had a different set of laws, fundamental constants, or initial conditions? What if we were to pick an alternative physical setup for the universe at random? Is our universe just *any old universe* within that set of possibilities?

The answer is a rather definitive no. If you prefer a universe with no structure, no galaxies, no stars, no planets, no nuclei, no atoms, no molecules, we've got plenty of those. A typical universe cannot support the complexity required by any yet-conceived form of life. Our universe is, in this precise sense, profoundly atypical.

Consider the following analogy. (Remember: all analogies are imperfect.) We're playing poker. On my last five deals, I dealt myself a royal flush. You'd be wise to raise an eyebrow and walk away from the table. I protest: any set of five hands is just as likely as any other, so you can't complain about my improbable royal flush. Obviously you shouldn't return to the table, but why?

All sets of poker hands are equally improbable *only if we assume* that I'm dealing fairly. But that is precisely what is in question. If we assume that I'm cheating, a royal flush is much more probable.

Similarly, one shouldn't dismiss fine-tuning because any set of parameters is just as likely as any other. That is true only if the values are *as if* random. Fine-tuning should encourage us to question that assumption.

In the case of the poker game, cheating makes the observed royal flush more likely. Does supposing that God exists make a life-permitting universe more likely? On theism, ultimate reality is a mind,[23] and so there are ultimate reasons for why the universe is what it is. For the omnibenevolent God of Christianity, these reasons will be moral (rather than practical). Our universe has moral value—it contains conscious agents who have freedom, responsibility, and opportunity. This is a morally valuable (though not necessarily morally perfect) universe, one that God has reason to create. This makes it much more likely than a universe with only empty space or black holes.

Answers to Objections

The fine-tuning argument, unsurprisingly, has been subject to criticism. For example, how can we know what God would want, and whether God is likely to create life? In reply, it is important to put this uncertainty in context. In the game of poker, suppose a cheater were to defend himself by saying, "You don't know me! You don't know if I'm a cheating kind of person."

This might be true, but it wouldn't change your mind. Why? Because you compare the probability of cheating to the probability of five consecutive royal flushes, which is about one in a hundred thousand trillion trillion.[24] Unless you believe that the prior probability of a cheater is similarly small, you've got a very good case for skullduggery. The same principle applies to the fine-tuning argument: the probability of life-permitting constants and initial conditions on naturalism is so small that it should swamp skepticism about a designer's intentions. Theists have long argued for the moral value of conscious life, so we can hardly be accused of ad hocery.

Another common objection is this: there is nothing surprising about fine-tuning because observers could only find themselves in a universe that supported the existence of observers. This is related to the anthropic principle, a term with a variety of contradictory definitions.[25] What should be uncontroversial is the weak anthropic principle, which is a tautology: physical observers can only find themselves in a universe that supports the existence of observers.

The anthropic principle explains why observers don't observe a universe with properties that would prohibit life, but it doesn't explain why a life-friendly universe exists at all. Philosopher John Leslie gives an excellent illustration of this point. Suppose you were about to be executed by a firing squad of fifty marksmen. "Ready, aim, fire!" yells their commander. As the smoke clears, you discover that they've all missed. You could just shrug your shoulders and say, "If they hadn't missed, I wouldn't be alive to wonder about it!" A more rational response, however, would be to consider the possibility that all the marksmen missed on purpose.

One explanation found in scientific literature for the concept of fine-tuning is the multiverse: there are vast numbers of other universes with different constants and initial conditions. Given enough variation, life would probably emerge *somewhere*. Applying the anthropic principle as a selection effect then makes it unsurprising that observers find themselves in one of the life-permitting universes.

This might sound like science fiction, but it is argued that multiverses are a natural consequence of (or reasonable extensions of) known physical and cosmological theories. These claims are controversial, but one can hardly expect perfect clarity at the cutting edge of science.

On the one hand, in most multiverse models, it is extremely unlikely that we *could* get direct evidence of other universes—the other universes are simply too far away for any signal to have reached us.

On the other hand, a multiverse theory does make predictions; specifically, it is supposed to predict the values of the fundamental constants and initial conditions of the universe of a typical observer. Luke and colleagues have recently published findings from supercomputer simulations of galaxy and star formation in universes with differing values of the cosmological constant (CC). Using these, we made predictions for CC for a given multiverse model. Based on the effect of the CC on galaxy and star formation, if we were part of a multiverse, we would expect the CC to be around 50 times larger than what is observed. The CC seems a bit too finely tuned for the theory.[26]

Why is being too fine-tuned a problem for a multiverse? Consider again the firing squad analogy: given enough firing squads shooting at random, eventually someone will survive. This scenario makes a prediction: if the marksmen were trying to kill you and missed by chance, we would expect the bullets to barely miss. If our "lucky" survivor sees that all the bullets missed by a couple of meters, he should suspect collusion, not coincidence.

There is one particularly interesting way that our universe could be too lucky for a multiverse. As noted earlier, our universe had plenty of useful energy at the beginning. But life doesn't need so much useful energy. As observers—which is what matters in a multiverse—we only need a star and our planet. Or just a human in a bubble of air in space. Or, simpler still, just a floating brain having a few thoughts. Because useful energy (orderliness) is rare, in many multiverses, most observers will observe that they are a floating brain surrounded by disorderly, useless energy. Our universe, with its useful energy and galaxies and planets and stars as far as the telescope can see, seems far too lucky to be a fluke in a multiverse.[27] Some multiverse theories may be able to avoid this problem, but this raises the specter of having a fine-tuned multiverse.

This brings us to the deepest problem with the multiverse as a response to the fine-tuning argument. Here's the question we're trying to answer: what would we expect if the universe had, at bottom, no purpose or design? We've suggested a useful approximation to this question: what would we expect if the constants and initial conditions of the universe had been chosen at random? The advantage of this question is that we can answer it in a systematic way rather than just checking every possibility that we can think of, and it stays as close as possible to the best physical theories that we have.

Can we use the theories of the multiverse to get a better approximation to our question? Can we systematically explore a set of possible multiverses? No, for several reasons. We have only a menagerie of toy models, proof-of-concept ideas with most of the important physics added by hand and no consensus from cosmologists about how to handle the probabilities. If a convincing, natural, elegant, glorious multiverse model appears tomorrow, then we'll pose a better approximate question and try to answer it. Until then, the multiverse isn't appealing to *evidence* that we have; it's appealing to a *theory* that we don't have.

Similarly, appealing to some as-yet-unknown deeper laws of physics will not help. If you've got some better version of the known laws of physics, then—after you've collected your Nobel Prize—we'll ask whether a life-permitting universe is likely or unlikely, given the physical possibilities of your idea. Until then, while some deeper law yet to be discovered may better describe our universe, assuming that such a law will overturn fine-tuning is simply begging the question.

Is the universe fine-tuned for life? Why does the universe seem to fortuitously smile on our existence? This question has puzzled physicists for decades, and the answers keep getting "curiouser and curiouser"! "'Well, I've often seen a cat without a grin,' thought Alice, 'but a grin without a cat! It's the most curious thing I ever saw in all my life!'"[28] In 2009, Vasily Belokurov of Cambridge University and colleagues discovered "The Cheshire Cat" group of galaxies in the Sloan Digital Sky Survey. In the image above, which combines X-ray and optical observations, you can see curved streaks around two central elliptical galaxies. These are distant galaxies, and the light from them has been distorted by gravitational lensing: the bending of light by a massive foreground galaxy, as predicted by Albert Einstein's theory of general relativity. (Courtesy of NASA)

What the Evidence Indicates

Let's return to Dawkins's quote in light of the evidence:

> The universe that we observe has precisely the properties we should expect if there is, at bottom, no design, no purpose, no evil, no good, nothing but blind, pitiless indifference.

This claim is false. A universe with, at bottom, no design and no purpose would be *dead*. Almost certainly. No structure, no useful energy, no galaxies, no stars, no planets, no chemistry, no complexity. Instead, as we look around us, we find a universe with something good at bottom: the capacity for life.

CHAPTER 13

REDISCOVERING THE DISCARDED IMAGE

PAUL M. GOULD

onsider a red kickball. A child sees the ball for the first time but has no idea what it is. She simply sees it. She is told it is a ball, and she comes to associate the word *ball* with this spherical object. After being encouraged to play with it, she further realizes that balls are objects that bounce and are fun to kick. There is a distinction, then, between "simple seeing" and "seeing as."[1] Initially the child simply sees the ball, but over time, she sees the ball *as* a ball.

Imagine now a Martian visiting Earth for the first time. Assume that Martians have the same perceptual and rational powers as humans and that, sadly, there are no red kickballs on Mars. When our Martian sees the ball, let's imagine it sees the ball *as* a tiny replica of its beloved planet. (The Martian is understandably not happy when the child cavalierly kicks it over the fence.) In both cases, we have a perceiver seeing one and the same thing, yet interpreting their experience differently. This thought experiment highlights a common phenomenon: Individuals often *see* and *understand* the world differently.

When it comes to seeing and understanding the physical universe, we can discern two basic ways of perceiving. Consider first the observations of Saint Augustine (AD 354–430) as recorded in his masterful spiritual autobiography *Confessions*.[2] Because heaven and Earth came into being and they now undergo change, wrote Augustine, "they cry aloud that they are made."[3] They also cry aloud that they were not self-made. They were made by Another: "You, Lord, who are beautiful, made them for they are beautiful. You are good, for they are good. You are, for they are."[4]

Considered in its totality, the universe is a "well-ordered harmony."[5] Each part, too, is beautiful. While humans are "a little piece of your creation," they are created with great dignity and value as God's image-bearers "because," as Augustine famously proclaimed, "you have made us for yourself."[6]

Let's fast-forward a millennium and consider the words of the reformer John Calvin (1509–1564). The universe, according to Calvin, is God's stage, "a dazzling theatre" in which his glory is on full display.[7] "Wherever you cast your eyes, there is no spot in the universe wherein you cannot discern at least some sparks of his glory."[8] Looking up into the night sky evokes awe of the Creator who "stationed, arranged, and fitted together the starry host of heaven in such wonderful order that nothing more beautiful in appearance can be imagined."[9] When considering the human person, God is seen there too: "Man [is] a microcosm…a rare example of God's power, goodness, and wisdom."[10] For Calvin, the universe and its denizens function like a mirror "in which we can contemplate God, who is otherwise invisible."[11] Man sees God in creation and, in seeing God, he finds himself and his place too.

Let's contrast this way of perceiving exhibited by Augustine and Calvin with a more modern approach. Two representative examples should suffice. Carl Sagan famously stated in 1980, "The cosmos is all that is or ever was or ever will be."[12] The physical universe "is rich beyond measure—in elegant facts, in exquisite interrelationships, in the subtle machinery of awe."[13] The order, beauty, and fittingness of the universe does not point to a God behind it all, however. That would require evidence! Certainly, Sagan argued, a deity *could* provide such evidence. If he existed and wanted to be known, "God could have engraved the Ten Commandments on the Moon."[14] Or perhaps God could have placed "a crucifix in Earth orbit."[15] But he didn't. "Why," Sagan asked, "should God be so clear in the Bible and so obscure in the world?"[16]

In this picture, humans are nothing special either. The idea that the universe was created by a loving God for the benefit of humans is a "delusion."[17] Science has revealed that "we live on an insignificant planet of a humdrum star lost between two spiral arms in the outskirts of a galaxy which is a member of a sparse cluster in which there are far more galaxies than people."[18] Take comfort still, for we are "children of the Cosmos"[19] even if the cosmos is a vast, horrible, awe-inspiring, purposeless amalgamation of matter and energy expanding into the void.

Sagan's books and immensely popular television series, *Cosmos: A Personal Voyage*, have shaped our culture's collective imagination regarding the physical universe and man's place within it. More recently, Neil deGrasse Tyson has assumed the mantle of cultural "de-creator" in his popular books and reboot of the *Cosmos* series.[20] Like Augustine, deGrasse Tyson thinks the universe began and undergoes change. But these facts do not "cry aloud" that all is made by God. "Some religious people assert," deGrasse Tyson allows, "with a tinge of righteousness, that something must have started it all...that something, of course, is God."[21]

But this is presumptuous, he says, an appeal to ignorance. All we can confidently assert is that "every one of our body's atoms is traceable to the big bang and to the thermonuclear furnaces within high-mass stars that exploded more than five billion years ago. We are stardust brought to life."[22] When we embrace the cold, hard truths of science and adopt a "cosmic perspective,"[23] man comes to understand his place in the universe. On the one hand, we are forced to see that the universe is not "a benevolent cradle designed to nurture life," but "a cold, lonely, hazardous place."[24] On the other hand, "we are participants in a great cosmic chain of being, with a direct genetic link across species both living and extinct...we are one with the rest of nature, fitting neither above nor below, but within."[25]

What is going on here? Augustine, Calvin, Sagan, and deGrass Tyson are looking at the same cosmos! It is true that technology has allowed us to learn more about the universe. But this alone cannot account for the two radically different ways of perceiving the universe and our place in it. The difference must be found elsewhere. I suggest the difference has to do with the *imaginative stories* and *philosophical assumptions* we *bring to* our perceptual experience. In other words, if we imagine the world as a closed system of inert matter in motion and assume the universe is indifferent to our existence, then it is little wonder that God's "dazzling theatre" is seen as a "Theater of the Absurd."[26]

In this essay, I will argue that a return to the older God-bathed and God-infused way of looking at the world is needed. The problem is not one of fitting modern science into the old wineskin of religion. Rather, the fix is both philosophical and imaginative. Even deeper, it is theological. To see reality accurately, we must see it as Jesus does. How does Jesus see reality? As sacred. As a gift. As enchanted.

In what follows, I aim to do three things. First, I will unpack the philosophical and imaginative underpinning to these two different ways of perceiving—on the one hand, by Augustine and Calvin, and on the other, by Sagan and deGrasse Tyson. Second, I will provide a philosophical argument in favor of the sacramental view of things. Then I will conclude with some practical advice on how, as individuals and the church, we can work to see and delight in reality as Jesus does and invite others to do the same.

Two Models of the Physical Universe

The Neo-Humean Model

Many today—even many Christians—are under the spell of an image of the world that can be aptly described as neo-Humean. In this picture, gifted to us by David Hume (1711–1776), the world is conceived as a vast mosaic of particles in motion. The world is regular—a grand mechanism—but there are no hidden dependencies to be found in it; there is just one little thing followed by another.[27]

A number of philosophical commitments support the neo-Humean picture. The theory of knowledge that guides this picture is called *scientism*. In its strongest form, scientism is the view that *all* knowledge comes from science. A weaker but still pervasive version of scientism (creatively dubbed *weak scientism*) views our *best* knowledge as coming from science. This theory of knowledge (in its strong or weak form), in turn, is thought to strongly support *materialism*, the view that everything that exists is material, made of stuff we can inspect with our senses in one way or another. While some don't make the connection between scientism and materialism (such as the Christian swept up the zeitgeist [spirit] of the age), many do. The Duke University philosopher of science Alex Rosenberg, for example, says that scientism entails materialism and materialism entails atheism.[28] For those who make the jump, we can add *atheism* as another philosophical underpinning to the neo-Humean picture.

Another philosophical commitment that shapes much of the theorizing in the neo-Humean mode is *reductionism*, the view that all of reality can be reduced to and understood in terms of microphysical parts. Sociology reduces to anthropology, which reduces to biology, which reduces to chemistry, which reduces to physics. Once we reach physics, we've reached rock bottom, the ground floor of reality. Scientism, materialism, and reductionism (and atheism) are philosophical theses, not commitments that are delivered to us from scientific discovery. Rather, we bring these commitments to our theorizing about the world, and these commitments, in turn, shape what we find and how we interpret the data.

A further philosophical presupposition that is often conjoined with scientism, materialism, and reductionism is *nihilism*, the view that there is no objective meaning and purpose to life and the universe. A corollary of nihilism that influences much of the scientific literature, and will be central to the discussion to follow, is the so-called *principle of indifference*, the view that nature is indifferent or unconcerned with humans. Man, in the neo-Humean picture, is nothing special. Minds are "late and local," the product of blind and purposeless evolution.[29] Humans are "blobs of organized mud"[30] that happen to exist for a brief time on (at least) the planet Earth. Summing up: In the neo-Humean picture, normativity, subjectivity, meaning, intentionality, and purpose "drain out" of the universe. The universe is rather empty; there is only one kind of thing—matter—jutting about in a cacophonic dance within the void.

The godless and empty universe is chillingly portrayed in Samuel Beckett's 1952 play *Waiting for Godot*.[31] This tragicomic story of the absurd depicts two days in the life of two lonely and lost souls who, obviously enough, are waiting for Godot. Godot, who arguably is a stand-in for God, never comes. The play ends as it began: with despair, loneliness, and a sense of dread. Throughout the play, Vladimir and Estragon try to pass the time, seeking to understand the meaning of life and their place in the universe. The problem is that the universe and our time within it is devoid of purpose:

> Vladimir [*sententious*] To every man his little cross. [*He sighs.*] Till he dies. [*Afterthought.*] And is forgotten.[32]

Man is not sustained by God's loving hands. Rather, man must make his own way—ultimately alone. There is no meaning to time. There are no sacred places: "Time flows again already. The Sun will set, the moon rise, and we away...from here."[33]

The Platonic-Aristotelian-Christian (PAC) Model

The neo-Humean picture of the world and man's place within it is depressing. It is also rather boring and unimaginative. What if the world is more complex, mysterious, wonderful, and exhilarating that we could ever imagine? What if time and place are invested with meaning and value? What if reality is God-bathed and God-infused? What if Calvin was right and the world is a "dazzling theatre" of God's glory? Can man reasonably hope, in the twenty-first century, for something better? Even in Beckett's *Waiting for Godot* there is a sliver of hope. The men are *waiting*. They haven't yet hung themselves.

Scene from the 1978 Avignon Festival performance of *Waiting for Godot*. (WikiCommons)

There is another picture of the world. This more ancient view, articulated by Augustine and Calvin and many others, captivated and informed man's collective imagination for more than 1,500 years. It, too, has a name: the Platonic-Aristotelian-Christian Synthesis of the High Middle Ages, or for short, the Great Tradition.[34] I'll simply refer to this second metaphor for understanding the world as the Platonic-Aristotelian-Christian, or PAC, model.

The *Platonic* part of PAC emphasizes the *participatory* nature of reality. The natural order participates in the sacred order; the real presence of God is manifest and mediated through that which he has made (Ephesians 1:23; Colossians 1:17). All things are *good things* because they participate in God's goodness. Reality is sacred, as Hans Boersma describes it, because it "participates in some greater reality, from which it derives its being and its value."[35]

The *Aristotelian* part of PAC emphasizes the *teleological* aspect of the natural order. The physical universe is not just matter in motion. Rather, there exist fundamental wholes—Aristotelian substances—that develop toward maturity according to their kind. Acorns develop into oak trees. Human fetuses into adults. Thus, substances—trees, dogs, humans, and more—are fundamental unities that have parts, properties, and powers by virtue of their nature or essence. The important contrast with the neo-Humean picture is this: As fundamental wholes, substances are not reducible to their constituent parts, properties, and capacities. The whole is prior to its parts. Substances are genuine objects in their own right.

Finally, the *Christian* part of PAC emphasizes the *hierarchical* and *rational* aspect of the physical universe. The substances found in the universe can be organized into a Great Chain of Being with God at the top and angels, man, beasts, plants, and inanimate matter dangling down. Everything that exists has its place. Everything fits together as intended by God. Moreover, because God exists and is the fount of all distinct reality, mind is prior to matter. Materialism is false. As C.S. Lewis colorfully put it, "Reason is older than Nature."[36]

The philosophical foundation of the PAC model stands in stark contrast with the philosophical foundation of the neo-Humean model. Instead of a rigid scientism there is a healthy respect for empirical facts as well as other sources of knowledge. In the place of materialism there is a dualism of mental and material. Instead of reductionism, nihilism, and atheism, we find antireductionism, teleology, and a sacramental order.

This model of the physical universe is nicely illustrated in another classic twentieth-century play from 1938, Thornton Wilder's *Our Town*.[37] Wilder's play helps us understand the sacredness of life. Rebecca and her brother George lie in bed talking:

> *Rebecca:* I never told you about that letter Jane Crofut got from her minister when she was sick. He wrote Jane a letter and on the envelope the address was like this: Jane Crofut; The Crofut Farm; Grover's Corners; Sutton County; New Hampshire; United States of America.
>
> *George:* What's funny about that?
>
> *Rebecca:* But listen, it's not finished: the United States of America; Continent of North America; Western Hemisphere; the Earth; the Solar System; the Universe; the Mind of God—that's what it said on the envelope.
>
> *George:* What do you know!
>
> *Rebecca:* And the postman brought it just the same.[38]

Wilder's *Our Town* helps us understand the *fittingness* of the universe. Everything hangs together in God. Nothing escapes God's loving gaze and tender care. The mundane is transformed into the sacred, the ordinary into the mysterious.

Scene from the 1938 Broadway production of the Pulitzer Prize-winning play *Our Town*. (WikiCommons)

Thus we have two competing models or metaphors that shape our perception and understanding of the world and our place in it: one characterized by absence and the other by presence, one by despair and the other by hope, one by destitution and the other by delight, one by ignorance and the other by mystery, one a dry desert and the other a rich cornucopia, one a cacophony and the other a symphony, one offering no peace and the other rest, one disenchanted and the other enchanted, one widely held today and the other a discarded image of a "prescientific age."

What is the difference between the two? The philosophical foundation and the imaginative metaphor erected upon that foundation to make sense of it all. Are there reasons to prefer one picture over the other? In the next section I provide an argument for why we should reject the neo-Humean model in favor of the Platonic-Aristotelian-Christian one.

The Principles of Indifference,
Human Flourishing, and God

Theoretical shaping principles guide our interpretation of the data.[39] So do the metaphors we live by.[40] If the principles that guide interpretation and the metaphors we live by are well motivated, then we have reason to think they serve as a clear lens to help us see things as they truly are. If not, we run the risk of looking out and up at the world (and within our hearts) through a dirty window.

If we are going to see reality correctly, a question of central importance is this: Are the guiding principles and metaphors that help us see and understand the world *reasonable*? Why think them true? If on balance the evidence points against a guiding principle or imaginative metaphor, then it should be rejected. I now argue that there are good reasons to reject a key principle that governs much of the thinking and perceiving in the neo-Humean mode, the principle of indifference. Recall that this principle states that nature should be indifferent to humans. Given this, it is no surprise that purveyors of disenchantment conclude that man is nothing special. The problem with this picture is that there are powerful strands of evidence—coming from science—that suggest nature is not indifferent to humans.

I will build my case in three steps. My first claim is that *there are no good scientific reasons to endorse the principle of indifference.* There are only *philosophical* reasons to adopt the principle of indifference: atheism, naturalism, nihilism, scientism, reductionism, and so on. But none of these philosophical *isms* are delivered to us from our observations of the natural world. They do provide a lens from which we can interpret the world and seek understanding. Yet they are not obvious and rational entailments from the physical evidence of the world. In fact, the *science* itself points in the other direction: Nature seems to conspire on behalf of humans! If so, then we find resources for a different and *theistic* shaping principle, the *principle of intentionality*: Nature should be favorable to human flourishing. What is the evidence coming from science that gives us reason to think the principle of indifference is false?

I offer two pieces of evidence that suggest nature is not indifferent to humans:

(E$_1$) The universe is finely-tuned for the *existence* of humans.

(E$_2$) The universe is finely-tuned for the *flourishing* of humans.

The fact that the universe, including its initial conditions and physical constants, is finely-tuned for the *existence* of humans is ably demonstrated by the cosmologists Luke Barnes and Allen Hainline in chapter 12. I'm more interested, for our purposes, in (E_2). Human flourishing goes beyond mere existence. It could have been that the universe is merely finely-tuned for our existence but is otherwise a rather hostile, cold, and uncharitable place. At least on Earth, however, this is not the case. Man not only survives; man can thrive too. There is the real possibility of human flourishing.

What does it mean to flourish? A flourishing life is one in which the full assortment of natural capacities are activated, employed, and perfected. Plants have nutritive and growth capacities and a flourishing plant actualizes these capacities to realize its own good. In addition to nutritive and growth capacities, dogs have sensory capacities, and to the degree that these capacities are actualized, we can speak of dogs flourishing. When it comes to humans we find a full panoply of capacities (in addition to growth and sensing) for reasoning, imagining, relating, acting, creating, moralizing, judging, and more. Many of our capacities are not needed, at least not obviously, to the extent (in range and depth) for mere survival. Yet we find those capacities present in us along with the genuine possibility of their actualization.

Consider full-fledged love of one person for another. That such love is possible I assume as obvious because it's actual (in my own life and the lives of many others). What does full-fledged love look like? A traditional answer is that love for another is composed of two desires: the desire for the *well-being* of the beloved and the desire for *union* with the beloved.[41] This kind of love goes far beyond what is required for survival. Personal and corporate survival of humans requires mutual interactions for the sake of companionship, provision, protection, and propagation. Whatever these strategic interactions might be, they fall well short of full-fledged love. Survival requires the *being* of others in relationship, not their *well-being*. The survival of the human species does require sexual union, but arguably this kind of union is neither the only nor the best kind of union for characterizing full-fledged love. Sexual union comes cheap and easy; full-fledged love and the desire of union with the beloved requires commitment, time, energy, and a kind of self-giving that is foreign to much of the hookup culture encouraged by the neo-Humean picture of the world.

What about art, beauty, and the human capacity to create? Evolutionary accounts, unsurprisingly, center on how aesthetics contribute to human survival: art signals (like a peacock's tail) the sexual fitness of the artist; art makes human groups feel special, creating a kind of social solidarity adventitious for life; art is pleasurable in ways analogous to other activities that contribute to survival; and so on.[42] The problem with these evolutionary accounts, and many more like them, is they don't go deep enough. Artists are often "evolutionary losers," laboring alone with meager financial reward or social recognition.[43] The sense of social solidarity and pleasure produced by art can be achieved in other ways—such as sporting events or religious activities—thus highlighting the inability of evolutionary accounts to explain the uniqueness of art, beauty, and the human capacity to create. There is a significant gap between what is needed for survival and the great works of art produced by, for example, Beethoven, van Gogh, and Shakespeare.

Finally, we see this same gap between what is needed for human survival and what is conducive to human flourishing in the ability to reason and gain knowledge of the world. Arguably, survival does require some level of cognitive ability: We need to be able to *navigate* in the world in order to survive.[44] But it is hard to explain on evolutionary grounds the human ability to do, for example, high-level mathematics or logics.[45] To share my own failures as a professor, all too often my logic students level the following complaint: "When will we ever need to do logical proofs in the real world?" I'm not unsympathetic in my reply: "It is true you can get by without doing higher-level logic, but having the ability to do so—and cultivating the mind—does contribute to your flourishing." That we can correctly do thirty-line logical proofs, all of which seem to have no obvious noncognitive benefit for survival, reveals a deep tension between what is required for humans to survive and what is required for them to flourish as intelligent beings in an intelligible universe.

The universe is clearly finely-tuned for the flourishing of humans. Fact (E_2) is nicely explained if we allow for the possibility that the Christian God exists. The ability for full-fledged love is grounded in the perfect love of the triune God, who creates humans to flourish in communion with himself and others. The human capacity for creativity is grounded in the *imago Dei*; man creates because he is made in the image of a creator God. So, too, with the human capacity for reason: Human minds exist because there is a divine mind who, in spreading his joy and delight, has created humans with the ability to know and understand God and the world he has made.[46]

The above considerations lead to my second claim: *Theism provides a plausible explanation for (E_1) and (E_2) and reason to adopt a different principle, the principle of intentionality.* In theism, man was made to be nourished on goodness, truth, and beauty. These great goods feed the soul and propel us toward the ultimate object of our longing and the source of all: God himself.

My third and final claim moves from the fittingness of theism to explain certain features of our world to the *truth* of theism. I now argue that theism is *rationally preferable* to naturalism (and the resultant neo-Humean picture) given (E_1) and (E_2). The following argument from fittingness helps us see the rational preferability of theism to naturalism.

1. The fact that the universe is finely-tuned for the *existence* and *flourishing* of humans is not surprising given theism.

2. The fact that the universe is finely-tuned for the *existence* and *flourishing* of humans is surprising given naturalism.

3. Therefore, it is probable that theism is true.

Much more can and ought to be said in elaborating and defending the argument from fittingness.[47] Assume the above argument is cogent. If so, then I suggest it's time to rehabilitate an old word and recapture a more ancient way of looking at things: The world is *sacred*. The universe points to *someone* beyond this world who has shaped it for our benefit. The cosmos speak to man's place in God's sacred order. How can we see the world in its proper light? How can we see the world as Jesus does: as a God-infused and God-bathed gift full of joy, delight, divine presence, mystery, and meaning? How can we recapture the Platonic-Aristotelian-Christian way of looking at things? In the next and final section, we'll explore the answer to these questions.

> The hope of eternal life is pictured for us every day and night as we look around and see the immensity, beauty, diversity, and fittingness of creation.

Rediscovering the Discarded Image

In 1 Corinthians 15, Paul wrote of the hope we have in Christ. One day all will be made new. Death will be defeated. Man will be raised to eternal life. This "living hope" (1 Peter 1:3) is real. Because Jesus was raised from the dead, one day we who are Christians will also be raised to new life. While this hope is real, it's hard to imagine, especially in a disenchanted age. How can we understand this living hope so that our lives are characterized and animated by it? Paul's answer is instructive:

> Not all flesh is the same: People have one kind of flesh, animals have another, birds another and fish another. There are also heavenly bodies and there are earthly bodies; but the splendor of the heavenly bodies is one kind, and the splendor of the earthly bodies is another. The Sun has one kind of splendor, the moon another and the stars another; and star differs from star in splendor. So will it be with the resurrection of the dead (1 Corinthians 15:39-42).

Paul helps us imaginatively understand the meaning of the universe. The hope of eternal life is pictured for us every day and night as we look around and see the immensity, beauty, diversity, and fittingness of creation. Just as the earthly and heavenly bodies each have their own splendor, so too (by analogy) will our imperishable bodies. Importantly, notice that the heavenly bodies—the Moon, the planets, the stars—perform for us a sacred duty, helping us to *imagine* a deep mystery, the mystery of our future resurrection in Christ.

By looking around and looking up with fresh eyes, we see the physical manifestation of the gospel story and the infinite happiness on offer for man. The heavens "declare the glory of God…Day after day, they pour forth speech" (Psalm 19:1-2), helping us to perceive how, as theologian Kevin Vanhoozer notes, "in the fullness of time, all things [will be] 'gathered up' into Christ (Eph 1:10, NRSV)."[48]

It's time to get practical. How can we see things as God intended? The answer is by entering into God's story—the gospel—and *seeing all things as part of God's unfolding drama*, a drama in which everything fits together in order to display the manifold wisdom, goodness, and power of God, who is "all in all" (1 Corinthians 15:28).

Calvin was right. The heavens and Earth are a "dazzling theatre" of God's glory. May we all take our place in this unfolding drama. May we see and delight in God and all that he has made. And then, as "sacred messengers" who "shine… like stars in the sky" (Philippians 2:15), may we invite others to do likewise.[49]

AFTERWORD

ASTRONOMY WITH
YOUR OWN TWO EYES

DANIEL RAY

For many who live in and around big cities, the wide swath of light generated by modern urban living virtually wipes out all but a handful of the
brightest stars. As popular astrophysicist Neil DeGrasse Tyson notes,

> I have never in my life seen the Milky Way galaxy from within the
> city limits of New York City, and I was born and raised here. If you
> observe the night sky from light-drenched Times Square, you might
> see a dozen or so stars, compared with the thousands that were visi-
> ble when [the seventeenth-century Dutch colonialist] Peter Stuyves-
> ant was hobbling around town. No wonder ancient peoples shared
> a culture of sky lore, whereas modern peoples, who know nothing
> of the night sky, instead share a culture of evening TV.[1]

In addition to the irresistible glow of a television, the science of modern
astronomy, with its daunting technological and mathematical aspects, makes
getting to know the stars overhead seem like an impossible—if not altogether
pointless—endeavor. Has not science charted and classified everything? What
use do the stars have for any of us? After all, most of us do not need the stars to
tell us when to plant or harvest. We can get apples and lettuce at the grocery
store year around. And we have the power of global positioning satellites in the
palms of our hands. Who needs the stars for navigation anymore?

Or maybe there is a general foreboding for believers that if we take a vested interest in the stars and constellations that somehow we are dangerously dabbling in astrological practices. We also do not have the resources of NASA at our disposal to build enormous telescopes or send probes to distant worlds. Plus, for many, the complicated mathematics just makes the whole stargazing business seem nearly pointless. In short, we can barely see the stars, we seem to have no use for them, we're not scientists, and we don't own a telescope. *Meh* on the cosmos, right?

What is necessary for all of us, as we've said in this book, is to recapture a vision of God's glory in the heavens. The skies above us are nightly telling of his glory, and yet like worms[2] burrowing through the dirt, we seem to have completely lost interest in whatever diadems of glory and wisdom we can glean from them. So what can be done?

Like the magi mentioned in Matthew's Gospel, we have to begin with a single star. It is really that simple. That star led them to Jesus. And I believe that is ultimately what the stars should do. Jesus is described in both the Old and New Testaments as a kind of "star" himself, at least in a poetic and metaphorical sense. He is the "sun of righteousness" in Malachi 4:2, "the bright Morning Star" of Revelation 22:16, "the light of the world" in John 8:12, and the "star… of Jacob" prophesied in Numbers 24:17. Not that one can look at the stars and immediately apprehend the wonders of Christ's love and mercy toward us, by any means. The point is not the star of Bethlehem or the stars in general, but to *whom* all the stars point. The stars are heavenly messengers who never tire of declaring the glory of God.

If you can get away from the industrial glow of modern city life, take a step toward doing some simple backyard astronomy you can do without a telescope. And start with just a single star. Any star will do. Figure out which of the four cardinal directions you are facing as you pick out a star (and if the star seems exceptionally bright, consider the possibility it might be a planet!). Then note any distinctive patterns of stars around the star you have chosen and make a rough sketch.

For this task I highly recommend the free and rather incredible software program Stellarium.[3] It is easy to access, easy to use, and gives you a remarkable facsimile of the heavens. Once the software is up and running, you can simply type in your zip code and the screen will give you a star-for-star visual of the sky above your town. There are also apps for your phone which do this too. You can compare your observations with the program and pinpoint the name of your star. The majority of more commonly known stars are all labeled in Stellarium, making learning star names quite easy and fun for the whole family. Through using this program, I myself have internalized the names and locations of several stars and hope to keep adding to the list and refreshing my memory of those I have already come to know.

Taken by the Hubble Space Telescope's Wide Field Planetary Camera 2,[4] this image shows the brilliant star Sirius A, the "Dog Star," and its smaller companion star Sirius B. The diffraction spikes seen here are reflections from within the telescope itself. (Courtesy of NASA)

I should add a brief thought here about why stars seem to "move": As you observe stars, you will note that they appear to change positions in the sky over time. And there are distinct patterns of stars that people have observed from time immemorial that regularly follow the same path in the sky. We call them the *zodiac*. This English word is based on the ancient Greek term *zoidiakos kyklos*, meaning "circle of little animals." This makes sense because most of these constellations (star patterns) are related to some sort of living creature. There is Leo the lion, Cancer the crab, Pisces the fish, Scorpius the scorpion, Aries the ram, and so on. These stars travel along the ecliptic, the "highway" if you will, of the Sun, Moon, and visible planets.

During the summer of 2018, Mars, Saturn, Jupiter, and Venus could all be seen together along the ecliptic. On a clear night, these four stunningly beautiful gems formed a graceful luminous arch from the eastern horizon to the west, making the ecliptic quite visible, much in the same way that the headlights and tail lights on automobiles as seen from an airplane at 30,000 feet indicate the presence of a highway. These constellations appear to "move" because of the rotation of Earth on its axis. The Sun also spends about a month in each of these constellations. Jupiter, on the other hand, from our terrestrial vantage point, spends approximately a year in each of them. As we orbit the Sun, we also spin like a top. This axial spinning affords us different glorious vistas of the heavens throughout the course of a year (one trip around the Sun).

You can think of the 12 constellations like a pie chart divided into 12 equal slices. You can imagine each of the slices having different star patterns. Projected onto the sky, it seemed to the ancients that this galactic pie chart spun around smoothly and regularly. The same slices would appear at the same time of year, "telling" the people to harvest, to plant, or to turn left or right on their journeys.

Stars thus served as guides for mankind and even helped the Apollo astronauts along their 480,000-mile trips to the Moon and back. Michael Collins, who piloted the lunar orbiter *Columbia* during the historic Apollo 11 mission, recalls how important learning star navigation was for their trip. Collins says, "A star sighting using the wrong star would be embarrassing at best, and could easily be disastrous."[5] He retells how he and his fellow crew would "Arc to Arcturus, Speed to Spica" as a means of navigating their spacecraft toward the Moon.

Though most of us will never find it necessary to refer to the stars to navigate our way to a destination, still, they serve an incredibly noble purpose to us. We were intended to contemplate and enjoy the heavens, to understand they have meaning and purpose in leading us to our Maker.[6] They enable us to consider that which is lovely, to give us pause to meditate and contemplate our existence, to revel in the beauty and awe they inspire. We do not have to be mathematicians or astrophysicists to derive encouragement and consolation from the regularity and beauty of the universe. They are reminders to us of God's love, of His steadfast faithfulness,[7] of His light shining in our darkness.

So take a step—a single step. Pick a spot in your backyard, or someplace away from the blinding lights of where you live, turn off the television for a few hours, and focus on a single star and follow its course. As you do so, consider that the one who made the heavens and the Earth came down to this celestial sphere and lived among us with a message of consolation for all of us: "Repent, for the kingdom of heaven is near" (Matthew 3:2 NET).

Soli Deo gloria.

An arm of our Milky Way Galaxy over the La Silla Observatory in northern Chile. The terms *Milky Way* and *galaxy* come from the Latin *via lactea*, or "the road of milk," a derivative of the more ancient Greek term *galaxias kyklos*, or "milky circle." A luminous reminder that Jesus is "the Way" and His Word is like pure milk (John 14:6; 1 Peter 2:2). (Courtesy of NASA)

CONTRIBUTORS

Dr. Luke Barnes is a postdoctoral researcher at the Sydney Institute for Astronomy. He earned a scholarship to complete a PhD in astronomy at the University of Cambridge. He has published papers in the field of galaxy formation and on the fine-tuning of the universe for life. He recently authored a Cambridge University Press book with Geraint Lewis entitled *A Fortunate Universe: Life in a Finely Tuned Cosmos.*

Dr. David Bradstreet is an astronomy and physics professor and chair at Eastern University. He has written more than 100 scholarly papers and coauthored *Star Struck* (Zondervan, 2016) and the *Binary Maker 3.0* software program that helps astronomical researchers worldwide calculate the characteristics of binary stars. In 2014, the International Astronomical Union named the asteroid 5896 Bradstreet in honor of his contributions to binary star research and innovative digital planetarium curriculum.

Dr. Brother Guy Consolmagno is the director of the Vatican Observatory and president of the Vatican Observatory Foundation. He has written more than 200 articles for scientific publications and is the author of a number of popular books, including *Turn Left at Orion* (with Dan Davis, Cambridge, 2011), and most recently *Would You Baptize an Extraterrestrial?* (with Father Paul Mueller, SJ, Image, 2014).

Dr. William Lane Craig is a research professor of philosophy at Talbot School of Theology and professor of philosophy at Houston Baptist University and author of more than thirty books and hundreds of referred articles. His most recent book is *God Over All* (Oxford, 2016).

Terry Glaspey is an adjunct professor of art and theology at Kilns College and the author of numerous books, including the award-winning *75 Masterpieces Every Christian Should Know* (Baker, 2015). He holds a master's degree in history from the University of Oregon and is a frequent lecturer at universities, churches, and conferences on the relationships between the arts, spirituality, theology, and history. Terry blogs at www.terryglaspey.com.

Dr. Paul M. Gould teaches philosophy and apologetics at the College of Graduate and Professional Studies at Oklahoma Baptist University. He is also the founder and president of the Two Tasks Institute. He is the editor or author of several books, including *Cultural Apologetics* (Zondervan, 2019). His website is paul-gould.com.

Dr. Guillermo Gonzalez is an assistant professor of astronomy and physics at Ball State University who specializes in astrobiology and stellar astrophysics. Guillermo has published more than 80 research papers in leading astronomy and astrophysics journals and is coauthor of *The Privileged Planet: How Our Place in the Cosmos Is Designed for Discovery* (Regnery, 2004).

Allen Hainline holds a bachelor's in physics from University of Texas, Austin and master's equivalent degree in systems and software engineering from the University of Texas, Continuing Engineering Studies. He is a former E-Fellow at Raytheon, where he led the team responsible for image processing for the world's first high-resolution satellite. He regularly presents seminars on fine-tuning in conference and university settings.

Dr. Holly Ordway is Professor of English at Houston Baptist University; she holds a PhD in English from the University of Massachusetts, Amherst. She is the author of *Apologetics and the Christian Imagination: An Integrated Approach to Defending the Faith* (Emmaus Road, 2017) and *Not God's Type: An Atheist Academic Lays Down Her Arms* (Ignatius, 2014). Her current project is *Tolkien's Modern Sources: Middle-earth Beyond the Middle Ages* (forthcoming from Kent State University Press). She is also a subject editor for the *Journal of Inklings Studies*. Her website is hollyordway.com.

Daniel Ray is a former middle- and high-school teacher and lay astronomer, and holds an MA in Christian apologetics from Houston Baptist University. Under the direction of Dr. Michael Ward, Daniel completed his thesis on the contemporary relevance of C.S. Lewis's cosmological imagination in The Chronicles of Narnia. *The Story of the Cosmos* is part of his professional and personal dream of creating a Christian response to the widely popular *Cosmos* series with Carl Sagan.

Dr. Sarah Salviander received her PhD in astrophysics from the University of Texas at Austin. She was a researcher at UT for sixteen years, where she specialized in the study of quasars, supermassive black holes, and galaxies. She is the author of several peer-reviewed journal papers and a comprehensive Astronomy & Astrophysics homeschool curriculum. She is currently writing books about the remarkable confluence between Christianity and modern science.

Wayne R. Spencer holds a master of science degree in physics from Wichita State University in Kansas. He is a former science teacher and has published peer-reviewed articles on a creationist view of planetary science. He also maintains the creationanswers.net website.

Dr. Melissa Cain Travis serves as an assistant professor of apologetics at Houston Baptist University and a contributing writer for *Christian Research Journal*. She is the author of *Science and the Mind of the Maker* (Harvest House, 2018) and the Young Defenders storybook series (Apologia Educational Ministries). She holds a PhD from Faulkner University and earned her MA in Science and Religion from Biola University, and a BS in general biology from Campbell University.

Dr. Michael Ward is Senior Research Fellow at Blackfriars Hall, University of Oxford, and Professor of Apologetics at Houston Baptist University. He is the author of the award-winning *Planet Narnia: The Seven Heavens in the Imagination of C.S. Lewis* (Oxford, 2010) and co-editor of *The Cambridge Companion to C.S. Lewis* (Cambridge, 2010).

SUBJECT INDEX

Scripture Index

Genesis
1:1 63, 183
1:14-16 269n6

Exodus
33:18-20 106

Numbers
24:17 236

Joshua
10 116

2 Samuel
6:14 68

Job
9:9 252n24
25:4-6 269n2
38:4 175
38:7 175
38:31 171, 252n24
38:33 89

Psalms
8 8, 269n6
8:4 10
19 11, 107, 164, 269n6
19:1 7, 10, 54, 63, 168
19:1-2 233
19:1-4 99, 132, 176
19:2 13
19:3 251n16
19:3-4 11
22:6 269n2
29 132
33:6 24
102:25 11
111 269n6
115:5-6 169
148 132
149:3 68

Ecclesiastes
3:11 252n41

Isaiah
40 269n6
41:14 269n2
45:12 89
65:17 256n32
66:22 256n32

Jeremiah
31 269n7

Amos
5:8 251n24

Malachi
4:2 236

Matthew
3:2 239
13:34 261n54
19:14 251n13
19:28 63

Luke
19:38 50
24:30-31 63
24:39-43 63

John
1:1-3 25
1:2-3 176
8:12 236
14:6 239
20:19 63
20:27 63

Acts
3:21 63

Romans
1 269n6

1:20 107, 168
3 269n2

1 Corinthians
15 28, 232
15:35-49 256
15:39-42 233
15:41 23

Ephesians
1:10 233
1:23 226

Philippians
2:15 233
3:21 63

Colossians
1:17 226

1 Thessalonians
5:21

Hebrews
1:2-3 89

1 Peter
1:3 232
2:2 239

2 Peter
3:13 256n32

Revelation
21 256n32
21:1-3 63
22:16 236

NOTES

Chapter 1—The Heavens Are Telling of the Glory of God

1. All Bible verses in this chapter are taken from the NASB.

2. C.S. Lewis, *The Inspirational Writings of C.S. Lewis: Reflections on the Psalm*s (New York: Inspirational Press, 1986), 163.

3. Sean Carroll, *The Big Picture: On the Origins of Life, Meaning and the Universe Itself* (New York: Dutton, 2016), 2.

4. Richard Norman, *On Humanism,* 2d ed. (London: Routledge, 2012), 89.

5. Neil DeGrasse Tyson, *Death by Black Hole* (New York: W.W. Norton, 2007), 46-47.

6. Carl Sagan, *Pale Blue Dot: A Vision of the Human Future in Space* (New York: Random House, 1994), 8.

7. Bertrand Russell, *A Free Man's Worship* (London: Routledge, 2009), 39.

8. John G. West, *Darwin Day in America* (Wilmington, DE: ISI Books, 2015), 385, and "Star Trek as Atheist Mythology—Brannon Braga," https://youtu.be/iJm6vCs6aBA?t=2m57s.

9. West, *Darwin Day in America,* 385.

10. Ray Villard, "Retiring Hubble Visualization Expert Blended the Best of Science and Art," http://hubblesite .org/news_release/news/2018-41.

11. "Beautiful Risk: 'Hubble Deep Field was a gamble,'" https://www.youtube.com/watch?v=EQlsX11I9hE. Quote begins around the 55-second mark.

12. "Beautiful Risk." The entirety of the quote begins at 1:15.

13. Matthew 19:14. In the original Greek text, "the heavens" are in plural form, τῶν οὐρανῶν.

14. "Hubble Deep Field," https://commons.wikimedia.org/wiki/File:HubbleDeepField.800px.jpg.

15. John Noble Wilford, "Space Telescope Reveals 40 Billion More Galaxies," https://www.nytimes.com/ 1996/01/16/science/space-telescope-reveals-40-billion-more-galaxies.html.

16. See Psalm 19:3.

17. "Q&A with Astrophysicist Anton Koekemoer," http://www.saintjohnsbible.org/promotions/news/pdfs/Sum mer16.pdf.

18. "Q&A with Astrophysicist Anton Koekemoer."

19. "Q&A with Astrophysicist Anton Koekemoer."

20. Stars themselves don't twinkle; it is Earth's atmosphere through which starlight passes that makes them appear as though they shimmer and twinkle.

21. Henry Wadsworth Longfellow, *Selected Poems* (New York: Penguin, 1988), 345-346.

22. "Hubble Team Unveils Most Colorful View of Universe Captured by Space Telescope," https://www.nasa.gov/ press/2014/june/hubble-team-unveils-most-colorful-view-of-universe-captured-by-space-telescope.

23. Jim Kaler, "Aldebaran," http://stars.astro.illinois.edu/sow/aldebaran.html.

24. See Job 9:9; 38:31; and Amos 5:8.

25. Munya Andrews, *The Seven Sisters of the Pleiades* (North Melbourne: Spinifex Press, 2013), 25.

26. Robert Burnham, Jr., *Burnham's Celestial Handbook: An Observer's Guide to the Universe Beyond the Solar System, Vol. 3, Pavo Through Vulpecula* (New York: Dover, 1978), 1868.

27. "Subaru Is Moving to Camden," https://www.subaru.com/camden.html. Scroll down to see "Origin of SUBARU."

28. Alfred Tennyson, *The Works of Alfred Lloyd Tennyson* (London: Wordsworth, 2008), 164.

29. Bryan Penprase, *The Power of Stars: How Celestial Observations Have Shaped Civilization* (New York: Springer, 2011), 3.

30. "3519. Kabowd," http://biblehub.com/hebrew/3519.htm.

31. Christopher W. Morgan and Robert A. Peterson, eds., *The Glory of God* (Wheaton, IL: Crossway, 2010), 77.

32. John North, *Cosmos: An Illustrated History of Astronomy and Cosmology* (Chicago: University of Chicago Press, 2008), 450.

33. Jane Austen, *Pride and Prejudice* (New York: Barnes & Noble Classics, 2004), 92.

34. James R. Hansen, *First Man: The Life of Neil A. Armstrong* (New York: Simon & Schuster, 2005), 35.

35. "About Our Hotel," http://www.palmerhousehiltonhotel.com/about-our-hotel/.

36. Roger Penrose, *Fashion, Faith and Fantasy in the New Physics of the Universe* (Princeton, NJ: Princeton University Press, 2016), xiii.

37. C.S. Lewis, *English Literature in the Sixteenth Century Excluding Drama* (Oxford: Clarendon Press, 1944), 3.

38. Terence Nichols, *The Sacred Cosmos: Christian Faith and the Challenge of Naturalism* (Grand Rapids, MI: Brazos, 2003), 14.

39. Jim Baggott, *Farewell to Reality: How Modern Physics Has Betrayed the Search for Scientific Truth* (New York: Pegasus, 2014), 11.

40. "John Archibald Wheeler's crazy ideas for a crazy world," https://www.youtube.com/watch?v=u4vvQfyUvXg. The quote begins at the opening of the video.

41. "He has made everything appropriate in its time. He has also set eternity in their heart, yet so that man will not find out the work which God has done from the beginning even to the end" (Ecclesiastes 3:11 NASB).

42. Abraham Kuyper, *Wisdom & Wonder: Common Grace in Science & Art* (Grand Rapids, MI: Christian's Library Press, 2011), 140.

43. Kuyper, *Wisdom & Wonder*, 144.

44. "Cosmic Collision Forges Galactic One Ring—in X-rays," https://www.nasa.gov/centers/marshall/history/cosmic-collision-forges-galactic-one-ring-in-x-rays.html.

45. J.R.R. Tolkien, *The Lord of the Rings,* 50th Anniversary One-Volume Edition (New York: Houghton Mifflin, 2004), 50.

46. Freeman J. Dyson, *Disturbing the Universe* (New York: Harper & Row, 1979), 250.

Chapter 2—A Glorious Resonance:
The Intelligibility of Nature and the *Imago Dei*

1. Quoted in Morris Kline, *Mathematics: The Loss of Certainty* (New York: Oxford University Press, 1980), 31.

2. Thomas F. Torrance, *The Ground and Grammar of Theology* (New York: T&T Clark, 1980), 1.

3. Thomas F. Torrance, *Christian Theology and Scientific Culture* (Eugene, OR: Wipf & Stock, 1980), 31, 58.

4. Torrance, *Christian Theology and Scientific Culture*, 62.

5. Carola Baumgardt, *Johannes Kepler: Life and Letters* (New York: Philosophical Library, 1951), 50.

6. Note that this is not to say that mathematics is an all-purpose tool for every kind of investigation into nature's orderliness. To be sure, there are nonmathematized aspects of the world that could be discussed in the context of divine rationality and creativity. This essay simply limits the scope of discussion to the natural sciences that are interwoven with mathematics.

7. "Milky Way Bulge," http://hubblesite.org/image/4101/gallery.

8. Cicero, *The Nature of the Gods* (New York: Oxford University Press, 2008), 13.

9. Plato, *Timaeus* (Indianapolis, IN: Focus, 2016), 14.

10. Plato, *Timaeus*, in Great Books of the Western World, vol. 6, 2d ed. (Chicago: Encyclopedia Britannica, 1990), 455.

11. A phase of Platonic thought that lasted from about the first century BC to about the third century AD.

12. Philo, "On the Creation," in *The Works of Philo*, trans. C.D. Yonge (Peabody, MA: Hendrickson, 1993), 4.

13. See William Lane Craig's treatment of this topic in "God and the Platonic Host," in *C.S. Lewis at Poet's Corner* (Eugene, OR: Wipf & Stock, 2016), 204.

14. Augustine of Hippo, *Sermons: 51-94* (Hyde Park, NY: New City Press, 1991), 225-226.

15. Augustine, *Eighty-three Different Questions* in *The Fathers of the Church*, vol. 70 (Washington, DC: CUA Press, 2010), 81.

16. Augustine, *On Genesis* (New York: New City Press, 2002), 246, 248.

17. Augustine, *Eighty-three Different Questions*, 81.

18. David Lindberg, *The Beginnings of Western Science* (Chicago: University of Chicago Press, 2007), 209.

19. John of Salisbury, *The Metalogicon* (Philadelphia, PA: Paul Dry Books, 2009), 29.

20. Salisbury, The *Metalogicon*, 133.

21. Salisbury, The *Metalogicon*, 227.

22. Salisbury, The *Metalogicon*, 41.

23. Carola Baumgardt, *Johannes Kepler: Life and Letters* (New York: Philosophical Library, 1951), 33-34.

24. Baumgardt, *Johannes Kepler*, 50.

25. Gerald Holton, *Thematic Origins of Scientific Thought* (Cambridge: Harvard University Press, 1988), 68.

26. Johannes Kepler, *Conversations with Galileo's Sidereal Messenger* (New York: Johnson Reprint, 1965), 43.

27. Max Planck, *Scientific Autobiography*, in Great Books of the Western World, vol. 56 (Chicago: Encyclopaedia Britannica, 1990), 110.

28. Planck, *Scientific Autobiography*, 116.

29. Planck, *Scientific Autobiography*, 116.

30. Max Jammer, *Einstein and Religion* (Princeton, NJ: Princeton University Press, 1999), 48.

31. Albert Einstein, *The World as I See It* (New York: Kensington, 2006), 31.

32. Albert Einstein, letter to Maurice Solovine dated Mar 30, 1952.

33. Albert Einstein, *Sidelights on Relativity*, trans. G.B. Jeffery and W. Perrett (London: Methuen, 1922), 28.

34. Albert Einstein, "Physics and Reality" (1936), reprinted in *Daedalus*, vol. 132, no. 4 (Fall, 2003), 24.

35. Albert Einstein, letter to Maurice Solovine dated Mar 30, 1952.

36. John Polkinghorne, ed., *Meaning in Mathematics* (New York: Oxford University Press, 2011), 44.

37. Polkinghorne, *Meaning in Mathematics*, 44-45.

38. Polkinghorne, *Meaning in Mathematics*, 41-42.

39. Polkinghorne, *Meaning in Mathematics*, 41.

40. Polkinghorne, *Meaning in Mathematics*, 43.

41. Max Tegmark, "The Mathematical Universe," *Found Phys* (2008), vol. 38, 108.

42. Alvin Plantinga, *Where the Conflict Really Lies: Science, Religion & Naturalism* (New York: Oxford University Press, 2011), 288.

43. Plantinga, *Where the Conflict Really Lies*, 228.

44. Plantinga, *Where the Conflict Really Lies*, 228.

45. Paul Davies, *Are We Alone?* (New York: Orion Productions, 1995), 85.

46. Plantinga, *Where the Conflict Really Lies,* 286.

47. Plantinga, *Where the Conflict Really Lies*, 287.

48. Thomas Nagel, *Mind and Cosmos: Why the Materialist Neo-Darwinian Conception of Nature Is Almost Certainly False* (New York: Oxford University Press, 2012), 17.

49. Nagel, *Mind and Cosmos*, 21.

50. Nagel, *Mind and Cosmos*, 121.

51. Thomas Nagel, *The Last Word* (New York: Oxford University Press, 1997), 130.

52. Paul Davies, *The Goldilocks Enigma* (Boston, MA: Houghton Mifflin, 2008), Kindle loc. 218.

53. Davies, *The Goldilocks Enigma*, Kindle loc. 218.

54. Davies, *The Goldilocks Enigma*, Kindle loc. 4780.

55. John Lennox, *God's Undertaker: Has Science Buried God?* (Oxford: Lion Books, 2009), 62.

Chapter 4—Eschatology of Habitable Zones

1. "The Extrasolar Planets Encyclopaedia," see at http://exoplanet.eu.

2. Wei Zhu et al., "About 30% of Sun-like Stars Have Kepler-Like Planetary Systems: A Study of Their Intrinsic Architecture," *The Astrophysical Journal*, 860.2 (2018): 101.

3. Michael Perryman et al., "Astrometric Exoplanet Detection with Gaia," *The Astrophysical Journal*, 797.1 (2014): 14.

4. "Tess: Transiting Exoplanet Survey Satellite," see at https://tess.gsfc.nasa.gov/science.html.

5. Brett Gladman et al., "Impact Seeding and Reseeding in the Inner Solar System," *Astrobiology*, 5 (2005): 483-496.

6. Michael Denton, *Nature's Destiny: How the Laws of Biology Reveal Purpose in the Universe* (New York: The Free Press, 1998).

7. One evolutionary biologist has proposed that the only way to save the naturalistic origin-of-life scenario is to invoke the multiverse: Eugene Koonin, "The cosmological model of eternal inflation and the transition from chance to biological evolution in the history of life," *Biology Direct*, 2 (2007): 15.

8. Guillermo Gonzalez, "Setting the Stage for Habitable Planets," *Life*, 4 (2014): 35-65.

9. Peter D. Ward and Donald Brownlee, *Rare Earth: Why Complex Life Is Uncommon in the Universe* (New York: Copernicus Books, 2000).

10. Not to be confused with the temperamental dwarfs of Tolkien's Middle-earth. They too are a little temperamental, though Tolkien wrongly called them dwarves. For more on Tolkien's Middle-earth, see Holly Ordway's chapter on "Recovering a Vision of the Cosmos: Tolkien's Creation Narrative in *The Silmarillion*." In the astronomical sense, a dwarf is a main sequence star that fuses hydrogen to helium in its core. Red dwarfs are near the dim end of the main sequence, and they tend to have longer-lasting flare activity.

11. René Heller and Michael Hippke, "Deceleration of high-velocity interstellar photon sails into bound orbits at α Centauri," *Astrophysical Journal Letters*, 835.2 (2017): L32-L37.

12. Ward S. Howard et al., "The first Naked-Eye Superflare Detected from Proxima Centauri," *Astrophysical Journal Letters*, 860.2 (2018): L30.

13. Even atheist/agnostic astronomers have grudgingly come to accept that modern cosmology points to a beginning. For example, Neil DeGrasse Tyson admits such in his recent book *Astrophysics for People in a Hurry*.

14. Anton-Hermann Chroust, "Aristotle's *On Philosophy*: A Brief Comment on Fragment 12 Rose, 13 Walzer, 13 Ross, 18 Untersteiner (Cicero, *De Natura Deorum* II. 37. 95-96)," *Laval théologique et philosophique*, 29.1 (1973), 19.

15. Carl Sagan, *Cosmos* (New York: Random House, 1980), 243.

16. For example, see Ann Gauger's story at https://evolutionnews.org/2018/06/beauty-leads-us-home/.

17. There is general consensus among science historians that modern science arose in Western Europe during the Middle Ages and nowhere else because of Christianity. An incomplete selection of recent works on this topic includes James Hannam, *The Genesis of Science: How the Christian Middle Ages Launched the Scientific Revolution* (Washington, DC: Regnery, 2011); Rodney Stark, *For the Glory of God: How Monotheism Led to Reformations, Science, Witch-Hunts, and the End of Slavery* (Princeton, NJ: Princeton University Press, 2003); Stacy Trasankos, *Science Was Born of Christianity: The Teaching of Fr. Stanley L. Jaki* (Titusville, FL: The Habitation of Chimham Publishing Company, 2014).

18. Nancy Forbes and Basil Mahon, *Faraday, Maxwell and the Electromagnetic Field—How Two Men Revolutionized Physics* (New York: Prometheus, 2014), 217.

19. Hans Blumenberg, *The Genesis of the Copernican Revolution*, trans. R.M. Wallace (Cambridge, MA: MIT Press, 1987), 3.

20. Guillermo Gonzalez and Jay Richards, *The Privileged Planet: How Our Place in the Cosmos Is Designed for Discovery* (Washington, DC: Regnery, 2004). Chapter 4 examines the atmosphere and how it permits clear views of the cosmos.

21. Robert Hazen, *The Story of Earth: The first 4.5 Billion Years, from Stardust to Living Planet* (New York: Penguin, 2012). Hazen argues that some two-thirds of Earth's approximately 5,000 mineral species are linked to the activities of living things. The Moon and the other terrestrial planets in the solar system have at most several hundred mineral species. This rich diversity of mineral species, easily accessible and concentrated in Earth's crust, is an important requirement for advanced technology.

22. Gonzalex and Richards, *The Privileged Planet*, chapter 3.

23. Pluto, which was classified as a planet until 2006, was not visited by a spacecraft until the probe *New Horizons* flew by in 2015.

24. Michael Hippke, "Spaceflight from Super-Earths Is Difficult," *International Journal of Astrobiology*, 2018, in press. For terrestrial planets larger than Earth, a larger mass of fuel must be employed to launch a given payload mass.

25. A. Abraham Loeb, "Interstellar Escape from Proxima b is Barely Possible with Chemical Rockets," *Scientific American*, 2018, in press. Note that a rocket that just reaches escape velocity from Earth (11 km/s) will slow down to zero velocity far from Earth. A rocket launched from Earth already has a speed relative to the Sun of 30 km/s (for free). With an additional 12 km/s, it can escape the solar system (42 km/s).

26. Michael Denton, *Wonder of Water: Water's Profound Fitness for Life on Earth and Mankind* (Seattle, WA: Discovery Institute Press, 2017).

27. David P. O'Brien et al., "The Delivery of Water During Terrestrial Planet Formation," *Space Science Reviews*, 214.47 (2018): 1-27.

28. The Wikipedia entry on asteroid mining is detailed and mostly up to date: https://en.wikipedia.org/wiki/Asteroid_mining.

29. I first made this point in Guillermo Gonzalez, "Extraterrestrials: A Modern View," *Society*, 35.5 (1998): 14-20.

30. The solar system's escape velocity from the asteroid belt is even less than it is from Earth, given the belt's greater distance from the Sun.

31. In 2007, N.T. Wright presented a careful new analysis of New Testament eschatology that contradicts popular ideas about heaven and the afterlife in *Surprised by Hope* (London: SPCK, 2007).

32. While Revelation 21 may be the clearest scripture about our postresurrection state, it is not the only one. Second Peter 3:13 as well as the Old Testament prophetic pronouncements Isaiah 65:17 and 66:22 also speak of the New Heaven and New Earth. Although the scope of Isaiah's prophecy may have been taken as local by his contemporary hearers, the New Testament passages are broader.

33. For example, see 1 Corinthians 15:35-49.

34. This is the view taken in the influential work by J. Richard Middleton, *A New Heaven and a New Earth: Reclaiming Biblical Eschatology* (Grand Rapids, MI: Baker, 2014).

35. Alberto A. Martinez, *Burned Alive: Giordano Bruno, Galileo, and the Inquisition* (London: Reaktion Books, 2018).

36. C. S. Lewis, "Dogma and the Universe," from *God in the Dock: Essays on Theology and Ethics*, ed., Walter Hooper (New York: Ballantine Books, 1990), 14.

37. Fred Adams, "The Future History of the Universe," in *Cosmic Update: Dark Puzzles, Arrow of Time, Future History*, eds. Fred Adams, Laura Mersini-Houghton, and Thomas Buchert (New York: Springer, 2012), 71-118.

Chapter 6—God, Black Holes, and the End of the Universe

1. A modern estimate of white dwarf density is far more absurd at almost 4,000,000 times the density of the Sun. A teaspoon of this matter would, in fact, weigh more than 22 tons on Earth.

2. *The Observatory*, 1935, vol. 58, 373.

3. Neutron stars were first proposed by astronomer Fritz Zwicky as the cause and byproduct of supernovae, the explosive deaths of massive stars. Oppenheimer considered Zwicky an unreliable scientist, and so based his work on Russian theoretical physicist Lev Landau's neutron core idea instead. As it turns out, Zwicky was right, but neutron stars and neutron cores are essentially the same object.

4. Oppenheimer and Volkoff also relied on mathematical work done by chemist-turned-physicist Richard Tolman to complete their calculations.

5. For this reason, physicists at the time referred to collapsed stars as "frozen stars."

6. Ray Monk, *Robert Oppenheimer: A Life Inside the Center* (New York: Anchor Books, 2014), 207-208.

7. Dennis Overbye, "John A. Wheeler, Physicist Who Coined the Term 'Black Hole,' Is Dead at 96," *The New York Times* (Apr 14, 2008), www.nytimes.com/2008/04/14/science/14wheeler.html.

8. Letter (Apr 9/10, 1599) to the Bavarian chancellor Herwart von Hohenburg. Collected in Carola Baumgardt and Jamie Callan, *Johannes Kepler Life and Letters* (New York: Philosophical Library, 1951), 50.

9. It is difficult to explain Finkelstein's unified frame of reference for imploding stars without a lot of technical language or illustrations. The interested reader is referred to chapter 6 of *Black Holes and Time Warps: Einstein's Outrageous Legacy* by Kip Thorne for a clever illustrated analogy of Finkelstein's resolution.

10. Albert Einstein, "Physics and Reality," *Journal of the Franklin Institute*, vol. 221 (Mar 1936): 349-382.

11. *Joannis Kepleri Astronomi Opera Omnia*, ed. Christian Frisch, vol. V (Frankfurt: Heyder & Zimmer, 1858), 224.

12. A radio instrument built for Bell Labs thirty years later would lead to the discovery of the cosmic background radiation, the final nail in the coffin of the eternal universe model.

13. So called because it was the 273rd object in the third Cambridge catalog of celestial radio sources.

14. Kip Thorne, *Black Holes and Time Warps: Einstein's Outrageous Legacy* (New York: W.W. Norton, 1995), 335.

15. Abraham Pais, *'Subtle is the Lord…' The Science and the Life of Albert Einstein* (New York: Oxford University Press, 1982), 113.

16. "*X* Structure at Core of Whirlpool Galaxy (M51)," http://hubblesite.org/image/68/gallery.

Chapter 7—Tycho Brahe and Johannes Kepler: The Gloriously Odd Couple of Astronomy

1. Max Caspar, *Kepler*, trans. C. Doris Hellman (New York: Dover, 1993), Kindle ed., 123.

2. Kitty Ferguson, *Tycho & Kepler: The Unlikely Partnership That Forever Changed Our Understanding of the Heavens* (London: Transworld, 2002), Kindle ed., 7.

3. James A. Conner, *Kepler's Witch* (New York: HarperCollins, 2008) Kindle ed., 23.

4. For a good discussion on the Julian versus Gregorian calendars at the time of Kepler, see Connor, *Kepler's Witch*, Kindle ed., 96-98.

5. Ferguson, *Tycho & Kepler*, 26-27.

6. Ferguson, *Tycho & Kepler*, 47 (bracketed portion from Ferguson).

7. "Tycho's Supernova Remnant," accessed October 10, 2018, http://chandra.harvard.edu/photo/2005/tycho/ and https://en.wikipedia.org/wiki/SN_1572#/media/File:Tycho-supernova-xray.jpg.

8. Arthur Koestler, *The Sleepwalkers: A History of Man's Changing Vision of the Universe* (London: Arkana, 1959), 296-297.

9. Koestler, *The Sleepwalkers*, 296-297.

10. James R. Voelkel, *Johannes Kepler and the New Astronomy* (Oxford: Oxford University Press, 1999), 22-23.

11. Voelkel, *Johannes Kepler and the New Astronomy*, 27.

12. Carola Baumgardt, *Johannes Kepler: Life and Letters* (New York: Philosophical Library, 1951), 27.

13. Voelkel, *Johannes Kepler and the New Astronomy*, 48.

14. Voelkel, *Johannes Kepler and the New Astronomy*, 77.

15. Johannes Kepler, *Harmonices Mundi*, or *The Harmony of the World*, 1619. Trans. Charles Glenn Wallis, 1939, Kindle ed., 6.

16. Baumgardt, *Johannes Kepler*, 34.

17. Caspar, *Kepler*, 381.

Chapter 8—The Cosmos and the Starry Night

1. Hugo of St. Victor, *Didascalicion*, Book VII, section 4. As quoted in Boudewijn Bakker, *Landscape and Religion from Van Eyck to Rembrandt* (Surrey, England: Ashgate Publishing, 2012), 25.

2. John Calvin, *The Institutes of the Christian Religion*, Book II, 6, 1.

3. Bakker, *Landscape and Religion from Van Eyck to Rembrandt*, 25.

4. Wikimedia Commons, public domain, see at https://commons.wikimedia.org/wiki/File:Jacob_Isaacksz._van_Ruisdael_-_Landscape_with_a_View_of_Haarlem_-_WGA20496.jpg.

5. William Wordsworth, "Ode on Intimations of Immortality."

6. Wikimedia Commons, see at https://commons.wikimedia.org/wiki/File:Caspar_David_Friedrich_-_Wanderer_above_the_sea_of_fog.jpg.

7. John Dillenberger, *The Visual Arts and Christianity in America* (New York: Crossroads, 1989), 98.

8. Wikimedia Commons, public domain, see at https://commons.wikimedia.org/wiki/File:Thomas_Cole,_The_Oxbow.jpg.

9. Eleanor Jones Harvey, *The Voyage of the Icebergs* (Dallas, TX: Dallas Museum of Art, 2002), 63.

10. Wikimedia Commons, public domain, see at http://www.hirschlandadler.com/galleries/frederic-edwin-church.

11. Wikimedia Commons, public domain, see at https://commons.wikimedia.org/wiki/File:Church_Heart_of_the_Andes.jpg.

12. Louis Legrand Noble, *Church's Painting: The Heart of the Andes* (New York: D. Appleton, 1859), 21.

13. *The New York Daily Tribune* (Jul 15, 1863).

14. Asher Durand, "Letters on Landscape Painting," in *The Crayon* (Jan 3, 1855).

15. See the discussion of his faith at http://www.newingtoncropsey.com/documents/JFC%20Biography%20web.pdf.

16. Wikimedia Commons, public domain, see at http://www.newingtoncropsey.com/documents/JFC%20Biography%20web.pdf.

17. Matthew Baigell, *Thomas Cole* (New York: Watson-Guptill, 1981), 54.

18. Earl A. Powell, *Thomas Cole* (New York: Harry N. Abrams, 1990), 129.

19. Wikimedia Commons, public domain, see at https://commons.wikimedia.org/wiki/File:Giotto_di_Bondone_-_Vault_-_WGA09168.jpg.

20. Wikimedia Commons, public domain, see at https://commons.wikimedia.org/wiki/File:Studying_astronomy_and_geometry.jpg.

21. Wikimedia Commons, public domain, see at https://commons.wikimedia.org/wiki/File:Flammarion_Woodcut.jpg.

22. Wikimedia Commons, public domain, see at https://commons.wikimedia.org/wiki/File:Frederic_Church_Meteor_of_1860.jpg.

23. Wikimedia Commons, public domain, see at https://commons.wikimedia.org/wiki/File:The_Sower_of_the_Systems_-_G._F._Watts.jpg.

24. Wikimedia Commons, public domain, see at https://www.tate.org.uk/context-comment/articles/gf-watts -symbolist-and-star-gazer.

25. Wikimedia Commons, public domain, see at https://www.missionjuno.swri.edu/junocam/processing?id=758.

26. Dante, *The Divine Comedy*, Paradiso, canto 33.

Chapter 9—Imagine There's No Heaven?: C.S. Lewis on Making Space for Faith

1. Letter dated 17 April 1961 to Alastair Fowler, *Collected Letters, Volume III*, ed. Walter Hooper (London: HarperCollins, 2006), 1257.

2. Later retitled by Walter Hooper as "The Seeing Eye" and republished in *Christian Reflections*, ed. Walter Hooper (London: HarperCollins, 1988).

3. C.S. Lewis, "The Seeing Eye," *Christian Reflections*, 209-213.

4. According to an interview with Valentin Vasilyevich, a close friend of Gagarin's: www.pravmir.com/did-yuri -gagarin-say-he-didnt-see-god-in-space/.

5. And Copernicus was not its first theorist; that honor goes to Nicolaus Cusanus (1401–1464), whose work Lewis knew well. Lewis wrote, "The work of the Renaissance was to substitute space (as a system of relations) for Place (as an aggregate of places) . . . Cusanus first made this possible by neutralizing space—emptying it of all quality: but Galileo's theory of motion actually carries it out" (Lewis's marginal commentary in his copy of Ernst Cassirer's *Individuo e Cosmo*, now held in the Wade Center, Wheaton College, IL). For further details, see my doctoral dissertation "The Son and the Other Stars: Christology and Cosmology in the Imagination of C.S. Lewis," pp. 253-254. Available online: https://research-repository.st-andrews.ac.uk/handle/10023/2783.

6. C.S. Lewis, *Out of the Silent Planet* (London: Pan, 1983), 35.

7. Garrett Green, *Theology, Hermeneutics, and Imagination* (Cambridge: Cambridge University Press, 2000), 15.

8. C.S. Lewis, *English Literature in the Sixteenth Century Excluding Drama* (Oxford: Clarendon Press, 1954), 3-4.

9. C.S. Lewis, "De Descriptione Temporum," in *Selected Literary Essays*, ed. Walter Hooper (Cambridge: Cambridge University Press, 1980), 1-2.

10. "In space no one can hear you scream," the tagline of the movie *Alien* (1979).

11. C.S. Lewis, "The Empty Universe," in *Present Concerns*, ed. Walter Hooper (Glasgow: HarperCollins, 1986), 81-83.

12. C.S. Lewis, *Miracles: A Preliminary Study* (Glasgow: HarperCollins, 1980), 18.

13. C.S. Lewis, *The Discarded Image* (Cambridge: Cambridge University Press, 1964), 222.

14. Lewis, *The Discarded Image*, 216.

15. C.S. Lewis, "De Audiendis Poetis," in *Studies in Medieval and Renaissance Literature*, ed. Walter Hooper (Cambridge: Cambridge University Press, 1966), 7.

16. "One happier look on your kind, suffering face, / And all my sky is domed with cloudless blue; / Eternal summer in a moment's space" (C.S. Lewis, *Poems*, ed. Walter Hooper [London: Fount, 1994], 123). A *moment's space*: a space that has temporal duration or even supra-temporal duration, for it admits "eternal summer," doubtless a glance at one particular "old poet," Shakespeare, and the famous line from his Sonnet 18: "But thy eternal summer shall not fade." William Blake had written of seeing "eternity in an hour"; here Lewis sees eternity in a moment. *Space*, which in this context means "time," can accommodate timelessness if we have the faculties to perceive it.

17. Lewis, "De Audiendis Poetis," 7.

18. Lewis, *English Literature in the Sixteenth Century Excluding Drama*, 50.

19. C.S. Lewis, *Mere Christianity* (Glasgow: HarperCollins, 1990), 10.

20. C.S. Lewis, "The Weight of Glory," in *The Weight of Glory and Other Addresses* (New York: HarperCollins, 2001), 25.

21. C.S. Lewis, *Studies in Words* (Cambridge: Cambridge University Press, 1960), 40.

22. Lewis, *The Discarded Image*, 99.

23. Lewis, *The Discarded Image*, 100.

24. Lewis, *The Discarded Image*, 100.

25. Lewis, *English Literature in the Sixteenth Century Excluding Drama*, 4.

26. Lewis, *The Discarded Image*, 111.

27. C.S. Lewis, *The Problem of Pain* (Glasgow: HarperCollins, 1983), 1.

28. Lewis, "The Salamander," *Poems*, 86-87. Lewis imagines a salamander peering out of the fire in his grate, likening its view of his room to that of men who once "looked out upon the skies." Little does the salamander perceive its true situation vis-à-vis the outside world. Let the reader understand.

29. Lewis, "Imagination and Thought in the Middle Ages," in *Studies in Medieval and Renaissance Literature*, 48.

30. C.S. Lewis, *Perelandra* (London: Pan, 1983), 151.

31. Lewis, *Miracles,* 57.

32. Lewis, "The Language of Religion," 164.

33. Lewis, "The Language of Religion," 165.

34. Lewis, "The Language of Religion," 165.

35. Lewis, "The Language of Religion," 171.

36. For example, "Nothing I can say will prevent some people from describing this lecture as an attack on science." C.S. Lewis, *The Abolition of Man* (Glasgow: HarperCollins, 1984), 45.

37. Percy Bysshe Shelley, "A Defence of Poetry" (1840).

38. Lewis, *The Abolition of Man*, 43.

39. C.S. Lewis, *Out of the Silent Planet* (New York: Scribner, 2003), 34.

40. Lewis, "The Salamander," 86-87.

41. "Orion Nebula," https://hubble25th.org/images/3.

42. Lewis, *Out of the Silent Planet*, 34.

43. Compare "the black womb of the unconsenting skies" in the poem, "Prelude to Space: An Epithalamium," first published in 1964. It was presumably a response to Arthur C. Clarke's 1947 novel *Prelude to Space*, which Lewis refers to in "On Science Fiction," an address he gave in Cambridge in 1955. Clarke's novel belongs to a sub-genre that Lewis calls the "fiction of Engineers" (he declares himself "completely out of sympathy with the projects they anticipate") and Lewis's poem is an epithalamium only in mockery: man's union with space as depicted here is no marriage, but rather a "rape." The poem pictures space exploration as a kind of "lust," man flinging "on space / The sperm of our long woes, our large disgrace." We can read its title in two ways: as a nod to Clarke's novel, but also as a description of what results from the "fierce," "grim," rapacious colonization that the poem portrays. While love would be the prelude to "one flesh" and a fruitful womb, the *libido dominandi* is merely the prelude to space.

44. Lewis, *Out of the Silent Planet*, 35-36.

45. Lewis, *Out of the Silent Planet*, 180.

46. C.S. Lewis, *Reflections on the Psalms* (Glasgow: HarperCollins, 1984), 56.

47. C.S. Lewis, *Spenser's Images of Life*, ed. Alastair Fowler (Cambridge: Cambridge University Press, 1967), 115.

48. C.S. Lewis, "Priestesses in the Church?," *God in the Dock*, ed. Walter Hooper (London: HarperCollins, 1982), 91-92.

49. Lewis, "Equality," in *Present Concerns*, 20.

50. Lewis, *The Abolition of Man*, 42f.

51. Lewis, *English Literature in the Sixteenth Century Excluding Drama*, 3-4.

52. Lewis, "Myth Became Fact," in *God in the Dock*, 42.

53. Lewis, *The Discarded Image*, 218.

54. Matthew 13:34.

55. Lewis, *The Abolition of Man*, 42.

56. Alasdair MacIntyre, *Whose Justice? Which Rationality?* (South Bend, IN: University of Notre Dame, 1988), 357.

57. C.S. Lewis, "The Empty Universe" *Present Concerns* (New York: Harcourt, 1986), 81.

58. Lewis, "Science-Fiction Cradlesong," in *Poems*, 71-72.

59. C.S. Lewis, *The Voyage of the Dawn Treader* (Glasgow: Fontana Lions, 1981), 159.

60. Owen Barfield, *Poetic Diction: A Study in Meaning* (Hanover, NH: Wesleyan University Press, 1984), 23.

Chapter 10—Recovering a Vision of the Cosmos:
Tolkien's Narrative in *The Silmarillion*

1. Tolkien wrote vastly more material for the legendarium of Middle-earth than appears in the single volume titled *The Silmarillion*, which was posthumously assembled and edited by his son and literary executor Christopher Tolkien. After the publication of *The Silmarillion* in 1977, Christopher prepared and published much more of his father's work on the legendarium in books such as *Unfinished Tales* and the complete *History of Middle-earth* (in ten volumes). As Rayner Unwin put it, "no other author has ever had the advantage of a literary executor with the sympathy, the scholarship, and the humility to devote half a lifetime to the task of unobtrusively giving shape to his own father's creativity. In effect one man's imaginative genius has had the benefit of two lifetimes' work." ("Early Days of Elder Days," in *Tolkien's Legendarium: Essays on The History of Middle-earth,* eds. Verlyn Flieger and Carl F. Hostetter [Westport, CT: Greenwood Press, 2000], 6.)

2. C.S. Lewis, *The Abolition of Man* (New York: HarperCollins, 1944), 18.

3. Lewis, *The Abolition of Man*, 19.

4. Lewis, *The Abolition of Man*, 65.

5. In *Apologetics and the Christian Imagination: An Integrated Approach to Defending the Faith* (Steubenville, OH: Emmaus Road, 2017).

6. Michael Ward, "The Good Serves the Better and Both the Best," in *Imaginative Apologetics*, ed. Andrew Davison (Grand Rapids, MI: Baker, 2012), 72.

7. "M45, The Pleiades," https://www.spacetelescope.org/projects/fits_liberator/fitsimages/davidedemartin_5/.

8. *Attacks of Taste,* eds. Evelyn B. Byrne and Otto M. Penzler (New York: Gotham Book Mart, 1971), 43.

9. Humphrey Carpenter, George Sayer, and Clyde S. Kilby, "A Dialogue," in *Minas Tirith Evening-Star*, vol. 13, no. 1 (Jan-Feb 1984), 20-24.

10. "Joanna Tolkien speaks at the Tolkien Society Annual Dinner, Shrewsbury, April 16, 1994," *Digging Potatoes, Growing Trees: vol. 2*, ed. Helen Armstrong (Telford: The Tolkien Society, 1998), 33.

11. J.R.R. Tolkien, "On Fairy-stories," in *Tolkien on Fairy-stories*, eds. Verlyn Flieger and Douglas A. Anderson (London: HarperCollins, 2014), 67.

12. Tolkien, "On Fairy-stories," 67.

13. Tolkien, "On Fairy-stories," 67.

14. Tolkien, "On Fairy-stories," 67.

15. Tolkien, "On Fairy-stories," 67.

16. Tolkien, "On Fairy-stories," 68.

17. Tolkien, "On Fairy-stories," 68.

18. J.R.R. Tolkien, *The Silmarillion*, ed. Christopher Tolkien, 2d ed. (Boston, MA: Houghton Mifflin, 2001), 15.

19. Tolkien, *The Silmarillion*, 16.

20. Tolkien, *The Silmarillion*, 17.

21. Tolkien, *The Silmarillion*, 17.

22. Tolkien, *The Silmarillion*, 20.

23. Tolkien, *The Silmarillion*, 20.

24. Tolkien, *The Silmarillion*, 21.

25. Tolkien, *The Silmarillion*, 22.

26. Tolkien, *The Silmarillion*, 15.

27. See John Garth, *Tolkien and the Great War* (Boston, MA: Houghton Mifflin, 2003) for an excellent account of the influence of Tolkien's war experiences on his writing.

28. Tolkien, *The Silmarillion*, 69.

29. C.S. Lewis, "Letter to Arthur Greeves, Oct. 18, 1931," in *Collected Letters, vol. 1* (London: HarperCollins, 2000), 977.

30. Tolkien, "On Fairy-stories," 78.

Chapter 11—Creation *Ex Nihilo:* Theology and Science

1. See chapters 1 and 2 of Paul Copan and William Lane Craig, *Creation out of Nothing: A Biblical, Philosophical, and Scientific Exploration* (Grand Rapids, MI: Baker, 2004).

2. Copan and Craig, *Creation out of Nothing*, chapter 3.

3. See William Lane Craig, *The* Kalām *Cosmological Argument* (London: Macmillan, 1979).

4. "Creator omnium invisibilium et visibilium, spiritualium et corporalium, qui sua omnipotenti virtute simul ab initio temporis, utramque de nihilo condidit creaturam, spiritualem et corporalem" (Concilium Lateranense IV, *Constitutiones 1. De fide catholica*).

5. Copan and Craig, *Creation out of Nothing*, chapters 4–6.

6. A. Einstein, "Cosmological Considerations on the General Theory of Relativity," in *The Principle of Relativity*, A. Einstein, et. al., with notes by A. Sommerfeld, trans. W. Perrett and J. B. Jefferey (New York: Dover, 1952), 177-188.

7. A. Friedman, "Über die Krümmung des Raumes," *Zeitschrift für Physik* 10 (1922): 377-386; G. Lemaître, "Un univers homogène de masse constante et de rayon croissant, rendant compte de la vitesse radiale des nébuleuses extragalactiques," *Annales de la Société scientifique de Bruxelles* 47 (1927): 49-59.

8. Gregory L. Naber, *Spacetime and Singularities: An Introduction* (Cambridge: Cambridge University Press, 1988), 126-127.

9. E. Hubble, "A Relation between Distance and Radial Velocity Among Extra-galactic Nebulae," *Proceedings of the National Academy of Sciences* 15 (1929): 168-173.

10. John A. Wheeler, "Beyond the Hole," in *Some Strangeness in the Proportion,* ed. Harry Woolf (Reading, MA: Addison-Wesley, 1980), 354.

11. P.C.W. Davies, "Spacetime Singularities in Cosmology," in *The Study of Time III*, ed. J.T. Fraser (New York: Springer Verlag, 1978), 78-79.

12. John Barrow and Frank Tipler, *The Anthropic Cosmological Principle* (Oxford: Clarendon Press, 1986), 442.

13. Principally the addition of an early inflationary era and an accelerating expansion.

14. William Lane Craig and James Sinclair, "The *Kalam* Cosmological Argument," in *The Blackwell Companion to Natural Theology*, eds. Wm. L. Craig and J.P. Moreland (Oxford: Wiley-Blackwell, 2009), 101-201; idem, "On Non-Singular Spacetimes and the Beginning of the Universe," in *Scientific Approaches to the Philosophy of Religion*, ed. Yujin Nagasawa (London: Macmillan, 2012), 95-142.

15. A. Borde, A. Guth, A. Vilenkin, "Inflationary Spacetimes Are Incomplete in Past Directions," *Physical Review Letters* 90 (2003): 151301, http://arxiv.org/abs/gr-qc/0110012.

16. Alexander Vilenkin, "Did the universe have a beginning?" http://www.youtube.com/watch?v=NXCQelhKJ7A. Cf. Audrey Mithani and Alexander Vilenkin, "Did the universe have a beginning?" arXiv:1204.4658v1 [hep-th] 20 Apr 2012, 1, where they state, "None of these scenarios can actually be past-eternal."

17. Alexander Vilenkin, "The Beginning of the Universe," *Inference: International Review of Science* 1/ 4 (Oct 23, 2015), http://inference-review.com/article/the-beginning-of-the-universe.

18. Robert Stewart, ed., *God and Cosmology: William Lane Craig and Sean Carroll in Dialogue* (Minneapolis, MN: Fortress, 2016), 70. The Greer-Heard Forum itself was held in 2014.

19. Stewart, *God and Cosmology*, 70.

20. Steward, *God and Cosmology*, 70.

21. Alan Guth to Daniel Came, Mar 19, 2017, cited by Came in our debate "Does God Exist?" at Trinity College, Dublin (Mar 23, 2017), available at https://www.facebook.com/reasonablefaithorg/videos/10154698973823229/ .

22. See Alexander Vilenkin, "Arrows of time and the beginning of the universe," arXiv:1305.3836v2 [hep-th], May 29, 2013; also Craig and Sinclair, "The *Kalam* Cosmological Argument," 157.

23. A.Vilenkin, cited in "Why physicists can't avoid a creation event," Lisa Grossman, *New Scientist* (Jan 11, 2012).

24. "If indeed all past-directed geodesics encounter a quantum spacetime region where the notions of time and causality no longer apply, I would characterize such a region as the beginning of the universe" (A. Vilenkin to William Lane Craig, personal correspondence, Dec 8, 2013).

25. Christopher Isham observes that although quantum cosmogonies "differ in their details they all agree on the idea that space and time emerge in some way from a purely quantum-mechanical region which can be described in some respects as if it were a classical, imaginary-time four-space" (C.J. Isham, "Quantum Theories of the Creation of the Universe," in *Quantum Cosmology and the Laws of Nature*, 2d ed., eds. Robert J. Russell et al. [Vatican City State: Vatican Observatory, 1996], 75). This feature of quantum cosmogony is very problematic, since diachronic emergence of time is obviously incoherent (J. Butterfield and C.J. Isham, "On the Emergence of Time in Quantum Gravity," in *The Arguments of Time*, ed. J. Butterfield [Oxford: Oxford

University Press, 1999], 111-68; Vincent Lam and Michael Esfeld, "A dilemma for the emergence of space-time in canonical quantum gravity," *Studies in History and Philosophy of Modern Physics* 44 [2013]: 286-293; Reiner Hedrich, "Hat die Raumzeit Quanteneigenschaften? –Emergenztheoretische Ansätze in der Quantengravitation," in *Philosophie der Physik*, ed. M. Esfeld [Berlin: Suhrkamp, forthcoming], 287-305). But how can one make sense of a synchronic emergence of time as a supervenient reality in the context of cosmogony? The authors cited do not tell us. The best sense I can make of it is to say that the Euclidean description is a lower-level description of classical spacetime prior to the Planck time. (One recalls Hawking's remark that when we go back to the real time in which we live, there still would be singularities.) So the same reality is being described at two levels. That implies that if the classical spacetime has a beginning, then so does the quantum gravity regime. For they are descriptions of the same reality. In the one a singularity is part of the description; in the other it is not. So what is prior to the Planck time is not the quantum gravity era as such; rather what is prior is the classical period of which the quantum gravity description is the more fundamental description. If this is correct, then given the beginning of the classically described universe, it is impossible for the universe as quantum gravitationally described to be without a beginning. For they just are the same universe at different levels of description.

26. Anthony Aguirre and John Kehayias, "Quantum Instability of the Emergent Universe" (Nov 19, 2013), arXiv:1306.3232v2 [hep-th]. They are specifically addressing the Ellis-Maarten model, but their point is generalizable.

27. Richard Schlegel, "Time and Thermodynamics," in *The Voices of Time*, ed. J.T. Fraser (London: Penguin, 1968), 511.

28. Ludwig Boltzmann, *Lectures on Gas Theory*, trans. Stephen G. Brush (Berkeley, CA: University of California Press, 1964), §90 (446-448).

29. Beatrice Tinsley, "From Big Bang to Eternity?," *Natural History Magazine* (Oct 1975), 103.

30. Duane Dicus et al., "The Future of the Universe," *Scientific American* (Mar 1983): 99.

31. Tinsley, "Big Bang," 105.

32. Paul Davies, "The Big Bang—and Before," The Thomas Aquinas College Lecture Series (Santa Paula, CA: Thomas Aquinas College, Mar 2002).

33. Lin Dyson, Matthew Kleban, and Leonard Susskind, "Disturbing Implications of a Cosmological Constant," http://arXiv.org/abs/hep-th/0208013v3 (Nov 14, 2002), 4. Their point of departure is Henri Poincaré's argument that in a closed box of randomly moving particles every configuration of particles, no matter how improbable, will eventually recur, given enough time; given infinite time, every configuration will recur infinitely many times. Eschewing a global perspective in favor of a restriction to our causally connected patch of the universe, they argue for the inevitability of cosmological Poincaré recurrences, allowing the process of cosmogony to begin anew. N.B. that even if bubble universes decay before the Poincaré recurrences could happen, there is still enough time for the invasion of Boltzmann brains, discussed below.

34. Roger Penrose, "Time-Asymmetry and Quantum Gravity," in *Quantum Gravity 2*, eds. C.J. Isham, R. Penrose, and D.W. Sciama (Oxford: Clarendon Press, 1981), 249; cf. Stephen Hawking and Roger Penrose, *The Nature of Space and Time*, The Isaac Newton Institute Series of Lectures (Princeton, NJ: Princeton University Press, 1996), 34-35.

35. Penrose, "Time-Asymmetry," 249.

36. Roger Penrose, *The Road to Reality* (New York: Alfred Knopf, 2005), 762-765.

37. For literature see Don N. Page, "Return of the Boltzmann Brains" (Nov 15, 2006), http://arXiv:hep -th/0611158.

38. Aron C. Wall, "The Generalized Second Law Implies a Quantum Singularity Theorem" (Jan 24, 2013), 38, http://arXiv: 1010.5513v3 [gr-qc].

39. Wall, "The Generalized Second Law," 4.

40. Paul Davies, "The Birth of the Cosmos," in *God, Cosmos, Nature and Creativity*, ed. Jill Gready (Edinburgh: Scottish Academic Press, 1995), 8-9.

41. All of these quotations are from Krauss's videos posted on YouTube, including his Asimov Memorial "Nothing Debate" 1:20:25; American Atheists lecture 26:23; Richard Fidler interview; discussion with Richard Dawkins at Arizona State Origins Project 37 min.; and Stockholm lecture 46:37.

42. David Albert, "On the Origin of Everything," critical notice of *A Universe from Nothing* by Lawrence Krauss, *New York Times Sunday Book Review* (Mar 23, 2012).

43. Alexander Vilenkin to Alan Guth, Mar 20, 2017. I am grateful to Daniel Came for sharing with me this correspondence, in which Vilenkin strongly rejects Guth's claim of a beginningless universe on the basis of time-reversal models.

44. Vilenkin, "The Beginning of the Universe."

45. From our debate posted at http://www.reasonablefaith.org/debate-transcript-what-is-the-evidence-for-against-the-existence-of-god#_ftn5; cf. Peter Atkins, *Creation Revisited* (New York: W.H. Freeman, 1992).

46. Christopher Isham, "Quantum Cosmology and the Origin of the Universe," lecture presented at the conference "Cosmos and Creation," Cambridge University (Jul 14, 1994).

47. Sean Carroll, "Does the Universe Need God?," in *The Blackwell Companion to Science and Christianity*, eds. J.B. Stump and Alan G. Padgett (Oxford: Wiley-Blackwell, 2012), 196.

48. "X-ray, Optical & Infrared Composite of Kepler's Supernova Remnant," https://en.wikipedia.org/wiki/Kepler%27s_Supernova#/media/File:Keplers_supernova.jpg and "NASA/ESA/JHU/R.Sankrit & W.Blair," http://www.nasa.gov/multimedia/imagegallery/image_feature_219.html.

Chapter 12—The Cosmic Coincidences of Fine Tuning

1. Richard Dawkins, *River out of Eden* (New York: Basic Books, 1995), 133.

2. Reductionism is the view that everything in the physical universe can in principle be explained completely and without remainder in terms of the arrangement and properties of the fundamental constituents of the universe. As Dawkins says in *The Blind Watchmaker*, "carburettors are explained in terms of smaller units… which are explained in terms of smaller units…which are ultimately explained in terms of the smallest of fundamental particles" (New York: Penguin Books, 1986), 17.

3. Dark matter is a type of matter that, unlike ordinary matter, does not interact with or emit light. We know of its existence through its gravitational effects.

4. Americans (such as Allen) refer to these bricks as LEGOs. The Lego Group has officially confirmed that this is incorrect, tweeting: "Please always refer to our products as 'LEGO bricks or toys' and not 'LEGOS.'…The word 'Lego' is an adjective, not a noun." While this debate was settled, no progress was made by Luke and Allen on the "math vs. maths" conundrum and the "aluminum vs. aluminium" debacle.

5. Most parents would especially appreciate toys that self-assemble!

6. By *physics,* we mean fundamental laws, constants, and initial conditions.

7. John von Neumann (1903–1957) was a Hungarian-American mathematician and physicist who contributed greatly to foundational aspects of mathematics and computer science. It was his work on cellular automata that showed the need for information storage to accomplish replication.

8. Geraint Lewis and Luke Barnes, *A Fortunate Universe* (Cambridge: Cambridge University Press 2016), 232.

9. While we avoid the technical term *entropy* here, we are using *orderly* as a synonym for *low entropy*, and *disorderly* for *high entropy*.

10. We don't think that this is the actual future of our universe, but it could be. And that's all that Penrose's argument requires.

11. Penrose proposed that there may be some unknown physics that constrains the beginning of the universe so that it must be smooth. He called this the Weyl Curvature Hypothesis. However, Penrose has noted that "simply as an assertion, the Weyl Curvature Hypothesis is perhaps more like a claim for 'an act of God' than a physical theory" (Roger Penrose, *Road to Reality* [London, Random House, 2004], 769). We would argue that it simply restates the problem rather than solving it.

12. The abundance of helium-4, helium-3, and deuterium are predicted to within 3-10% (Coc, Uzan and Vangioni, 2014: arxiv.org/pdf/1307.6955.pdf). However, the predicted abundance of lithium-7 is too high by a factor of three. In another proud moment for scientific creativity, cosmologists call this "the lithium problem." (If you're rusty on chemistry: a deuterium nucleus consists of a proton and a neutron. Two protons and one neutron makes helium-3, and two protons and two neutrons makes helium-4.)

13. It is possible that, due to a physical theory known as supersymmetry, the CC might naturally cancel to 70 decimal places. There would still be, conservatively, fine-tuning to one part in 10^{30} (if 100 decimal places is a minimum for a universe with structure). As of 2018, no evidence of supersymmetry has been found despite the extensive efforts of the Large Hadron Collider and other particle physics experiments. And the mass scale of supersymmetry may still need to be fine-tuned.

14. Lewis and Barnes, *A Fortunate Universe*, 268.

15. Recent work in this area by Fred Adams and Evan Grohs, and Luke and Geraint Lewis, has refined many of the existing fine-tuning claims about stars.

16. Luke A. Barnes, "Binding the diproton in stars: anthropic limits on the strength of gravity," *Journal of Cosmology and Astroparticle Physics* 2015.12 (2015): 050.

17. Because Newton's gravitational constant G has units, we must specify exactly how we intend to change its value. Here, we fix Planck's constant (h) and the speed of light (c), and some fundamental mass scale, such as the electron mass. Equivalently, we could fix h, c, and G, and "increasing the strength of gravity" would be the same as increasing the masses of the electron, proton, and neutron by the same factor.

18. You may think that even if photon energy levels were significantly different, evolution could simply favor different molecules, but this fails to recognize the constraints imposed by physics. George Greenstein discusses this point in detail in *The Symbiotic Universe*, noting that "within broad limits all molecules absorb light of similar colors…the general scale of energy required…is the same no matter what molecule you are discussing" ([New York: William Morrow, 1988], 97). Evolution would also rely on this coincidence in photon energy levels before it can select for helpful light-sensitive molecules.

19. The mathematically-squeamish should look away now: $\left(\dfrac{G}{\hbar c}\, \dfrac{m_{\text{proton}}^{6}}{m_{\text{electron}}^{4}} \right)^{1/8} \sim \alpha^{3/2}$

20. W.H. McCrea and Martin Rees, *Large Numbers and Ratios in Astrophysics and Cosmology: Discussion*, Philosophical Transactions of the Royal Society of London Series A, 310 (1983): 317.

21. For example, the proton is unstable unless the strength of electromagnetism is finely tuned to be more than counterbalanced by the difference in the quark masses making up protons and neutrons (the mass of the down quark needs to exceed the mass of the up quark by more than this).

22. Technical details and references to the scientific literature can be found in Luke's comprehensive review article: Luke A. Barnes, *The Fine-Tuning of the Universe for Intelligent Life* (Publications of the Astronomical Society of Australia, 2012), 29, 529-564.

23. Or at least more like a mind than anything else with which we are familiar.

24. The probability of this happening is about 1 in 10^{29} in five-card stud. Technically, we compare the product of the prior probability and the likelihood of the evidence for each hypothesis.

25. There are several flavors of this principle, including Martin Gardner's "Completely Ridiculous Anthropic Principle" or CRAP. Martin Gardner, "WAP, SAP, FAP & PAP," *New York Review of Books* 33 (May 8, 1986): 22-25. See the discussion in chapter 1 of Lewis and Barnes, *A Fortunate Universe*, 15.

26. Luke A Barnes, Pascal J. Elahi, Jaime Salcido, et al., "Galaxy Formation Efficiency and the Multiverse Explanation of the Cosmological Constant with EAGLE Simulations," *Monthly Notices of the Royal Astronomical Society*, 477 (2018): 3727-43.

27. This is known as the Boltzmann brain problem.

28. Lewis Carroll, *The Annotated Alice: The Definitive Edition*, ed. Martin Gardner (New York: W.W. Norton, 2000), 67.

Chapter 13—Rediscovering the Discarded Image

1. For a nice discussion of this distinction, see J.P. Moreland and Garrett DeWeese, "The Premature Report of Foundationalism's Demise," in *Reclaiming the Center*, eds. Millard J. Erickson, Paul Kjoss Helseth, and Justin Taylor (Wheaton, IL: Crossway, 2004), 81-107. Importantly, as Moreland and DeWeese point out, our concepts, thoughts, and conceptual schemes don't cut us off from seeing reality. Rather, they function "as a sort of swiveled neck brace that directs the subject's attention but does not cut off the object from the subject by standing between them" (103).

2. Augustine, *Confessions*, trans. Henry Chadwick (Oxford: Oxford University Press, 1998).

3. *Confessions*, XI. iv, 224.

4. *Confessions* XI. iv, 224.

5. *Confessions* XIII. xxviii, 299.

6. *Confessions* I. I, 3.

7. John Calvin, *Institutes of the Christian Religion*, ed. John T. McNeill and trans. Ford Lewis Battles (Louisville, KY: Westminster John Knox Press, 1960), 1.5.8, 61.

8. *Institutes* 1.5.1, 52.

9. *Institutes* 1.14.21, 181.

10. *Institutes* 1.5.3, 54.

11. *Institutes* 1.5.1, 52-33.

12. Carl Sagan, *Cosmos* (New York: Random House, 1980), 4.

13. Sagan, *Cosmos*, 4.

14. Carl Sagan, *The Varieties of Scientific Experience*, ed. Ann Druyan (New York: Penguin, 2006), 167.

15. Sagan, *The Varieties of Scientific Experience*, 167.

16. Sagan, *The Varieties of Scientific Experience*, 167.

17. Carl Sagan, *Pale Blue Dot* (New York: Random House, 1994), 17.

18. Sagan, *Cosmos*, 193.

19. Sagan, *Cosmos*, 242.

20. The language of "de-creator" is from Philip Rieff, *My Life Among the Deathworks* (Charlottesville, VA: University of Virginia Press, 2006).

21. Neil deGrasse Tyson, *Astrophysics for People in a Hurry* (New York: W.W. Norton, 2017), 32.

22. Tyson, *Astrophysics for People in a Hurry*, 33.

23. Tyson, *Astrophysics for People in a Hurry*, 205.

24. Tyson, *Astrophysics for People in a Hurry*, 206.

25. Tyson, *Astrophysics for People in a Hurry*, 199, 201.

26. The phrase was originally coined by Martin Esslin to describe post-World War II plays that wrestled with the question of meaning in a godless universe. See Martin Esslin, *The Theatre of the Absurd* (New York: Anchor Books, 1961).

27. The late philosopher David Lewis (1941–2001) was a powerful defender of this Humean picture. According to Lewis, the world is composed of a "vast mosaic of local matters of particular fact, just one little thing and then another...And that is all" ("Introduction," in *Philosophical Papers, vol. 2* [Oxford: Oxford University Press, 1986], ix).

28. "If we're going to be scientistic, then we have to attain our view of reality from what physics tells us about it. Actually, we'll have to do more than that: we'll have to embrace physics as *the whole truth about reality*. Why buy the picture of reality that physics paints? Well, it's simple, really. We trust science as the only way to acquire knowledge. That is why we are so confident about atheism." Alex Rosenberg, *The Atheist's Guide to Reality: Enjoying Life Without Illusions* (New York: Norton, 2011), 20.

29. The phrase "late and local" is from Graham Oppy, "Conflict Model," in *Four Views on Christianity and Philosophy*, eds. Paul M. Gould and Richard Brian Davis (Grand Rapids, MI: Zondervan, 2016), 30.

30. Sean Carroll, *The Big Picture* (New York: Dutton, 2017), 3.

31. Samuel Beckett, *Waiting for Godot* (New York: Grove Press, 2011).

32. Beckett, *Waiting for Godot*, 52.

33. Beckett, *Waiting for Godot*, 68. This line is from Vladimir.

34. Hans Boersma, *Heavenly Participation* (Grand Rapids, MI: Eerdmans, 2011), 21. Boersma emphasizes the Platonic-Christian synthesis but it is more accurate to speak of the Platonic-*Aristotelian*-Christian synthesis.

35. Boersma, *Heavenly Participation*, 24. Elsewhere Boersma states, "The entire cosmos is meant to serve as a sacrament: a material gift from God in and through which we enter into the joy of his heavenly presence" (9).

36. C.S. Lewis, *Miracles* (New York: Touchstone, 1996), 34.

37. Thornton Wilder, *Our Town* (New York: HarperCollins, 1998).

38. Wilder, *Our Town*, 46.

39. The philosopher of science Jeffrey Koperski speaks of a three-layered triangle to the academic discipline of science: observation and data at the bottom, theories and laws at the middle, and metatheoretic shaping principles (MSPs) at the top. "MSPs help determine what good theories, laws, and models look like as well as how one should proceed in their discovery and development" (in *The Physics of Theism* [Malden, MA: Wiley Blackwell, 2015], 26-27).

40. This is one of the central insights in Kevin J. Vanhoozer, *Pictures at a Theological Exhibition* (Downers Grove, IL: InterVarsity, 2016).

41. For an excellent canvass on the debate over the nature of love, including a defense of the view, held notably by Thomas Aquinas, that love consists in the desire for the well-being of and union with the beloved, see Eleonore Stump, *Wandering in Darkness* (Oxford: Oxford University Press, 2010), chapter 5.

42. See Roger Scruton, *Beauty: A Very Short Introduction* (Oxford: Oxford University Press, 2009), 29-32 and Raymond Tallis, *Aping Mankind* (Durham, NC: Acumen, 2011), 286-306.

43. Tallis, *Aping Mankind*, 300.

44. While there are significant challenges to the claim that reason can emerge from a neo-Humean world, I'll assume in this paragraph for the sake of argument that it has. The tension I'm highlighting, again on the assumption that minds have evolved, is the gap between what is needed for our survival, cognitively speaking, and the actual cognitive faculties found in humankind. For a sustained argument that evolution plus naturalism gives us reason to doubt our cognitive faculties' ability to deliver truth, see Alvin Plantinga, *Where the Conflict Really Lies* (Oxford: Oxford University Press, 2011), chapter 10 and Thomas Nagel, *Mind and Cosmos: Why the Materialist Non-Darwinian Conception of Nature Is Almost Certainly False* (Oxford: Oxford University Press, 2012), chapter 4. For an argument that naturalism (without or without evolution) is incompatible with the existence of minds, see C.S. Lewis, *Miracles* (New York: Touchstone, 1960), chapter 3.

45. As the scientist-turned-theologian John C. Polkinghorne puts it, "[survival] does not begin to explain why highly abstract concepts of pure mathematics should fit perfectly with the patterns of the subatomic world of quantum theory or the cosmic world of relativity, both of which are regimes whose understanding is of no practical consequence whatsoever for humankind's ability to have held its own in the evolutionary struggle (*Science and Creation* [Philadelphia, PA: Templeton Foundation Press, 1988], 30).

46. For more on these themes, see Norman Kretzmann, "A Particular Problem of Creation," in *Being and Goodness*, ed. Scott MacDonald (Ithaca, NY: Cornell University Press, 1991), 229-249.

47. For more on the argument from fittingness, see the discussion of the fine-tuning argument in chapter 2. See also Robin Collins, "The Teleological Argument," in *The Blackwell Companion to Natural Theology*, eds. William Lane Craig and J.P. Moreland (London: Blackwell, 2009), 202-281 and Geraint F. Lewis and Luke A. Barnes, *A Fortunate Universe* (Cambridge: Cambridge University Press, 2016).

48. Vanhoozer, *Pictures at a Theological Exhibition*, 24.

49. The idea of "sacred messengers" is nicely unpacked by Philip Rieff in chapter 5 of his *My Life Among the Deathworks* (Charlottesville, VA: University of Virginia Press, 2006).

Afterword: Astronomy with Your Own Two Eyes

1. Neil DeGrasse Tyson, *Death by Black Hole and Other Cosmic Quandaries* (New York: W.W. Norton, 2007), 321.

2. See Isaiah 41:14; Job 25:4-6; Psalm 22:6; Romans 3.

3. Stellarium, see at http://stellarium.org/.

4. The Dog Star Sirius and its Tiny Companion," http://hubblesite.org/image/1820/gallery.

5. Michael Collins, *Carrying the Fire: An Astronaut's Journey* (New York: Farrar, Straus and Giroux, 1974, 2009), 286. *Disastrous* literally means "against the stars." Collins, I'm thinking, was doing a bit of wordplay here!

6. See Genesis 1:14-16; Psalm 8; 19; 111; Isaiah 40; Romans 1.

7. See Jeremiah 31, especially verses 35-37, where God compares His faithfulness to the "fixed order" of the heavens.

To learn more about Harvest House books and
to read sample chapters, visit our website:

www.harvesthousepublishers.com

HARVEST HOUSE PUBLISHERS
EUGENE, OREGON